COMPLETE CONDITIONING FOR FOOTBALL

Aaron Wellman, PhD, CSCS
Editor

Cameron Josse, Peter Remmes,
Justin Collett, Jordan Hicks
Contributors

HUMAN KINETICS

Library of Congress Cataloging-in-Publication Data

Names: Wellman, Aaron, 1974- editor.
Title: Complete conditioning for football / Aaron Wellman, PhD, CSCS,
  Editor.
Description: First edition. | Champaign, IL : Human Kinetics, [2024] |
  Includes bibliographical references and index.
Identifiers: LCCN 2022040900 (print) | LCCN 2022040901 (ebook) | ISBN
  9781718214453 (paperback) | ISBN 9781718214460 (epub) | ISBN
  9781718214477 (pdf)
Subjects: LCSH: Football--Training. | Physical education and training. |
  Sports--Physiological aspects. | Sports injuries--Prevention. | BISAC:
  SPORTS & RECREATION / Football | SPORTS & RECREATION / Coaching /
  Football
Classification: LCC GV953.5 .C64 2024 (print) | LCC GV953.5 (ebook) | DDC
  796.33207/7--dc23/eng/20220901
LC record available at https://lccn.loc.gov/2022040900
LC ebook record available at https://lccn.loc.gov/2022040901

ISBN: 978-1-7182-1445-3 (print)

The web addresses cited in this text were current as of August 2022, unless otherwise noted.

Managing Editor and Permissions Manager: Hannah Werner; **Copyeditor:** Michelle Horn; **Indexer:** Kevin Campbell; **Senior Graphic Designer:** Sean Roosevelt; **Cover Designer:** Keri Evans; **Cover Design Specialist:** Susan Rothermel Allen; **Photograph (cover):** Randy Litzinger/Icon Sportswire via Getty Images; **Photographs (interior):** Photo on page 1 © Matthew Holst/Getty Images. Photo on page 7 © Joe Robbins/Icon Sportswire via Getty Images. Photos on pages 39, 169, and 219 © Jamie Sabau/Getty Images. Photo on page 67 © Corey Perrine/Getty Images. Photo on page 109 © Greg Fiume/Getty Images. Photos on pages 145 and 265 © Jeremy Hogan/SOPA Images/LightRocket via Getty Images. Photo on page 247 © Justin Casterline/Getty Images. Photo on page 287 © Steven Branscombe/Getty Images. All other photos © Human Kinetics, unless otherwise noted; **Photo Asset Manager:** Laura Fitch; **Photo Production Specialist:** Amy M. Rose; **Photo Production Manager:** Jason Allen; **Senior Art Manager:** Kelly Hendren; **Illustrations:** © Human Kinetics, unless otherwise noted; **Printer:** Versa Press

We thank Indiana University in Bloomington, Indiana, for assistance in providing the location for the photo shoot for this book.

Human Kinetics books are available at special discounts for bulk purchase. Special editions or book excerpts can also be created to specification. For details, contact the Special Sales Manager at Human Kinetics.

Printed in the United States of America   10   9   8   7   6   5   4   3   2   1

The paper in this book is certified under a sustainable forestry program.

Human Kinetics
1607 N. Market Street
Champaign, IL 61820
USA

United States and International
Website: **US.HumanKinetics.com**
Email: info@hkusa.com
Phone: 1-800-747-4457

Canada
Website: **Canada.HumanKinetics.com**
Email: info@hkcanada.com

E8714

Contents

Foreword

To be able to perform at the highest level, a football player must possess the physical characteristics of speed, strength, and power, and he must utilize those characteristics through intense and repeated contact when playing the game of football. To best develop these attributes, players must put themselves through strict physical training—pushing themselves to their limits. There is a tremendous amount of trust built between an athlete and the coach going through this process together, and there is no one I trust more with our players in the training process than Coach Aaron Wellman and his staff.

Dr. Aaron Wellman started his career as a graduate assistant at Indiana University (1997-1998), and I was beyond ecstatic when he decided to bring his 25 years of expertise in the field of strength and conditioning back to Bloomington. Coming to us from a four-year stint with the New York Giants, where he was working with many of the premier NFL athletes in the game of football, Aaron established himself as one of the top sport performance strength and conditioning specialists in the country. I knew he was exactly the type of person Indiana Football needed to move this program to the next level.

Aaron and I share many passions; among those passions is our desire to use our knowledge of the game of football to build up young men physically, mentally, and spiritually. Coach Wellman spent 13 years of his career in the Big Ten, a league that prides itself on its stout, physical play. We both knew the quality of our strength and conditioning program would be the difference maker when it came to preparing our athletes to compete in this league.

As senior assistant athletic director for football performance here at Indiana University, Coach Wellman provides professional expertise derived from his master's degrees in sport science and nutrition science and doctoral degree in sport science. Coach Wellman possesses strength and conditioning certifications from both the CSCCa and NSCA, and he also holds certificates in performance nutrition from ISSA.

Coach Wellman's greatest asset, though, is his ability to care deeply for the individual and develop an individualized performance program for each athlete at all stages of their development (from beginner to the highest level of professional athlete). These programs develop the individual's maximum speed, strength, and power, all while mitigating the risk of injury.

In *Complete Conditioning for Football*, Coach Wellman and his staff have combined their proficiency in strength and conditioning to provide coaches with a comprehensive guide for how to develop a full-year program, complete with scope and sequence for each phase of training. The attention to detail and straightforward guidance in this book help make training each essential physical attribute and implementing the full scope of the program seamless. This is the type of information that will improve any football program and give it an edge over the competition. After seeing how our players develop to their maximum physical potential under Coach Wellman's training and expertise, there is no doubt that your players can too!

Tom Allen
Head Football Coach
Indiana University

Preface

I would like to thank you for purchasing what we believe to be one of the most comprehensive and pragmatic books on training football players that has been published in the last 10 years. Over the previous 26 years of my career, 18 of which include serving as a head strength coach, I have made my share of mistakes, learned several lessons, discarded many methodologies, and adopted several more. Like most of you, I am a lifelong learner who recognizes that as I continue to evolve and improve my knowledge and abilities as a coach, my athletes become the direct benefactors. As coaches, leaders, and educators, we are obligated to constantly upgrade our skills in every area that may contribute to the health, welfare, and improved performance of our athletes. This book is designed to support those obligations.

This book was written out of my desire to provide practical recommendations to coaches at all levels to assist in the design and implementation of safe and effective training programs that yield exceptional results. Our athletes deserve our best, and it is our responsibility to ensure that is exactly what we deliver.

My formal education includes two master's degrees, in applied sport science and nutrition science, along with a PhD in sport science. These formal learning opportunities have provided insights that I could not have gained solely in the trenches. The relationships I have developed with colleagues and the coaches with whom I have been blessed to work have all contributed to my development and continue to sharpen me as a coach.

Complete Conditioning for Football is the culmination of approximately 18 months of writing and a career spanning 26 years across both Division I college football and the NFL. Our entire performance team at Indiana University has poured countless hours into writing, reviewing, and bringing this project to life. Similar to the work we do with our athletes every day, this book has been a labor of love as we worked to deliver a logical, evidence-based resource for performance coaches at every level of competition. We want to provide coaches with a simple, easy-to-understand program that provides actionable steps to implement immediately within the existing performance program.

We left no stone unturned in describing and outlining every physiological characteristic that must be addressed when designing and implementing a performance program for football. Chapters 2 through 4 define and describe our approach to improving the linear speed, agility, and change-of-direction ability of athletes, and the chapters provide practical drills to address these areas. Chapters 5 through 7 outline specific resistance training methodologies to improve the strength and power of football players, with an entire chapter dedicated specifically to hypertrophy training. Comprehensive chapters on conditioning (chapter 8), nutritional strategies for peak performance (chapter 9), and training for athletes recovering from injury (chapter 10) are also included. We saved the best for last! Chapter 11 ties together all physical qualities, outlining a yearly training program for maximizing the performance of football players.

Complete Conditioning for Football is a user-friendly guide designed to optimally prepare football athletes in an evidence-based, progressive manner leading up to, and continuing throughout, the competitive season. It is our hope that this book not only makes an immediate positive contribution to your performance program but also will be a valuable resource and tool for you for years to come.

Chapter 1

Game Plan for Training

Our program's performance conditioning plan is system-based. We prefer to use the word *system* as opposed to *philosophy* to convey the dynamic and holistic nature of our training game plan. Our system is constantly evolving, consistently upgraded, and frequently evaluated. It is based on my 25 years of experience with Division I athletes and NFL players, the vast experience of our performance staff, countless conversations with colleagues, hundreds of books, thousands of research papers, and too many mistakes to count. Our system is informed by science and guided by best practice, and it places the needs of athletes before our own biases.

The principles underlying our approach are as follows:

- The program progresses throughout the year based on "what's important now." During phases that are farther away from the competition period, such as the winter off-season phase, we push athletes' performance ceilings higher and emphasize more general abilities such as maximal strength, linear acceleration, top speed, general aerobic endurance, and explosive power. As the competition period draws closer, it becomes more important to emphasize the qualities needed to sustain the loads imposed on the players in practice and in games, so the emphasis may shift more in favor of agility and change-of-direction training and specific endurance qualities that better resemble the actions of the football game while maintaining previously developed abilities.

- The training process should be monitored using objective measures. A coach can use several performance tests to monitor an athlete's progress against a goal, including tests for jump height, jump distance, sprint times, and strength testing, to name a few.

- Training with the same emphasis should not continue for so long that an athlete's adaptive reserves are depleted. Know when to de-load or modify the training stimulus.

- An athlete's buy-in to the system is critical to overall success.

- An athlete is limited by his body's ability to recover. Sleep, nutrition, and hydration are an athlete's three biggest allies in the recovery process.

- Training is intense by nature, but it does not have to be complex. Always program the minimum effective dose. Remember, the goal is to train optimally, not maximally.

This chapter is an overview of the key components that make up our training system from a philosophical and scientific view. Subsequent chapters will go into further detail as we discuss the specific exercises we incorporate as well as how we organize all these factors into one holistic training program that shifts as the year goes on.

PERIODIZING TRAINING EFFECTIVELY

Few sport performance dimensions are as discussed, debated, and enveloped in historical myth as periodization. Periodization is nothing more than a plan or road map—and even the most well-intentioned plans change. As performance coaches, we do not have a crystal ball. We cannot possibly predict the individual responses that may occur over an 8-week training program in our athletes. Professor and performance coach Mel Siff once described periodization as an exercise in stress management, and in many regards, this description is accurate.[1]

As performance coaches, we subject our athletes to stressors in the form of exercises, volumes, intensities, and frequencies. Subsequent stressors are typically then applied in a preprogrammed fashion for the duration of that particular block of training. If the optimal amount of stress is applied to each athlete, positive adaptation occurs in the form of increased performance, improved well-being, and reduced injury risk. If the stressors prove to be inappropriate, maladaptation manifests as a decrease in performance and an increased injury risk.

The periodization paradigm is built on the implicit assumption that mechanical loading parameters directly dictate training adaptations. Mechanical training stressors serve as the primary stimulus for adaptation; however, they are not the sole drivers of adaptation. All training programs, by nature, are incomplete. As coaches, clamoring that a "perfect" or even "best" periodization model exists is not realistic, unless humans respond to imposed training stress in predictable patterns and consistent time frames and can conform to predictable dose-response relationships.[2] Years of experience confirm that none of these suppositions are accurate.

As performance coaches, we must remember that the value of the training plan is interwoven with the athlete's perceptions, expectations, doubts, and beliefs associated with the plan. Training adaptations are influenced by the psycho-emotional constructs that are typically tied to the plan. While no "best practice" exists for periodized training, implementing a periodization model for planning purposes appears to have little downside, as long as we appreciate the constraints of any model and remain mindful of the errors, oversights, and misconceptions implicit in periodization's underpinnings.

The main goal of a training program is to improve the on-field performance of an athlete, so performance coaches must have a comprehensive understanding of each player's position-specific demands. Football is a high-intensity anaerobic sport, placing heavy demands on the athlete, and is characterized by brief, intense bursts of work during plays and short rest periods between plays. On-field success has its roots in technical and tactical skills and physical characteristics like speed, change-of-direction ability, strength, and power. Football players must possess an adequate aerobic capacity to provide power intermittently over a long duration and recover quickly in short intervals.

Players will need a high maximum anaerobic power so they can perform the powerful movements of repeated acceleration and deceleration throughout competitive games. These high-intensity movement demands, and the repeated blunt-force trauma during the high-impact collisions and repetitive contact inherent to the sport, provide additional stress unique to football.

While a plethora of periodization models exist, including linear, undulating, block, and conjugate, the single "best" periodization model does not exist. The "best" model is the one that fits the current needs of your situation and your athletes. As a coach, I've always struggled with the idea of labeling our periodization model. In football athletes, several physical qualities need to be developed concurrently. In our system, all physical qualities are trained throughout the calendar year. Consequently, training components are not completely removed; they simply get deemphasized at certain times of the year.

Regardless of the training methodology implemented, coaches are often constrained by external factors, including the number of athletes in each group, the time allotted for each session, the number of weekly training sessions, available equipment, and several other factors. The training program should be progressive and should have a general direction. This means that the plan should proceed logically, allowing each subsequent training period to build upon the period before.

MONITORING ATHLETES' RESPONSE TO TRAINING

Monitoring the training process involves not only objectively quantifying the volume and intensity of physical activity completed but also each athlete's response to the stress associated with training. Frequently monitoring the individual response to the training program provides a level of objectivity from which adjustments to the training program may be made.

We do not designate specific days for testing to be completed; the testing simply becomes part of the training program. On a day when we work up to a heavy set of 2-3 repetitions on a strength exercise like the bench press or squat, we may simply use velocity-based training (VBT) to measure the speed of the bar during the lift and take the fastest repetition of the set to determine the athlete's current 1-repetition training maximum. We will cover VBT in more detail in chapter 5.

If a coach does not have access to technology that accurately measures bar speed, an alternative such as repetitions in reserve (RIR) may be used to determine an athlete's training maximum on a given day. While RIR is a more subjective measure than bar velocity, an experienced coach or experienced lifter may be able to determine how many repetitions with a given load could have been performed. The closer to failure the athlete takes the set, the more accurately they can gauge an accurate number of RIR. Because of the inherent daily variability in athletic performance due to psychological and physiological fluctuations in sleep, stress, nutrition, and hydration, RIR provides a valid and cost-effective method of monitoring athlete progress. This is especially important during the in-season period when maximum strength testing may not be practical.

MODIFYING TRAINING APPROPRIATELY

No matter how well designed a training plan is on paper, modifications are typically made daily. In a team sport, there will always be players returning from an injury, players dealing with nagging tightness or pain, and players experiencing mobility-based restrictions. These are all areas of concern that may contraindicate some exercises for these players, so we will have to find a modification that allows them to train. In addition, we are always at the mercy of what occurs with our players when they are away from us or participating in activity beyond our control outside of football practice. So, it is our responsibility to consistently pay attention to the current state of our players and find ways to achieve desirable training outcomes. This may mean manipulating the overall training intensity or volume, exercise sequencing, or exercise modifications. However, we must also remember that too much change can result in negative consequences, such as adaptation stiffness, where a novel stimulus actually puts the body in an unfamiliar position and may result in increased tightness or soreness. So, there's always a delicate balance to modifying the training and ensuring that we stay on track and work around the potential setbacks as best we can.

GETTING ATHLETES TO BUY IN TO THE PROGRAM

Like the modification process, no matter how well designed a training plan is on paper, positive effects will be absent if the football players simply do not believe in the training regimen. We are constantly in a battle for every player's mind, body, and spirit, educating them in small chunks along the way so that they understand *why* we have them engage in certain activities. Additionally, we openly communicate to our players that our doors are always open and questions are welcome. Every player is keenly aware that they have the right to understand the purpose behind our protocols. Additionally, taking performance measures along the way and sharing those measures with the players allows them to see their own progress, which can have a significant positive impact for building buy-in. Overall, we want our athletes to understand that we are here for them as a support network and that their health, improvement, and well-being are our primary concerns.

PROMOTING POSITIVE ATHLETE SELF-CARE PRACTICES

Along with educating players on the whys of our program, we also aim to educate them about how to live a healthy lifestyle and take responsibility for their own recovery. As we will discuss in greater detail later, the two self-care practices that we preach ensure our players are aware that they need to aim for at least 7 hours of sleep each night and devote some time to considering their nutritional intake. Sleep and nutrition are at the top of our list for promoting positive athlete self-care practices. Additionally, we show our players ways that they can help manage their bodies daily by using targeted mobility, stretching, foam rolling, or other movement-based strategies to promote activation before training and practice as well as for cooling down after training and practice. Lastly, we aim to help our players pay attention to how they speak to themselves or to other people, how they carry themselves in terms of their body language, and the habits they build each day to ensure they are able to make it to all their appointments while still finding time for eating, hydrating, resting, and recovering.

CONCLUSION

Training is a long-term process for which no magical program exists. Individual, positional, and bioenergetic demands must be considered. The goal of training is to increase output, which means to improve and optimize all body systems, but most importantly to improve outputs of the specific movement, exercise, or sporting activity. It is important for the performance staff to identify the key objectives of the training program and the practical methods of monitoring the progress of these objectives to determine program efficacy and identify when modifications need to be made.

Chapter 2

Movement Preparation

Movement preparation involves preparing the body to perform a specific workload or set of activities. Commonly called a *warm-up*, movement preparation forms a key part of the overall structure for enabling athletes to perform at a high level. Along with helping prepare athletes for their training sessions and sports practices, the movement preparation period may also help reduce the chance of injury by properly activating and priming the body to perform work. Football is a very intense sport with high outputs of strength, power, and speed along with contact or collision, so injuries are a reality of the game. However, with proper movement preparation, some injury risks that come with playing the game may be mitigated because the body will be in a better state to perform the actions of the game.

Other key benefits of movement preparation include enhanced blood flow to the muscles through an increased heart rate, a rise in core body temperature, and an improvement in range of motion for the joints. As blood is pumped to the muscles, it helps promote tissue healing, which can improve pliability and allow it to move more seamlessly through different ranges of motion. This is vital because football will require various body postures and positions, some with a wide range of motion, depending on the specific movement being performed. It is our responsibility to ensure that our movement preparation exposes players to these different ranges as best as possible before they take part in subsequent training.

COACHING MOVEMENT PREPARATION

Movement preparation is not about just "going through the motions." It's an important part of the training process, so we have to be dialed in and enforce proper mechanics and body positions to help our players expand movement capacity. Movement preparation is largely based on enhancing player mobility, and we tell our players that mobility is a skill, just like strength, power, or speed. Thus, mobility must be trained purposefully and with intention. Just moving around aimlessly will do nearly nothing for developing broader ranges of movement.

Movement preparation can be a dynamic, living assessment each day. If players appear to struggle to attain the positions they are normally capable of attaining with little trouble, it may be a clue for us as coaches that the players are dealing with fatigue, soreness, mental stress, or some other form of under-recovery. So, we have to be mindful during the training session, even though it may only be 10-15 minutes. Every minute of it counts. So, it's important that we convey to the players that the movement preparation period is part of the training and should not be seen as "just a warm-up," where they see it as something outside the "actual training." Movement preparation is a skill.

FIELD-BASED MOVEMENT PREPARATION

Before starting a training session on the field, we have our players perform a field-based movement preparation routine. Typically, this will have three separate parts in a specific order:

1. Walking mobility
2. Ground-based mobility
3. Nervous system activation

Walking Mobility

Walking mobility has low-intensity, dynamic mobility exercises (meaning there is constant movement) that are used primarily to promote blood circulation, transport heat to the muscles of the arms and legs, and improve tissue pliability. Walking mobility is done at a designated distance that the coach determines. Each movement is usually performed for 10-15 yards, after which a 10- to 15-yard stride may be performed to further elevate heart rate and promote blood flow. Exercises follow that we will incorporate into this portion of the field-based movement preparation.

Knee Hugs

Knee hugs are a simple way to start improving hip extension mobility by challenging the athlete to remain in an upright, neutral posture as the arms hug one thigh toward the chest. The stance leg must remain straight and fully extended. If performed properly, the stance leg glute will be activated to promote hip extension while the hip flexors are extended and stretched.

Execution

1. Start standing upright, with the feet facing forward (see figure *a*).
2. Bend one knee and pull it up to the chest by hugging it with the arms (see figure *b*).
3. While hugging the knee, stay upright and stand tall without leaning or hunching.
4. Set that leg down and take 3 steps before hugging the opposite leg and repeating the same movement.
5. Continue until crossing the designated line.
6. Turn around and perform the next movement the opposite direction.

Figure 2.1   Knee hugs.

Leg Cradles

Leg cradles are similar to knee hugs, but the leg is turned into an external rotation of the hip so that the foot of the leg being lifted is tilted toward the stance leg. In this position, the athlete will put one hand under the heel or around the toes and the other hand under the knee and lift the leg up toward the chest to feel a stretch in the external rotator muscles of the hip. Again, it is paramount that the upper body remain upright and neutral during the execution of this exercise to maximize mobility benefits, so if athletes round at the spine, they will not only miss out on improving mobility but may be negatively affecting their posture and putting their spines and lower backs at risk.

Execution

1. Start standing upright, with the feet facing forward (see figure *a*).
2. Bring one leg up so it is parallel to the ground by grabbing the heel or toes with one hand and the knee with the other hand (see figure *b*).
3. While standing tall, pull the foot and ankle as high as possible.
4. After completing a repetition on one leg, take 3 steps and do the same thing with the opposite leg.
5. Continue until crossing the designated line.
6. Turn around and perform the next movement the opposite direction.

Figure 2.2   Leg cradles.

Straight-Leg Kicks

Straight-leg kicks are a simple way to improve the mobility of the hamstring muscle. Start with an upright, neutral posture and kick one leg up in the air, keeping both the kicking leg and the stance leg straight. This way, there is a big thigh separation between the swing leg and the stance leg, which, when performed properly, can open up the hamstring in the kicking leg while improving hip extension of the stance leg. If the athlete rounds the spine during this process, these benefits may not be achieved.

Execution

1. Start standing upright, with the feet facing forward and one leg staggered behind the body (see figure *a*).
2. While keeping the chest and shoulders upright, kick the rear leg up as high as possible with the opposite arm extended in front (see figure *b*).
3. After kicking one leg up, take 3 steps and do the same thing with the opposite leg.
4. Continue until crossing the designated line.
5. Turn around and perform the next movement the opposite direction.

Figure 2.3   Straight-leg kicks.

Reverse Lunge and Reach

The reverse lunge and reach improves hip extension mobility while also stretching the muscles along the lateral line of the body to improve trunk mobility. By reaching and fully extending the arms overhead and leaning away from the back knee, this lateral line is extended all the way from the knee to the fingertips and causes a pronounced hip extension stretch. Athletes who do not reach with extended arms or do not lean away from the back knee will not achieve this potent stretch and may not fully extend the hip. So, these are the focal points when coaching this exercise as part of movement preparation.

Execution

1. Start standing upright, with the feet facing forward (see figure *a*).
2. Step backward with one leg, dropping the back knee toward the ground by bending both legs. Then, fully extend the arms and lean the torso away from the rear leg to intensify the stretch in the hips (see figure *b*).
3. Push backward through the lead leg so that the feet come back together, then take 3 steps and do the same thing with the opposite leg.
4. Continue until crossing the designated line. No extra steps should be taken in between each lunge.
5. Turn around and perform the next movement the opposite direction.

Figure 2.4   Reverse lunge and reach.

Forward Hip Circles

Forward hip circles explore the end ranges of the hip joint through a rotational movement while standing upright and moving forward. The movement is initiated by extending the hip back and swinging the leg out to the side until it rotates all the way to the front. The athlete should be encouraged to maintain an upright, neutral posture while attempting to rotate the leg through as big of a range of motion as possible. Two coaching points that we use with this exercise are to have the athletes imagine they walk over an imaginary set of hurdles on either side of their bodies or think about drawing the biggest circle that they can with their kneecaps.

Execution

1. Start standing upright, with the feet facing forward and one leg staggered behind the body (see figure *a*).
2. Bring the rear leg up and out to the side of the body, keeping the toes dorsiflexed and driving the knee as high as possible (see figure *b*).
3. Keep the dorsiflexion in the toes and knee as high as possible while bringing the leg around to the front of the body (see figure *c*).
4. Place the foot back on the ground, then take 3 steps and do the same thing with the opposite leg.
5. Continue until crossing the designated line.
6. Turn around and perform the next movement the opposite direction.

Figure 2.5   Forward hip circles.

Backward Hip Circles

Backward hip circles have all the same benefits of forward hip circles, but the entire motion is done in reverse order. So, the movement is initiated by driving the knee forward and up in front of the body before swinging the leg out to the side of the body until it rotates into extension in the back. Again, the athlete should be encouraged to maintain an upright, neutral posture while attempting to rotate the leg through as big of a range of motion as possible.

Execution

1. Start standing upright with feet facing forward.
2. Bring one knee up in the air in front of the body.
3. With the toes dorsiflexed and the knee up in the air, circle the knee laterally to the side of the body.
4. Place the foot back on the ground, then take 3 steps and do the same thing with the opposite leg.
5. Continue until crossing the designated line.
6. Turn around and perform the next movement the opposite direction.

Quad Stretch and Reach

This exercise promotes flexibility around the knee and quadriceps in addition to adding extension through the torso. The athlete will use one hand to grab the same-side ankle with the leg bent and actively pull the knee into greater flexion. This is where the quad stretch will be felt. The opposite arm and hip are fully extended to provide a lengthening effect. It's important that the hips be extended during this exercise because the hip extension will increase the intensity of the quad stretch, which is desirable to properly warm up the knee.

Execution

1. Start standing upright, with the feet facing forward.
2. Bring the heel of one foot to the butt and grab it with the same-side hand.
3. With the opposite hand, reach up as high as possible.
4. While reaching up, push through the toes on the down foot, flexing the calf muscle and getting tall on the ball of the foot.
5. After performing one repetition on that leg, take 3 steps and do the same thing with the opposite leg.
6. Continue until crossing the designated line.
7. Turn around and perform the next movement in the opposite direction.

Lateral Lunge

The lateral lunge is used to emphasize various forms of mobility in the hips and ankles. The athlete will step out to the side and aim for a wide base of support between the feet, typically much wider than shoulder-width. The lead leg will achieve deep hip flexion, where the athlete shifts the center of mass backward through the hips before sitting down deep through the knees. At the same time, the lead foot should remain flat on the ground to challenge the dorsiflexion mobility of the ankle. The trailing leg will remain extended so that as the athlete sinks down through the lead leg, the trailing leg groin will be stretched. The torso should remain in a neutral posture, but as the hips drop down through the lead leg, the chest may begin to drop toward the ground. As long as the spine is kept in a neutral position, this will not be an issue and may be common for players who have very long legs relative to the length of their torsos.

Execution

1. Start standing upright with feet facing forward (see figure *a*).
2. Step out laterally to the side and bend the knee to sink into a squat position through the lead leg, with the rear leg extended (see figure *b*).
3. While lunging, keep the back flat and keep both heels on the ground.
4. Coming up, take a crossover step with the rear leg and repeat the lateral lunge action.
5. Repeat until crossing halfway, then face the opposite direction and repeat the lateral lunge movement until crossing the designated line.

Figure 2.6   Lateral lunge.

Ground-Based Mobility

The ground-based mobility portion of our field-based movement preparation is used for some of the body parts most important for mobility in football, like the hips, groin, and ankles. These areas tend to be problematic when athletes have major restrictions in these areas. So, by consistently touching on ground-based work for these areas, we can positively influence mobility capacity over time. The exercises are typically performed for time, 20-30 seconds for each exercise. The following are some of our favorite ground-based mobility activities.

90/90 Hip Rotations

These hip rotations promote external and internal rotation of the hips, the latter of which is a common restriction in our players and an important movement capacity requirement to properly extend the hips in activities like sprinting. Athletes should have a square shoulder and torso position so that the emphasis is on the movement at the hips, not compensations occurring when the trunk twists.

Execution

1. Sit on the ground with the legs bent at approximately 90 degrees, the feet flat on the ground, the arms behind the body, and the palms flat on the ground just behind the hips. The distance between the feet should be at least shoulder-width.

2. Keeping the shoulders square and the head facing forward, rotate one leg inward toward the body while rotating the opposite leg away from the body so that both knees drop to the ground in the same direction.

3. Lower the knees as close to the floor as possible while keeping the shoulders square. If trunk-rotating compensations occur, do not go beyond this point. Hold for 2-3 seconds at the end range of motion.

4. Continue keeping the shoulders square and reverse the motion of the legs in the opposite direction.

5. Repeat until the allotted time has expired.

Push-Up Position Alternating Groiners

Push-up position alternating groiners promote a combination of hip flexion with external rotation on one leg while promoting hip extension and internal rotation with the other. Being able to demonstrate adequate mobility in this exercise assures us as coaches that an athlete has the mobility to achieve full hip extension in actions like sprinting or changing direction at speed. It's important to look for how the trunk moves in relation to the hips and legs during this exercise. The hips should move independently of the trunk, where the trunk can maintain a neutral posture as the legs move back and forth. Athletes who are limited in this capacity will start to compensate at the trunk through a rounding of the spine, which is a dead giveaway that more mobility work needs to be done. This is another example of how movement preparation can serve as a consistent, dynamic movement screen.

Execution

1. Set up in a push-up position with the arms and legs extended, aiming for a straight-line posture from the base of the head down through the feet (see figure *a*).

2. Bring one foot forward by flexing the hip while keeping the back leg extended. The front foot should be placed on the ground right next to the hands to exhibit sufficient mobility (see figure *b*).

3. Once the foot is on the ground, the hips may be lowered slightly and the chest lifted up, maintaining neutral posture by emphasizing extension through the back leg and deeper flexion through the lead leg.

4. Return the front foot back to reset in a push-up position before moving the opposite leg forward in the same manner.

5. Continue alternating legs and repeat until the allotted time has expired.

Figure 2.7   Push-up position alternating groiners.

Push-Up Position Alternating Hip External Rotation

The push-up position alternating hip external rotation also promotes hip extension through the back leg but with a stronger focus on hip external rotation of the lead leg. As the lead leg comes forward, the leg is rotated so that the foot turns toward the midline of the body and the knee turns to the outside of the body before the leg rests down on the ground on the outside shin. Again, the hips should move independently of the trunk, where the trunk can maintain a neutral posture as the legs move back and forth.

Execution

1. Set up in a push-up position with the arms and legs extended, aiming for a straight-line posture from the base of the head down through the feet.

2. Bring one foot forward by flexing the hip while keeping the back leg extended. The front heel should rotate in toward the midline of the body while the knee rotates toward the outside. This is an external rotation motion of the hip. The lower leg is then placed on the ground on the outside shin in between the hands.

3. Once the leg is on the ground, the hips may be lowered slightly and the chest lifted up, maintaining neutral posture by emphasizing extension through the back leg and a deeper range of motion through the lead leg.

4. Return the front foot back to reset in a push-up position before moving the opposite leg forward in the same manner.

5. Continue alternating legs and repeat until the allotted time has expired.

Figure 2.8   Push-up position alternating hip external rotation.

Pike Position Calf and Ankle Mobilization

The pike position calf and ankle mobilization prioritizes ankle dorsiflexion mobility in addition to actively lengthening the calf muscle. Of all the ground-based mobility exercises we use, we perform this exercise for the shortest duration, typically only for 10 seconds on each side. We want to ensure we get some activation and lengthening at the calf and ankle but not too much because that could negatively affect field-based activities like sprints or plyometrics. Those exercises are based on a spring-like stiffness at the ankle. But, of course, too much stiffness is a problem as well, so we have found that 10 seconds on each foot is sufficient as long as the player is actively and intensely driving the heel to the ground during the stretch portion of the exercise.

Execution

1. Set up in a push-up position with the arms and legs extended, aiming for a straight-line posture from the base of the head down through the feet.
2. From here, lift the hips up into the air while actively driving through the palms to fold the body up into the pike position, where the heels flatten to the ground.
3. Cross one leg over the other and drive through the ball of the foot on the stance leg.
4. Once the heel is fully lifted off the ground, drive it back down to the ground in a controlled manner until the heel is fully on the ground.
5. Repeat until the allotted time has expired and then switch legs.

Figure 2.9　Pike position calf and ankle mobilization.

Nervous System Activation

The nervous system activation part of the field-based movement preparation is used to activate the central nervous system with more intensive exercises that feature higher speed and power outputs. The goal is to build off the enhanced movement ranges of the walking and ground-based mobility routines and essentially "wake the body up" by stimulating the legs before moving into an intense field-training session to follow. Each of these exercises should be performed for 10-15 yards before aggressively accelerating into a sprint for an additional 10-15 yards. The following exercises are incorporated into this portion of the field-based movement preparation.

A-Skip

The A-skip is one of the most basic drills incorporated into a sprinting-based warm-up and is used to build a sense of coordination, timing, and rhythm using postures that emulate those found in high-speed running. The contact of the feet into the ground should be "springy" and "bouncy" where the athlete appears to be at peace but also exhibits aggressive power into the ground through the ball of the foot. As the legs move back and forth in relation to each other, the ground force application should also be quick and efficient, timing up well with the flexing of the opposite thigh in one swift movement when the stance leg extends. The relation of the movements in the hips and legs with the arms is an important one, and they should interact in an opposite and reciprocal fashion—the right arm and left leg move to the front of the body together and vice versa for the opposite limbs. If the coordination, rhythm, or timing is off, then the exercise will not be performed in a way that properly activates the nervous system. However, these are relatively complicated to master for an athlete who lacks experience performing this drill, so patience and time are also required by us as coaches when implementing this drill.

Execution

1. Start standing upright, with the feet facing forward (see figure *a*).
2. With a slight forward lean and the chest over the ball of the foot, drive one of the knees up to at least waist high, keeping the ankle dorsiflexed (see figure *b*).
3. Once the bottom leg is fully extended and the opposite leg is above the waist, drive the top leg down to the ground behind the center of mass, putting force into the ground to propel forward (see figure *c*).

4. Once the top leg drives through the ground, drive the opposite leg up above the waist and repeat the steps until reaching the prescribed destination (see figure *d*).

Figure 2.10   A-skip.

Straight-Leg Skip

The straight-leg skip is performed with the same rhythm and timing of the A-skip, but instead of bending at the knee as the lead leg is driven toward the front of the body, the lead leg stays straight. So, only the hip will flex as the leg comes forward. Again, attacking down and back into the ground through the ball of the foot is the objective when propelling forward, and the athlete should not strike the heel first. This is a coordination challenge because the athlete may intuitively assume that the heel hits first since the leg is extended. We must coach the athlete to achieve enough "bounce" from the previous ground contact to attain the necessary flight time to get the leg under the body and prepare to land on the ball of the foot first.

Execution

1. Start standing upright, with the feet facing forward.
2. With a slight forward lean and the chest over the ball of the foot, keep one leg straight and kick it forward at least waist high while the bottom leg extends at the hip, knee, and ankle (see figure *a*).
3. Once the bottom leg is fully extended and the opposite leg is above the waist, drive the top leg down to the ground below the center of mass (see figure *b*).
4. Once the top leg drives through the ground, drive the opposite leg up above the waist (see figure *c*).
5. Repeat the steps until reaching the prescribed destination.

Figure 2.11   Straight-leg skip.

Shuffle Jacks

Shuffle jacks are very simple in appearance and in execution, but they can serve a potent function to activate the outside muscles of the hips and the muscles around the ankle complex, and get some more movement through the upper body to activate the muscles around the shoulder girdle. When coaching this exercise, we emphasize not letting their heels click together so that the athletes achieve an effective lateral push and maintain an athletic base in terms of how their feet are aligned in relation to their hips. If the feet are always around hip-width or slightly wider, the athlete can theoretically move or accelerate in any direction out of that base. If the feet contact each other, it will be much more difficult to have coordination and rhythm because the athlete may then trip or stumble. We also emphasize a big arm swing so that we ensure the shoulder is properly activated and a dynamic stretching effect takes place.

Execution

1. Start standing upright, facing perpendicular to the starting line so that the initiation of movement will be to the side instead of to the front (see figure *a*).
2. Shuffle laterally while moving the arms in a jumping jack movement (see figures *b-c*).
3. Continue until reaching the prescribed destination.

Figure 2.12 Shuffle jacks.

Carioca

The carioca exercise is used to train coordination, rhythm, and timing in multiple planes. The athlete will be moving laterally (to the side), and the hips will rotate both to the left and to the right. Although the specific execution of the exercise and the muscle firing patterns differ from the A-skip or other rhythmic drills that are performed linearly, the intent for the athlete is similar. For example, when the knee drives up and forward in an A-skip, the opposite leg is extended and pressed powerfully into the ground. A similar phenomenon occurs in the carioca as one leg is driven up and across the body, leading with the knee, while the other leg extends and pushes the body laterally in a crossover pattern. Therefore, the rhythm and timing are largely the same, but the coordination changes. Helping our players find these areas of connection between various movements is another bonus of taking the time to really coach during the movement preparation period.

Execution

1. Start standing upright, facing perpendicular to the starting line so that the initiation of movement will be to the side instead of to the front (see figure *a*).
2. While standing tall and not hunching, cross the rear leg behind the body, allowing the hips to rotate but keeping the torso and gaze facing forward (see figure *b*).
3. Reposition the lead leg back to the side of the body and press it down into the ground, extending the hip and pushing the body to the side as the rear leg knee is driven up and across the midline of the body (see figures *c-d*).
4. When landing on the crossing swing leg, push toward the other leg to momentarily uncross the legs.
5. Repeat the steps of the entire cycle until reaching the prescribed destination.

Figure 2.13 Carioca.

Backward Run

The backward run helps athletes develop coordination using another movement solution (moving backward), which is more common for defensive players like cornerbacks, safeties, and linebackers but serves as a nice variation to develop general movement literacy for all athletes. This exercise also helps activate the muscles around the knees and shins, which are largely important for deceleration and change of direction, so it's imperative that we promote nervous system activation and blood flow to these areas before participating in a field-based training session.

Execution

1. Start standing with knees slightly bent and the torso tilted slightly forward while maintaining a neutral spinal posture (see figure *a*).
2. Bring the heel of one foot to the butt, then extend it out (see figure *b*).
3. With the opposite foot, push up and backward off the ball of the foot.
4. Land on the ball of the foot and repeat with the other heel (see figure *c*).
5. Continue until reaching the prescribed destination.

Figure 2.14 Backward run.

High-Knee Run

The high-knee run is used to activate the muscles of the posterior chain (e.g., glutes, hamstrings, and calves) to perform work powerfully in a "bouncy" or "spring-like" fashion to replicate the positions and ground-contact times of upright, high-speed running. We emphasize driving the lead knee up to where the thigh should be approximately at the same height as the front of the hip as the stance leg extends powerfully into the ground. The pelvis should remain in a neutral position, facing forward and not tilting down toward the ground. As the athlete pushes into the ground with each step, the hip height should not drop, something commonly seen when athletes have poor reactive strength and start to buckle at the knee or at the ankle. The legs should scissor back and forth with speed but not at the expense of achieving the proper range of motion when flexing and extending at the hips. The arms should swing naturally in relation to the legs, as they would during high-speed running. Performing this exercise properly daily during movement preparation can have a significant positive effect on high-speed running mechanics over time, so it's imperative that coaches pay attention to how it's being performed.

Execution

1. Start standing upright, with the feet facing forward (see figure *a*).
2. Using proper running mechanics, accelerate away from the line and drive the knee forward and the heel toward the butt.
3. Keep an upright torso without leaning or hunching.
4. Continue this action, alternating swiftly from one leg to the next until crossing the designated finish line (see figures *b-c*).

Figure 2.15 High-knee run.

WEIGHT ROOM MOVEMENT PREPARATION

The movement preparation in the weight room activates the body for training and features high levels of muscle tension against substantial resistance. The bulk of the work done in a weight room is based on developing muscular strength and hypertrophy with slower movements that allow the athlete to consciously focus on generating muscular tension. So, in the movement preparation period, we aim to use a similar strategy with more rudimentary movements and exercises where we want our players to really lock in mentally and feel what their body is doing, how their muscles fire, and what positions they exhibit.

Upper-Body Weight Room Preparation

The upper-body weight room preparation typically means using various body weight, low-resisted, or band-resisted movements to prepare the muscle groups around the shoulder, elbow, and wrist joints. In particular, the muscles around the rotator cuff are targeted as well as exposing the anterior shoulder and pectoral muscles to tension and stretch before performing heavy pressing exercises. Here are a few examples of upper-body weight room preparation exercises that we include in our program.

Push-Up Plank Shoulder Taps

Push-up plank shoulder taps are used to activate the muscles of the anterior shoulder while also activating the core in an anti-rotational manner, meaning that the athlete has to stay strong through the trunk to prevent rotational swaying as one arm comes off the ground at a time. We like to incorporate this exercise before moving into some form of horizontal press during the main training session.

Execution

1. Start with arms locked in a push-up position.
2. Keep the arms underneath the shoulders and feet about shoulder-width apart.
3. Raise one hand up and tap the opposite shoulder.
4. Pause for about a 2-second count, then place the hand back on the ground in the push-up position.
5. Repeat with the other hand and continue alternating until the designated time or reps are completed.

Isometric Push-Up Hold

The isometric push-up hold is used to challenge shoulder stability in a deep-range shoulder extension pattern, as seen at the bottom of a bench press. In this position, the pectoral muscles will be stretched but the isometric component indicates that the athlete has to actively hold this joint position for a given time period, typically for 20-30 seconds. In this way, the athlete is challenged to find strength and stability through the pectoral muscles while they are in a lengthened state, which can have a positive effect on nervous system activation when moving into a horizontal pressing motion during the main training session. The core also has to stay engaged to fully stabilize the trunk so that the hips stay in line with the shoulders and do not drop excessively to the floor or rise excessively into the air.

Execution

1. Start with the arms locked in a push-up position.
2. Keep the arms underneath the shoulders and the feet about shoulder-width apart.
3. Lower the chest to approximately 3 inches from the ground.
4. Hold that position for the designated time, usually 20-30 seconds.

Figure 2.16   Isometric push-up hold.

Plate Halos

Plate halos are performed with a 25-pound weight plate and are used to activate the muscles around the shoulders and upper back. The aim is for the athlete to keep the head still and achieve the rotational movement by using the arms, not compensating by swaying at the trunk or neck. One cue that we use is to move the plate around the head; don't move the head around the plate. If performed properly, this exercise can help promote blood flow and heating of the tissues associated with overhead shoulder positions, so it can be beneficial to incorporate before overhead or incline pressing exercises in the main training session.

Execution

1. Start with holding the designated weight plate in front of the face.
2. Going in one direction, circle the head with the plate, starting with passing the ear, going around to the back of the head toward the other ear, and back to the front of the face.
3. Continue for the designated time or reps, usually 15-20 seconds or 4-5 reps.
4. Once the time or reps is completed, repeat in the opposite direction.

Plate Cuban Press

The plate Cuban press is used to activate the muscles of the rotator cuff as well as perform a pressing motion to prepare the shoulder joints for any overhead or incline pressing movements to follow. A weight plate is held in each hand—typically 5-pound plates, but 10-pound plates may be used with stronger athletes and 2.5-pound plates may be used for athletes who need rotator cuff strength development. The two biggest mistakes made in this exercise are allowing the elbows to drop below the shoulders and letting the wrists bend backward. When pulling and rotating the arms, a 90-degree elbow bend should be maintained except when extending into the press overhead. Also, the wrists should be kept in a straight line with the forearms so that the work is emphasized at the shoulder joint, not allowing for energy leaks by breaking at the wrist.

Execution

1. Start with the arms down to the sides, palms facing back. Hold a 5-pound plate in each hand (see figure *a*).
2. Bring the elbows up toward the ceiling until the elbows are at 90 degrees (see figure *b*).

3. Rotate at the shoulders, keeping the elbows at 90 degrees until the palms face forward (see figure *c*).
4. Press the 5-pound plates up by extending the arms straight up in the air (see figure *d*).
5. Lower the elbows down to 90 degrees, the palms now facing forward.
6. Rotate at the shoulders, keeping the elbows at 90 degrees until the palms face backward.
7. Lower the weight to the starting position.
8. Repeat for the designated reps, usually 8-12.

Figure 2.17   Plate Cuban press.

Plate Incline T-Y-W

The plate incline T-Y-W exercise series activates the posterior muscles of the rotator cuff as well as the upper back in various positions. In our program, we emphasize horizontal and vertical pulling exercises like dumbbell row and chin-up variations, and we enforce proper positioning of the shoulder blades to maximize the tension across the back muscles. For an athlete with poor posterior rotator cuff strength, this can be challenging, so including posterior rotator cuff exercises like the plate incline T-Y-W in each movement preparation routine can help develop this strength over time.

Execution

1. Set a bench to a 30-degree incline.
2. Lay facedown with a 5-pound weight plate in each hand.
3. Raise the arms straight out to the side with the thumbs up toward the ceiling (see figure *a*).
4. Pause for a 2- to 3-second count, then lower the arms while controlling the movement to the starting position.
5. Continue for the designated reps, usually 6-10.
6. After performing incline Ts, stay facedown on the bench. With a 5-pound weight in each hand, raise the arms toward the head at a 45-degree angle, with the thumbs up. This should look like the letter *Y* (see figure *b*).
7. Pause for a 2- to 3-second count, then lower the arms while controlling the movement to the starting position.
8. Continue for the designated reps, usually 6-10.
9. After performing incline Ys, stay facedown on the bench. With a 5-pound weight in each hand, drive the elbows up until they are 90 degrees and parallel to the ground (see figure *c*). Rotate at the shoulders until the palms face the floor, keeping the elbows at 90 degrees (see figure *d*). Rotate back to the elbows at 90 degrees and parallel to the ground. Return to the starting position.
10. Continue for the designated reps, usually 6-10.

Figure 2.18   Plate incline T-Y-W.

Lower-Body Weight Room Preparation

The lower-body weight room preparation typically means using various body weight, low-resisted, or band-resisted movements to prepare the muscle groups around the hip, knee, and ankle joints. In particular, the muscles around the glutes are targeted and expose the hip flexors and calf and ankle complex to tension and stretching before performing heavy squatting, lunging, or hinging exercises. Here are a few examples of lower-body weight room preparation exercises that we include in our program.

Isometric Split Squat Hold

The isometric split squat hold is used to challenge the stability of the hips, knees, and ankles in a deep-range hip flexion and extension pattern, as seen at the bottom of a deep lunge. In this position, the back leg hip flexor muscles will be stretched, but the isometric component indicates that the athlete has to actively hold this joint position for a given time, typically 20-30 seconds. The calf and Achilles of the lead leg and the feet and toes of the back leg will be stretched in a similar manner. In this way, the athlete is challenged to find strength and stability through the hips, knees, ankles, and feet while they are in a lengthened state, which can have a positive nervous system activation effect when moving into deep-range resistance exercises like a barbell lunge or barbell squat. The core also has to stay engaged to fully stabilize the trunk so that the hips stay in a neutral posture in a split position, whereas an unstable athlete will tend to sway to the side.

Execution

1. Start in a split squat with the front heel under the hips and the back knee on the ground about 6 inches behind the front heel.
2. Drive the front knee toward the front toe and lift the back knee 1-3 inches off the ground while keeping the hips and torso in a neutral position.
3. Hold that position for 30 seconds while keeping the hands off the legs. Keep the chest up and shoulders back.
4. Perform on each leg.

Figure 2.19 Isometric split squat hold.

Cook Hip Lift

The Cook hip lift is a basic exercise to isolate and activate the gluteal muscles of the leg on the ground. By hugging one leg in toward the chest, the range of motion is restricted to keep the low back from hyperextending, which helps to better isolate the gluteal muscles. Engaging this muscle group can help prime the body for primary lower-body exercises like barbell squats, Romanian deadlifts, hip thrusts, lunges, or any other lower-body strength exercise.

Execution

1. Lie on the back with the feet flat on the floor.
2. Raise one knee up toward the chest as high as possible and hold the leg in that position with the arms (see figure *a*).
3. With the down foot, push down on the ground with the whole foot, dispersing even pressure from the heel to the ball of the foot.
4. Extend the hips off the ground while squeezing the glutes and keeping the core tight at the top position (see figure *b*).
5. Hold at the top position for 2-3 seconds.
6. Lower the hips back to the bottom position.
7. Continue for the designated number of reps, usually 8-10.
8. When finished, repeat with the opposite side.

Figure 2.20   Cook hip lift.

Mini Band 3-Way Hip External Rotation

The mini band 3-way hip external rotation activates the gluteal muscles, primarily the external rotators of the hip. Much like bridging movements (e.g., Cook hip lift), engaging this muscle group can help prime the body for primary lower-body exercises like barbell squats, Romanian deadlifts, hip thrusts, lunges, or any other lower-body strength exercise.

Execution

1. Place a mini band around both knees.
2. Stand with the feet shoulder-width apart and slightly bend the knees.
3. Keep the chest upright and the shoulders back, and maintain good posture.
4. With the feet flat on the ground, rotate the left knee outward without lifting the foot.
5. Hold the outward position for 1-2 seconds while squeezing the glutes.
6. Next control the knee back to the starting position.
7. Once finished with one leg, do the same with the other leg.
8. For the last variation, rotate both knees outward simultaneously without lifting the feet.
9. Hold the outward position for 1-2 seconds while squeezing the glutes and then control the movement of the knees back to the starting position.
10. Do each variation for the designated number of reps, usually 8-12.

Figure 2.21   Mini band 3-way hip external rotation.

PREPRACTICE AND PREGAME MOVEMENT PREPARATION

The prepractice movement preparation routine that we incorporate is one that has to fit within a 10-minute window because this is the time that our coaching staff provides for us to warm up our players. So, we have to consider the minimal effective dose of how to prime our players' bodies for the next activity in the practice script. Fortunately, in football, the practice periods that tend to follow the movement preparation period are those associated with individual skills and drills that serve as a nice, extended primer for the more intensive periods of practice, where players will interact with each other in units and as a team.

In our program, the prepractice warm-up will be very similar to any field-based movement preparation routine, except that we rearrange the order of the parts to the following:

1. Walking mobility + nervous system activation
2. Ground-based mobility

We use the combination of walking mobility and nervous system activation for heart rate elevation and overall stimulatory effect so the players' bodies essentially "wake up" before we put them on the ground to mobilize their warmed tissues and give them an opportunity to regain some control of their breathing and allow their heart rates to decrease and stabilize. In this way, we aim to have them feeling flushed and fresh when entering the remainder of the practice session. So, our typical prepractice movement preparation routine will look like the following:

Walking Mobility + Nervous System Activation

1. Hip circles—15 yards forward, 15 yards backward
2. Lateral lunge—10 yards left, 10 yards right, then stride 10 yards
3. Shuffle jacks—15 yards left, turn, then 15 yards right
4. A-skip + straight-leg skip—15 yards + 15 yards
5. Carioca left—15 yards, turn, then stride 15 yards
6. Carioca right—15 yards, turn, then stride 15 yards
7. Backward run—30 yards
8. Walking straight-leg kicks—15 yards, then stride 15 yards
9. High-knee run—30 yards
10. Two-point start—15 yards sprint, maintain speed for another 15 yards (see chapter 3)

Ground-Based Mobility

1. 90/90 hip rotations—20-30 seconds
2. Push-up position alternating hip external rotation—alternate legs for 20-30 seconds
3. Pike position calf and ankle mobilization—10 seconds each side
4. Push-up position alternating groiners—alternate legs for 20-30 seconds

For pregame movement preparation, we use the same prepractice movement preparation routine, but the main difference is that we may incorporate some preparation exercises in the locker room before going out to the field. These exercises will resemble the ones we use before our weight training sessions before a lower-body resistance training session. So, we may have our players perform some work to activate the gluteal muscles, like the Cook hip lift or mini band 3-way hip external rotation. Our reason for incorporating these exercises as a sort of premovement preparation is to help dial in our players' focus by giving them some basic, familiar activities on which to concentrate and hopefully reduce some excessive psychological anxiety associated with game day. Additionally, the players will be wearing game-day uniforms that are never worn in practice, so it gives the players more time to adjust to the fit and feeling of the game uniforms before they take the field. We are always looking for ways to be mindful and help our players have the best physical and psychological readiness on game day.

CONCLUSION

In summary, the movement preparation periods are designed to help stimulate the body for the primary work that follows. Whether this is work done in a field-based training session or a weight room training session, we have to be mindful of how to prepare and prime the body to enter a favorable state to maximize each part of the session. It's also important to monitor *how* these exercises are performed, knowing the proper positions, postures, muscles to be worked, and the desired feelings and experiences of the athlete rather than simply going through the motions to fill up time. In our view, the movement preparation doesn't have to be too complicated, but it does have to be purposeful, coached properly, and considered a vital component of the entire training process.

Chapter 3

Speed Training

In the past, football was played in a fairly constricted area with run-heavy offensive schemes like the Pro Set, Power I, Wishbone, T-Formation, and others that were characteristic of players crowding around the line of scrimmage. During that era, players had less space to cover, and the biggest, strongest, and most powerful players were typically the most productive. Now, football is much more dynamic. Spread offenses send players across the whole field, and defenses are forced to counter them. This evolution has put pressure on players to move faster than ever, from sideline to sideline and vertically up the field. Speed is now an essential asset in our sport.

Many football plays result in players covering less than 30 yards, so most speed efforts involve acceleration and not top speed. This is why coaches keep track of "explosive plays," statistics for how many offensive plays go for 20 yards or more. It's understood that these plays are rare and influence the score of the game. However, when an explosive play opportunity arises, it is crucial for players to be able to call on their top speed capability to dominate in these moments. Thus, while acceleration will make up most of the work when training for speed qualities in football, top speed preparation cannot be ignored.

The only way to truly improve speed performance is to expose players to sprinting. Sprinting at maximal effort is arguably the most intensive exercise that the human body can perform. It's vital for us to understand how to build the capacity in our players so they can handle high-speed running. In this chapter, we will identify the biomechanical aspects of acceleration and top speed, how to test and monitor these qualities, and how to program to develop them.

COACHING ACCELERATION AND SPEED

Acceleration is at the forefront of speed training considerations because every position on the field will require great acceleration ability. The differences in positions will be based on *how far* the player needs to accelerate based on positional tasks. For example, an offensive lineman may only need to accelerate within a 5-yard area throughout the game. On the other hand, a wide receiver may far exceed this distance on explosive offensive plays or when covering and returning kicks and punts. So, every position must learn to effectively accelerate, but the player position will determine how much overall sprint training is necessary.

During acceleration, when the foot touches the ground, the angle of the shin tells a clear story of how well a player can accelerate forward. We look for a positive shin angle, a position where the knee is ahead of the toe when the foot touches the ground. A positive shin angle indicates that the "push" back into the ground will effectively project the player's body forward in a horizontal direction, which is desirable during acceleration. A positive shin angle can be seen in figure 3.1.

When the knee is instead over or behind the foot, this is a negative shin angle. This common mistake is found in an athlete who has not been properly trained in sprinting and who believes he must attain his stride length by reaching out with the foot rather than pushing back through the hip. In this case, the player will land more on the heel than the ball of the foot, putting tremendous strain on the hamstring and risking injury. Figure 3.2 shows an athlete with this fault.

In addition to shin angle, it's important to transmit force and power generated at the hip down through the foot and into the ground with each step. If a player has weak ankles and feet, the ankle will collapse on

Figure 3.1 Positive shin angle when transmitting force into the ground.

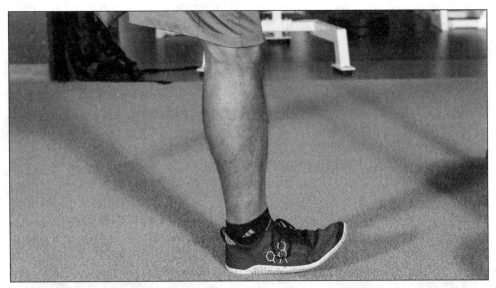

Figure 3.2 Reaching out with the lead foot, leading to heel striking and more negative shin angle on ground contact.

ground contact, dissipating energy that would otherwise be used to add to the propulsion. To accelerate at a high level, a player must have strong ankles on ground contact.

Another acceleration skill is the ability to rapidly switch or "scissor" the legs back and forth after each push-off. This thigh-switching speed ties in to expansion and contraction, which is illustrated in figure 3.3. Expansion means that when the athlete pushes through the ground to accelerate his body forward, he expands his arms and legs through big ranges of motion. The trail leg is extended to near maximal extension, ideally falling into a straight line from the top of his head, through his torso and hips, and on down through to the ball of the foot. At the same time, the opposite leg drives forward, leading with the knee, until the thigh is approximately at the level of the hip in front of the body and the foot sits underneath the top of the hamstring in a positive shin angle. Thus, there is a wide split between the thighs, as illustrated by the points of the triangle in frames 1, 3, and 5 in figure 3.3.

Once the back foot leaves the ground, contraction becomes the focal point, which refers to the thighs rapidly closing back in toward each other to prepare for the next ground contact. In figure 3.3, this is illustrated by the points of the triangle in frames 2, 4, and 6. The triangle points in the frames of expansion remain constant, and the triangles in the frames of contraction become more condensed with each step, indicating that the athlete is scissoring the thighs faster with each step, which is ideal.

Many football players struggle with effective thigh movement and tend to push too much, as figure 3.4 illustrates. Here, the athlete forces himself to stay low and tries to attain each sprint stride by reaching out in front of his body rather than pushing back and down into the ground. The points of the triangle are nearly the same in every frame, indicating that the athlete is stuck in a perpetual cycle of expansion with no contraction. This not only leads to poor performance but also puts tremendous strain on the hamstrings and can risk injury.

The movement principles of acceleration and top speed will tend to overlap, but the movement displays will be different. This difference is because the body should naturally rise to an upright position as the athlete achieves greater sprinting speeds. Therefore, when force is put into the ground at high speeds, it will be mostly downward, whereas it is more

Figure 3.3 Good expansion and contraction from step to step in early acceleration.

Figure 3.4 Expansion without contraction, leading to poor performance and excessive strain on the hamstrings.

"down and back" during acceleration. When entering top speed, proper technique is crucial for not only enhancing speed performance but also reducing the risk of soft-tissue injury. Common biomechanical aberrations seen in football players who sprint at top speed include the following:

- *A pelvis that is rotated too much toward the ground.* A common display of this is a "duck butt" position, where the athlete is overarching or forcing a forward lean instead of being upright with a neutral posture.
- *Too much butt-kicking behind the body.* The heel collides with the buttocks far behind the midline of the body, presenting a "butt kicking" technical fault. This tells us that the athlete is trying to "push" down the field too much rather than "bouncing" down the field at top speed.
- *Not enough front side lift.* The knee of the lead leg does not approach the height of the hip as the leg swings through to the front side of the body.
- *Overstriding by casting the foot out in front of the hips.* The athlete won't be able drive the foot down as effectively and will strike with the heel first rather than the ball of the foot.
- *A collapse of the ankle, knee, and hip on ground contact.* If the ankle, knee, and hip lack the elastic strength and coordination as a unit, they will collapse and force will dissipate rather than being transmitted through the ground.

The sequence in figure 3.5 is an example of an athlete showing inefficient mechanics when running at high speed (e.g., a segment between 30 and 40 yd of maximal effort sprinting). Notice the previously mentioned factors that are present, such as casting the foot out and leading with the heel and not enough front side lift.

Figure 3.5 Inefficient mechanics at high running speeds—anterior pelvic tilt, excessive butt-kicking behind the body, casting out with the lead foot.

Instead, we want to see athletes sprinting at top speed with the following:

- *An upright, neutral posture.* The pelvis is facing forward, allowing for efficient hip movement.
- *Less butt-kicking behind the body.* The trail leg should extend backward just enough to allow for a powerful "bounce" into the ground before moving forward again.
- *More front side lift.* The knee should be in line with the hip at the end of the forward leg movement and the thigh is near parallel to the ground.
- *The foot driving down into the ground under the hips.* The foot should not cast out too far in front of the hips. Contact should be on the ball of foot.
- *Stiff, powerful ground contact.* The ankle, knee, and hip should not excessively deform, ensuring that the power being generated at the hip can successfully transmit through the knee, ankle, and foot into the ground.

The sequence in figure 3.6 shows an athlete with efficient mechanics at top speed. We can see a more neutral posture and more front side lift.

Figure 3.6   Efficient mechanics at high running speeds—neutral pelvis, greater front side lift, and striking the ground near the center of mass.

All the efficient mechanics at top speed coincide with each other. So, proper posture and pelvic position allow the hips to properly extend and achieve front side lift. The front side lift allows the foot to attack down and back into the ground. Sprinting properly over time will help develop the requisite timing of the hip, knee, and ankle so they don't collapse on ground contact. These factors help athletes sprint more efficiently at high speeds, reducing the strain on muscles like the hamstrings, hip flexors, and groin. When performed properly, athletes look like they are bouncing down the field rather than forcefully straining their way.

Resisted Sprinting

Resisted sprinting is a simple and effective way to improve horizontal strength, power, and early acceleration. For players to accelerate, they have to overcome their own body weight and other forces like gravity and inertia to propel themselves forward. The strongest and most powerful players in the horizontal plane will be the best accelerators. This is exactly what resisted sprinting aims to improve. Resistance can be a plate-loaded sled or other specialized pieces of equipment like cable or rope systems that resist against the athlete when they sprint straight ahead with speed. Another common practice is sprinting up a hill, where gravity provides the resistance. Coaches may incorporate whatever equipment they may have available to them.

The next question is always how much resistance should be used. Well, the answer is based on what you're trying to improve. For example, traditional track and field practices incorporate loads that are somewhere between 10% and 20% of body weight on the sled, or a load that corresponds to about 90% of highest unloaded speed for a given distance. The idea is to slow the athlete down enough to allow him to feel some friction but still be able to hit relatively high speeds and keep his technique intact. This can be very effective for improving mid to late acceleration, and the resistance allows the player to continue applying horizontal force into the ground for longer periods of time before getting fully upright.

However, lately, much heavier resisted loads are incorporated to maximize the very early acceleration capability of football players (e.g., first three steps or first 5 yd). The idea is that we can expose players to the environment of a very short sprint, like 5 yards, and spread it out over 10-15 yards by using very heavy resistance to keep them in an exaggerated forward lean like that seen in the first few steps of unloaded acceleration. This can give players more exposure to high horizontal forces and challenge them to produce the necessary acceleration to overcome those forces with speed.

In these cases, when using a plate-loaded sled, the additional load may be as heavy as between 80% and 100% of body weight. So, for a 200-pound player, the load may be 160-200 pounds of resistance. It should be noted that going this heavy has a very specific purpose: to improve maximum horizontal strength and power during early acceleration. If a coach expects to see massive increases in top speed from using very heavy resistance, they may be disappointed.

Acceleration Sprinting

While there are great benefits to using resisted sprinting for football players, it is simply not logical to exclusively use resistance when aiming to improve player speed outputs. Ideally, unloaded acceleration will be included throughout the entire training cycle so that players are able to experience their bodies moving freely in space and can begin to coordinate their sprinting with any increases they attain in strength, power, or mobility.

Given that sprinting is a complex skill and that most positions in football (perhaps with the exception of the offensive line) will use it during the game, it's necessary to take the time to practice improving it. And there's simply no other way for the human body to generate the same intensity of movement speed than when sprinting in a straight line. Unloaded acceleration provides a potent training stimulus for the body. It's especially important for young male athletes during junior high to high school (e.g., 11-17 years old) because this has been shown to be a very sensitive period in the natural development of movement speed and explosive abilities.[1] However, the improvement of speed as a skill may continue well beyond high school.

So, we can have players perform unloaded accelerations of various distances (typically ≤30 yd) and progress by using shorter distances (e.g., 5-15 yd) during the early phases of a training program and gradually progress toward longer sprint efforts (e.g., 20-30 yd) as the program unfolds. This allows the players to adapt to ever-increasing speeds and intensities in a natural progression. Some positions, like offensive line or interior defensive linemen, may not need to exceed 15-20 yards per effort due to the demands of the position. It may be better to spend additional training time getting faster at shorter distances because this will be more like what they do in the game.

We can also have the players perform sprints from various positions, such as standing, kneeling, from a 3-point stance, or lying facedown on the ground. To add more variety, these same positions can be performed facing forward, to the side, or to the rear, with the latter two requiring the athletes to turn the body before accelerating forward. Varying the starting positions can help replicate the variety of positions that may occur while playing football and teach the players to coordinate themselves and accelerate their bodies from various angles.

Top Speed Sprinting

Top speed training is different from acceleration training because an athlete can accelerate over a given distance at maximum intensity, but the movement speed attained may not be the athlete's top speed capability. For example, if a wide receiver sprints at full speed for 10 yards but needs at least 30 yards to reach his top speed, then it doesn't matter how many 10-yard sprints he performs because his top speed will not change. Since the distance is so short, he may only attain a little over 80% of his top speed capability. In this case, he will need to sprint over longer distances to have the time and space to reach higher sprinting speeds.

For top speed training, we tend to use a 95% rule, where we aim for our players to reach at least 95% of their maximum speed when training to improve top speed. To accomplish this, the sprint distance must be long enough to allow for maximal running speeds. In football, it's been found that for NFL combine participants, a distance of 20 yards may be enough space to achieve between 93% and 96% of top speed regardless of position, as long as the sprint effort is performed with maximal effort.[2]

TESTING AND MEASURING ACCELERATION AND TOP SPEED

As with other performance abilities, it's important that we periodically test and monitor changes to acceleration and speed performances. When our players start an off-season training program, we test them in these areas as a baseline and then test them again, ideally every 4 weeks. Acceleration and speed outputs can fluctuate significantly on a weekly basis, so going every 4 weeks allows training adaptations to take place so that we can see changes in performance from a broader perspective over time.

The most common sprint test in football is the 40-yard dash. This is the test used at the NFL combine and has been the standard in assessing player speed for decades. Given how well-integrated the 40-yard dash is for coaches and players alike, it's sure to stay around. However, it has limitations. For one, there are various ways to time a 40-yard dash, including timing with a stopwatch, timing with a fully automatic measuring device, and semi-automatic timing where the start is triggered manually and the finish is calculated by a device. This is an important consideration when looking at testing results because if two athletes were timed in different ways, it can be difficult to determine who performed better.

Given the budget constraints of different programs, especially at the junior high and high school levels, coaches are ultimately left to use what they have available to them. It's better to test and monitor changes in speed by using a stopwatch than to not monitor speed at all. However, if we are just looking at a spreadsheet of different 40-yard dash times, we need to question how those times were measured. When football coaches scout prospective players, they need to be aware of how the "verified" times were collected. To compare a player who was measured solely by a stopwatch against a player who was measured using fully automatic technology is like comparing apples to oranges.

Measuring Different Sprint Segments

In the 40-yard dash, we get a good idea of how fast a player was able to travel from 0-40 yards. But, what about 0-10 yards? How well does the player transition from 10-20 yards in a 20-yard sprint? As we've discussed throughout this chapter, different sprinting distances will give athletes a very different experience due to the forces they must overcome, the speeds reached within the available space, and the position (or positions) of their bodies at different speeds (e.g., forward lean versus being upright). If we are only measuring 0-40 yards, we are unable to get a clear picture of how that 40-yard time was accomplished. Did the player have an explosive start at the beginning but struggle to continue accelerating toward the end? Did the player have a poor start but show great ability to spread out acceleration over the second half of the sprint? These important questions help us understand where each athlete's strengths and deficiencies lie for how they perform over a long acceleration effort like 40 yards.

By measuring different sprint segments, we begin to see a clearer picture. In figure 3.7, we see an athlete who runs a 4.50-second 40-yard dash. If we look at the segments for 10-20 yards, 20-30 yards, and 30-40 yards, we see that the time to cover each of those 10-yard segments is getting lower (e.g., from 1.06 sec to 0.93 sec), indicating that the athlete is continuing to accelerate every 10 yards through the finish at the 40-yard line.

By comparison, in figure 3.8, we see an athlete who hits the same sprint times up to the 30-yard mark before decelerating in the final 30-40 yards. We know this athlete has started decelerating because at 20-30 yards, the time was 0.96 seconds, and at 30-40 yards, it was 1.03 seconds. Due to this deficiency, the second athlete runs a slower 40-yard dash, accomplishing a time of 4.60 seconds and being a 10th of a second slower than the first athlete. So, from this observation we see that the second athlete struggles to continue accelerating at very high speeds and will need more top speed training to improve.

Comparing segment times is most useful when comparing players in the same position group. We can observe the fastest players at each position and look at how they organize their sprint segments, giving us a target

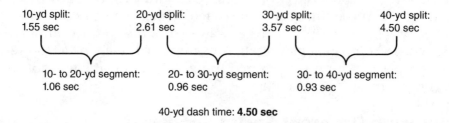

Figure 3.7 40-yard dash segments showing gradual acceleration.

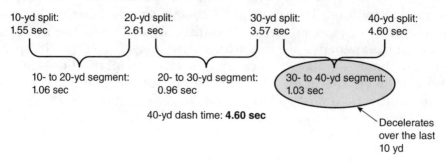

Figure 3.8 40-yard dash segments showing deceleration after 30 yards.

for the other players in that position. As another example, we might see a defensive end struggle in the first 10 yards when compared to the other defensive ends, telling us that this player may need more work on starts or heavy-resisted sprinting to help build the requisite horizontal strength and power to fire off the line.

Automated systems with timing gates make these segments easier to measure because we can place a timing gate at each 10-yard increment. This way, we can get multiple segments measured from one sprint. If timing gates are unavailable, another option is simply to take a stopwatch and have the athlete perform a 10-yard sprint, a 20-yard sprint, a 30-yard sprint, and so on. Then, we can subtract the 20-yard time from the 10-yard time to get the segment for 10-20 yards and do the same for the other segments. Again, even though this is not ideal, we believe it's better to attain the information using the available equipment than not getting any information at all.

Measuring Top Speed

Even though sprint and segment times can reflect an athlete's ability to accelerate, it is still worth considering an athlete's top speed to understand just how fast the athlete can move at maximum intensity. This is especially important for players who have to perform during game-breaking plays, like wide receivers, defensive backs, running backs, tight ends, and linebackers. If we resort to physics, we learn that speed is expressed as distance over time:

$$Speed = Distance\ /\ Time$$

Technically speaking, any unit of distance over any unit of time can be used (e.g., miles per hour, feet per second, kilometers per minute), but the unit used in the metric system (and most commonly found in sport science) is meters per second (m/sec). In most sports across the world, the distances measured are in meters. This is not the case in American football, which, of course, measures the game in yards. Thus, if we calculate speed for any sprint effort using distance over time, the units will be in yards per second (yd/sec) rather than in meters per second.

Additionally, in the United States, it has become commonplace to discuss a football player's speed in the unit of miles per hour (mph). This is becoming more popular thanks to NFL Next Gen Stats and other reporting on television where player speeds are publicized as a measure of miles per hour. So, to keep the conversation universal, it is important that we convert speed calculations from yards per second to miles per hour so that we may gain a better perspective of how fast these players are in relation to high-level college and professional players. The conversion from yards per second to miles per hour is as follows:

$$1\ yd/sec = 2.05\ mph$$

The next step is to measure a relatively short segment where the player is sprinting at maximum speed. This means that, in this situation, the athlete would already be accelerating before the measurement start line. In other words, the athlete would be measured "on the fly." Thus, the common measurement for top speed is a "flying sprint" test, typically either a flying 10-yard sprint or flying 20-yard sprint.

In this test, the athlete has a specific entry distance allowing for the attainment of near-maximum speed and is then measured over a designated 10- or 20-yard segment farther down the field. Figure 3.9 illustrates a testing design for a flying 10-yard sprint assessment using timing gates. If timing gates are unavailable and the coach has only a stopwatch to record, we recommend using a flying 20-yard sprint assessment instead (see figure 3.10), since the flying 10-yard sprint may be too fast to measure accurately with a stopwatch.

You might ask why we can't just take our 40-yard time and divide it against a distance of 40 yards to get our speed measurement. Well, consider the same sprint data from figure 3.7, where we would have the following calculation:

40 yards (distance) / 4.5 seconds (time) = 8.9 yd/sec

8.9 yd/sec multiplied by 2.05 (conversion to mph) = 18.2 mph

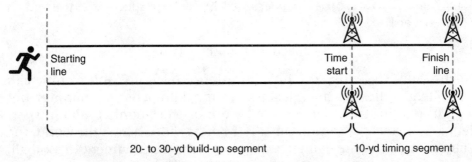

Figure 3.9   Flying 10-yard sprint assessment using timing gates.

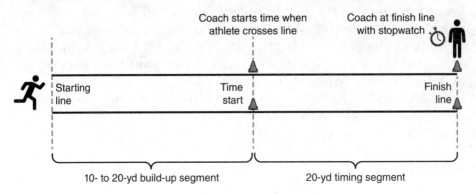

Figure 3.10   Flying 20-yard sprint assessment using a stopwatch.

The problem with this approach is that the speed of 18.2 mph reflects the average speed over a very broad distance of 40 yards. Instead, we can look at the segment for 30-40 yards, which is 0.93 seconds, and get a different calculation:

$$\text{10 yards (distance of segment for 30-40 yards)} / \text{0.93 seconds (time)} = 10.8 \text{ yd/sec}$$

$$10.8 \text{ yd/sec multiplied by 2.05 (conversion to mph)} = 22.1 \text{ mph}$$

So, by measuring a shorter segment that's closer to the point at which the player is operating at maximum speed, we get a much different picture of that athlete's true top speed. Although the calculated speeds will be lower when measuring a flying 20-yard sprint versus a flying 10-yard sprint, the metrics will still prove useful for monitoring changes over time. If the speeds increase, the athlete is getting faster and raising their top speed capability.

We like to use 20-30 yards for the run-up leading into a flying 10-yard sprint. Of course, it's possible that players with slower overall top speeds (offensive and defensive linemen, for example) hit their relative top speeds sooner than faster players, so we will typically use a 20-yard run-up for offensive and defensive linemen and a 30-yard run-up for all other players. Table 3.1 provides speed goals based on results from flying 10-yard sprint testing for each position at both the high school and collegiate or professional level.

Table 3.1   Flying 10-Yard Sprint Standards for Various Football Positions

Positions group	High school player		College or pro player	
	Flying 10-yd sprint time goal (sec)	Associated max speed goal (mph)	Flying 10-yd sprint time goal (sec)	Associated max speed goal (mph)
Wide receiver Defensive back	<1.00	>20.5	<0.95	>21.5
Tight end Linebacker Running back Dual-threat quarterback	<1.10	>18.5	<1.00	>20.5
Offensive line Defensive line Pro-style quarterback	<1.20	>17.0	<1.10	>18.5

EXERCISES AND DRILLS TO DEVELOP ACCELERATION AND SPEED

Various exercises and drills are used to develop acceleration and speed. The list we have compiled is a collection of the drills we feel are the most valuable, where minimal equipment is required and large performance gains can be attained. The acceleration exercises are based on various "starts," which refers to how the player initiates a speed effort. Starting from various positions and angles and incorporating implements like medicine balls can all help a player's coordination and teach the player to find a sense of stability when accelerating from various positions when playing football. Resisted sprinting is used to enhance the amount of force and power a player can put into the ground to enhance the ability to explosively project his body forward when sprinting. Lastly, upright sprinting exercises are incorporated to teach players how to perform when upright and running at high speeds, aiming to push the top speed higher.

Drop-In Start

The drop-in start is used to train acceleration without having to overcome the inertia of a dead-stop position. This is advantageous because momentum leads into the accelerative effort, so players can hit speed over shorter distances, and it is less stressful to the body since there will be less overall strain. We like to use drop-in starts when we want to emphasize high speed, but it is also a way to introduce new distances into the program, such as progressing from 10-yard sprints to 20-yard sprints. The first exposure to the 20-yard distance can be performed with a drop-in start for a few weeks before transitioning to another dead-stop starting position later.

Execution

1. Begin standing 1-2 yards away from the starting line in an upright position.
2. Either walk or skip toward the goal line and then immediately drop the hips down into an acceleration position.
3. Accelerate forward for a predetermined distance at maximum intensity.

2-Point Start

This is the most basic starting position for acceleration. For our purposes, it's a simple way to get the player in the correct stance, foot on a line, and have him simply accelerate his body forward. Although the initiation of the sprint is from a dead stop, the body angle will be higher than with lower starting positions, so the acceleration forces required will be relatively low, similar to the drop-in start. Therefore, the 2-point start is a great position to use for acceleration efforts during early training periods.

Execution

1. Begin in a 2-point stance with the front foot on a line and the back foot lined up to allow for balance. Body weight is distributed across both feet.

2. Shift the body weight so that most of the weight is on the front foot—we typically say about 70% of the weight on the front foot and 30% of the weight on the back foot.

3. The weight distribution should allow a positive shin angle of the front leg, and the hips should be low enough that the body is coiled like a spring, ready to drive forward.

4. From a dead stop, accelerate forward for a predetermined distance at maximum intensity.

Figure 3.11   2-point start.

Half-Kneeling Start

The half-kneeling start is used to challenge a player to overcome his own body weight from a low position with an emphasis on the lead leg. The player will have to shift his body weight favorably toward the front leg, achieve a positive shin angle, and then propel himself forward. Those with poor mobility of the hips and ankles or poor horizontal strength will struggle with this exercise. However, this position is vital for football players, not only for sprint acceleration but also for other scenarios like driving through a form tackle.

Execution

1. Begin in a half-kneeling position with the front foot on a line and the back foot lined up somewhere near the front heel. Body weight should be distributed across both feet.
2. From a dead-stop position, the weight should be shifted forward onto the front leg so that the knee drops down, the heel lifts up, and the shin takes on a positive angle.
3. Explode through the front leg to get the body to propel forward into a low, smooth acceleration angle.
4. Accelerate forward for a predetermined distance at maximum intensity.

Figure 3.12   Half-kneeling start.

Push-Up Start

The push-up start is used to practice a self-organizing, very low starting position for acceleration. The "self-organizing" component refers to how the player will have to organize the position of the legs while pushing up from the bottom position so that a smooth acceleration angle is achieved. If the foot drives too far forward and the first push is from a neutral shin angle and flat foot, the overall acceleration will be thrown off. The player must learn through feedback from the body which hip, knee, shin, ankle, and foot positions are most helpful for maximizing a sprint acceleration.

Execution

1. Begin at the bottom of a push-up position with the fingertips on a line and the head slightly over the line.
2. From a dead-stop position, push to the top of a push-up position while driving one of the legs forward. Contact the ground so the body weight is heavily shifted forward onto the front leg and the knee is low, the heel is up, and the shin angle is positive.
3. Explode through the front leg while maneuvering the arms into a sprinting rhythm to get the body to propel forward into a low, smooth acceleration angle.
4. Accelerate forward for a predetermined distance at maximum intensity.

3-Point Start

The 3-point start is one of the most argued-about positions for acceleration because of the influence of the NFL combine and so many coaches trying to maximize the 40-yard dash. We will simply present our opinion based on our research into combine preparation and conversations with track and field coaches. We believe the most important aspect of the 3-point start is setting the body up in a position that will not only maximize the first step but also allow the player to experience a gradual rhythm and rise as he accelerates as far as 40-50 yards from this position. Thus, while many coaches feel it's worth teaching the players to "crowd the line" and try to "make a 10-yard sprint into a 9-yard sprint," we believe that this can cause the shin angles to be too vertical at the start, leading to a vertical projection on the first step where we want a horizontal projection. We will admit that sometimes crowding the line can lead to a better 10-yard time, but we are concerned with what happens after the first 10 yards as well. Therefore, we subscribe more to the technique that has the front shin at a 45-degree angle and the back shin relatively parallel to the ground so that the player can have a smooth first step and subsequent gradual building of rhythm and rise with each step thereafter. The execution we will describe is how we set up our players in this position.

Execution

1. Begin with both feet on the starting line, about hip-width apart.
2. Shift the lead foot back until the toes of that foot are in line with or 1-2 inches behind the heel of the other foot.
3. Move the trailing foot behind the lead foot and go into a half-kneeling position, where the trailing leg's knee is about at the instep of the front foot (near the middle).
4. The front foot and back foot can be manipulated from here based on how the legs are built. For example, someone with very short shins might be able to crowd the line a little more, whereas someone with very long shins might have to shift back farther.
5. Once the feet are set, lean forward toward the front foot and turn the hands sideways along the front of the start line.
6. Raise the hips until the front leg is bent at about 90 degrees and the trail leg is somewhere around 135 degrees. Also, ensure that the front shin achieves about a 45-degree angle from the floor. If it doesn't, adjust the feet.
7. Lift the hand on the same side as the lead leg to the hip of the lead leg to achieve a 3-point stance. Hold this position for 3 seconds before taking off into a sprint.
8. Accelerate forward for a predetermined distance at maximum intensity.

Figure 3.13   3-point start.

Medicine Ball Chest Pass Into Sprint

This exercise is similar to the drop-in start, where the goal is to get some momentum going into the accelerative effort. However, this time we want to emphasize the initial push of the first two steps, so we incorporate a 10-pound medicine ball that is launched forward horizontally. The player attempts to carry this momentum into the rest of the acceleration. This drill is best used with distances of 10-15 yards where the goal can be to launch the ball forward as powerfully as possible and then chase after to catch up to it. The emphasis is on accentuating the power of the initial steps of a short acceleration.

Execution

1. Begin in a 2-point stance (described previously) while holding a medicine ball at chest level.
2. From a dead stop, rapidly extend the hip through the front leg while launching the ball forward along a horizontal path. Use a pressing motion to emulate a "chest pass" maneuver.
3. Once the ball has been released, accelerate forward for a predetermined distance at maximum intensity.

Medicine Ball Knee Punch Run

The medicine ball knee punch run is used to help players understand good front side lift while sprinting in an upright position. The player holds a light medicine ball (5-10 lb) in front of his torso and is instructed to sprint forward while attempting to punch the front knee toward the medicine ball so that the front thigh contacts the ball. Even if the thigh does not fully contact the medicine ball, the exercise can help the player understand what good front side lift feels like. Also, having the weighted ball in the front of the body allows for feedback where the player's body realizes it cannot hunch forward or it will be sent into a forward roll, so it helps reinforce good pelvic position and core activation.

Execution

1. Begin in a 2-point stance (described previously) while holding a medicine ball at the level of the navel, slightly above the hips.
2. Accelerate into a 2-point start while attempting to drive the front thigh toward the medicine ball, with the goal of contacting the ball.
3. Due to the nature of the exercise, the body will become upright sooner, so the goal is then to continue accelerating in this position while contacting the ball with the thigh.
4. Accelerate forward for a predetermined distance at maximum intensity.

Light-Resisted Sprint

Light-resisted sprinting refers to resistance that slows a player down to 85%-90% of unloaded maximum speed. Typically, this occurs when a plate-loaded sled weighs 10%-20% of a player's body weight. The sled load should include the weight of the sled itself, so a 200-pound player would sprint against a total sled load of 20-40 pounds. The greatest benefit of using light resistance is that the player is slowed down just enough that he is able to feel his body move in space more than when unloaded, but the speed can still be high enough that he is able to attain the same technique of unloaded sprinting. So, it's loaded technique training but also a way to safely train at high speeds, especially for skill players like wide receivers and defensive backs.

Execution

1. Resistance is typically used with a plate-loaded sled and a waist harness but can include a waist harness attached to large chains that drag along the floor or any number of cable- or rope-based systems that are available. If all else fails, finding a hill that's not too steep and allows for high speeds is another option to provide some resistance.

2. Various starting positions can be used, such as a 2-point start, 3-point start, or half-kneeling start.

3. Acceleration and effort should be maximal for a predetermined distance, typically 15-20 yards.

Figure 3.14   Light-resisted sprint.

Heavy-Resisted Sprint

Heavy-resisted sprinting refers to resistance that slows a player down to about 50% of unloaded maximum speed. Typically, this occurs when a plate-loaded sled weighs 80%-100% of a player's body weight. The sled load should include the weight of the sled itself, so a 200-pound player would sprint against a total sled load of 160-200 pounds. Naturally, for linemen, this can be 300 pounds or higher, so it may be more useful to incorporate a push sled for them to load enough resistance. The greatest benefit of heavy resistance in the horizontal direction is the ability to develop maximum horizontal power to positively influence the first 5-10 yards of a sprint start. So, it's actually horizontal power training, not technique training, and the overall goal is to expose players to very high horizontal forces and ask them to overcome these forces as fast as possible.

Execution

1. Resistance is typically used with a plate-loaded sled and a waist harness but can include a push sled if necessary, especially if higher loads are required. If all else fails, finding a very steep hill is another option.
2. Because the resistance is so heavy, only 2- or 3-point starts are used with heavy-resisted sprints.
3. Acceleration and effort should be maximal for a predetermined distance, typically 10-15 yards.

Figure 3.15   Heavy-resisted sprint.

High-Knee Build-Up Run

The high-knee build-up run is used to get a player into a good upright sprint position with front side lift; set the rhythm of upright sprinting with quick, springy steps; and attempt to add horizontal acceleration while maintaining the front side lift and step rhythm. Essentially, we work backward from an acceleration into an upright position and instead put the players in the upright position first and then ask them to accelerate and add horizontal power. This helps players feel the optimal combination of horizontal-to-vertical forces being applied to the ground when sprinting upright so they can feel more comfortable when transitioning to top speed.

Execution

1. Begin upright behind a starting line and perform a high-knee run while in place.
2. Once the knee height and rhythm have been established, maintain them while accelerating forward past the starting line.
3. Continue accelerating gradually across a predetermined set of segments (e.g., every 5 yd or every 10 yd) for a predetermined total distance, typically 30-50 yards total.

Build-Up Sprints

Build-up sprints teach players the transition from acceleration to top speed, so they emphasize rhythm and rise in late acceleration.

Execution

1. Begin with a drop-in start (explained previously) and begin accelerating at 70%-75% of maximum effort.
2. Continue accelerating gradually across a predetermined set of segments (e.g., every 5 yd or every 10 yd) for a predetermined total distance, typically 30-50 yards total.
3. By the final segment, a goal can be given in terms of intensity—for example, "Build up to about 90% speed by the final 10 yards."

Curved Sprints

Curved sprints serve two primary functions for developing speed in our program. One, curved sprinting helps load the lateral hamstring a bit more so we can expose this muscle to unique lines of stress that also occur in the game of football, such as during punt or kick coverage. The other benefit of curved sprinting is that it allows us as coaches to monitor technique more effectively while the athlete is performing maximally because the curved pattern will lead to naturally less speed than the athletes are capable of achieving, similar to a resisted sprint. So, as coaches, we can stand "in the curve" and watch each player progress through the curve and then comment on his technique after, if necessary. The curve is set up across a given distance, typically 20-40 yards total, and has a gradual bend so the players are able to achieve a proper upright sprinting technique.

Execution

1. Begin with a drop-in start (explained previously) and accelerate maximally across the entire curve.
2. Top speed posture should be attained somewhere around halfway through the curve and then maintained through the finish.

Flying Sprints

Flying sprints are not just for testing and monitoring—they are also very potent as a training exercise. Flying sprints may be used to expose a player to speeds very close to top speed in a way that includes a gradual, more relaxed build-up to maximum intensity. They are similar to a build-up sprint, but the acceleration rate is much higher and the speed effort in the "flying" window is maximal.

Execution

1. Begin with a drop-in start (explained previously) and accelerate maximally toward a set of cones that are set 20-30 yards away.
2. Gradually pick up speed before reaching the cones, and once the starting cones are crossed, sprint with maximal effort through the finish cones, which are typically 10-20 yards away.

Sprint-Float-Sprint

We believe it helps our players to learn to manipulate their speed efforts because in the game of football, they will have to learn to manipulate tempo by speeding up or slowing down based on what the game is showing them. The sprint-float-sprint drill emphasizes a player's ability to accelerate maximally across a given segment (sprint), hold that speed for the next segment (float), and then accelerate even more across the final segment (sprint). This is a potent drill for teaching skill players how to hit another gear of acceleration while they are already sprinting very fast, which may just be the training stimulus they need to develop the difference between getting caught from behind or scoring a touchdown on a long run.

Execution

1. Begin with a drop-in start (explained previously) and accelerate maximally toward a set of cones that are 15-20 yards away.

2. After crossing the set of cones, maintain the current speed as much as possible while heading toward another set of cones 15-20 yards away.

3. When crossing the next set of cones, again maximally accelerate in the upright position to finish through the final set of cones 15-20 yards away.

4. Segments are typically 15-20 yards each, so the player will cover 45 or 60 yards of distance per repetition.

ACCELERATION AND SPEED TRAINING PROGRAM

When we consider what happens during football, we see that players may need to sprint at any time. Therefore, consistent speed exposure of various intensities may be warranted for two primary reasons:

1. When football players have a greater exposure to high-quality sprint training, it can enhance the skill acquisition of acceleration and getting faster.

2. Football players need the capacity for explosive efforts at any given moment throughout the week across the entire season.

Rest and Recovery Between Maximum Intensity Sprints

When performing sprint training, it is important to understand the recovery time needed between each repetition. This will depend on the intensity we are emphasizing. For example, if we want to push the ceiling higher on acceleration or top speed, we must ensure that the players are receiving full recovery periods between repetitions. By definition, if players are not fully recovered, they will not be able to operate at their maximum intensities because fatigue will naturally slow them down. So, a good rule is to incorporate 30-60 seconds of rest for every 10 yards covered at maximum intensity. Table 3.2 displays recovery ranges for different distances covered with one sprint repetition.

Table 3.2   Recommended Recovery Time Between Sprint Efforts Based on Distance Covered

Sprint distance	Recommended recovery time between repetitions
10 yd	30-60 sec
20 yd	1-2 min
30 yd	1.5-3 min
40 yd	2-4 min

Total Volume of Sprint Work

If we keep execution quality high, the total yardage of linear sprint exercises doesn't need to exceed 300 yards in one workout. The upper volume range for skill positions like wide receivers and defensive backs might be 200-300 yards in a speed session. Other skill-oriented positions, like linebackers, tight ends, running backs, and quarterbacks, might have an upper volume range of 150-250 yards. Offensive and defensive linemen might have an upper volume range of 100-200 yards. Depending on the team's playbook, these volumes might change if the quarterback hardly runs or defensive ends are expected to cover in passing zones, for example.

It's important to emphasize that "sprint work" is a different consideration than just "running." Portions of our workouts will be devoted to slower, more extensive running to help improve aerobic fitness, but this work will not be considered "sprinting" because the intensity is low. We consider anything over 80% of maximum speed or anything where the athlete is performing at 100% maximum effort as sprint work. We can perform sprint work 3-4 days a week, so we are able to spread out the exposure to speed across the week. Table 3.3 illustrates the ranges of total sprint yardage covered in one session as well as weekly volume ranges for each position group.

Table 3.3 Maximal Effort Sprint Training Upper Range Volume Guidelines Based on Position

Position group	Session total sprint volume	Weekly total sprint volume
Wide receiver Defensive back	200-300 yd	600-1,200 yd
Tight end Linebacker Running back Dual-threat quarter- back	150-250 yd	450-1,000 yd
Offensive line Defensive line Pro-style quarterback	100-200 yd	300-800 yd

In terms of purely linear, maximal intensity sprinting, players might only perform four to six total sprints in one workout. Since speed is present on most days throughout our training week, we believe that a little goes a long way when aiming to keep quality high. We also have to consider all the other work being done in the same workout session, which could include any mix of change-of-direction, agility, endurance, explosive power, or weight room strength training. Also, when we perform sprint testing, we always aim for the lower end of total volume ranges because the intensity will be as high as possible.

The player's position group will also determine the distance of each sprint effort. This affects total volume. For example, linemen can perform the same number of repetitions as skill players do but not travel as far. On a testing day, a skill player might perform three 40-yard sprints to achieve a volume of 120 yards, whereas a lineman might perform three 20-yard sprints to achieve a volume of 60 yards.

Varying Resisted Sprint Loads to Improve Sprint Phases

Using heavy-resisted loads in sprinting may specifically target the sprint start and early acceleration but may not be as potent for targeting the later phases of sprint acceleration or top speed. In developing maximum velocity, we can assume that we should not use resistance and all exercises aimed at improving this phase should be unloaded. Figure 3.16 lays out a basic progression of loaded and unloaded sprint training.

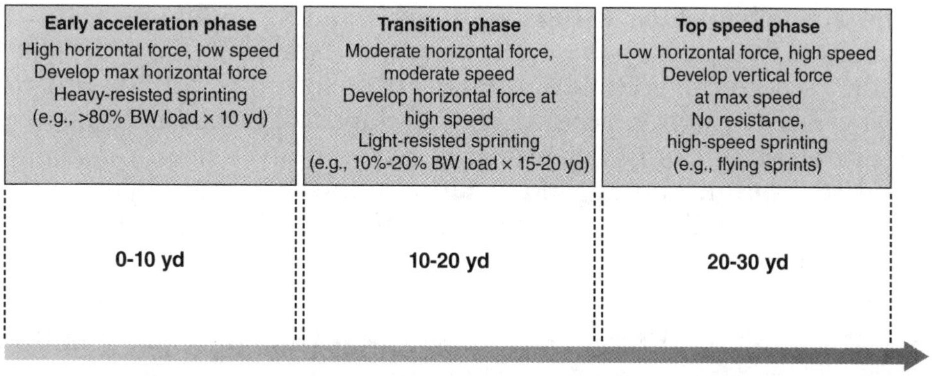

Early acceleration phase	Transition phase	Top speed phase
High horizontal force, low speed Develop max horizontal force Heavy-resisted sprinting (e.g., >80% BW load × 10 yd)	Moderate horizontal force, moderate speed Develop horizontal force at high speed Light-resisted sprinting (e.g., 10%-20% BW load × 15-20 yd)	Low horizontal force, high speed Develop vertical force at max speed No resistance, high-speed sprinting (e.g., flying sprints)
0-10 yd	10-20 yd	20-30 yd

Figure 3.16 Basic progression of loaded and unloaded sprint training.

Sample Training Week for Speed Development

In off-season training, we can design progressive speed training to achieve gradual exposure to higher intensities of sprinting. Table 3.4 shows a sample sprint training template we might use for the first half of off-season summer training. In this example, the rationale is to introduce sprint training at reduced volumes where the focus is on building intensity over the first 3-4 weeks. So, we would perform sprinting for 3 days during the week.

Table 3.4 Summer Off-Season Linear Sprint Training Block 1 (4 Weeks)

Monday	Tuesday	Wednesday	Thursday	Friday
Acceleration	No running	Resisted sprinting Acceleration Top speed technique	Resisted sprinting Acceleration	No running

The sprinting emphasis in this phase is on short acceleration (e.g., 10-20 yd per repetition), resisted sprinting (both heavy and light resistance), and introductory top speed exercises (e.g., high-knee build-up runs, build-up sprints, and curved sprints). The top speed emphasis is on building upright sprinting technique at lower intensities to prepare the body for more intense top speed training in the next phase.

The second half of the off-season summer training might resemble what is presented in table 3.5. As we get closer to fall training camp, the goal is to increase both the volume and intensity of sprinting. So, the first step is to increase the number of sprinting sessions to 4 days across the week. The overall emphasis is still primarily acceleration, but we can remove the resisted sprint training, add distance to the acceleration efforts (e.g., progress from 10-20 yd to more repetitions of 20-30 yd), and add more exposure to top speed.

Table 3.5   Summer Off-Season Linear Sprint Training Block 2 (4 Weeks)

Monday	Tuesday	Wednesday	Thursday	Friday
Acceleration	Acceleration Top speed technique	Acceleration	Acceleration Top speed development	No running

With this design, the sprinting done throughout the week will start to resemble in-season practice, where faster, more intense days are at the start of the week and intensity is somewhat reduced toward the end of the week. Top speed exposure becomes important to prepare the players for highly intense, competitive situations in practice, like a wide receiver and defensive back both chasing after a deep ball. We can progress the top speed training toward more volume of flying sprints and sprint-float-sprint designs. Longer acceleration efforts will also help shift the overall emphasis of training toward faster sprinting.

CONCLUSION

Linear speed is directly tied to performance in football and is a skill that needs to be developed over time. While much of the game is short acceleration, being skillful and having the physical capacity to operate at a high level from first step to top speed is paramount to high performance during explosive plays that may exceed 10 yards of running. It's not enough just to include sprinting in a training program; the sprint work must be deliberately included with a defined purpose and devoted coaching to foster speed enhancement. When it comes to increasing speed, quality is vital and must be protected. Speed development is not a "quick fix" that can be placed in the program for a few weeks and then big changes occur. Speed requires time and exposure for adaptation. It's necessary to keep some aspect of speed training present throughout the entire training year so that we can give our athletes the best opportunity to become faster.

Chapter 4

Agility and Change-of-Direction Training

As football has evolved to spreading players out across the field, the need to stop and change direction from high speeds has also drastically increased, both in intensity and volume. Players must be able to create separation or track down opponents in larger field spaces, requiring the ability to move in multiple directions with efficiency and handle a lot of physical stress. In addition, when the game was more constricted, it was easier for players to read what was happening in front of them, since more bodies were within their line of sight. Now, players must dial in on the most important "keys" that serve as perceptual triggers to help guide them in movement decisions since they are far less capable of seeing the entire field.

Linear speed remains an important player attribute, but agility and change of direction are more significant determinants of game speed in football. True agility involves a synergistic relationship between brain and body, a continuous cycle between perception and action that will ultimately determine how players behave in the game environment. Agility is a rapid whole-body movement with change of velocity or direction *in response to a stimulus*.[1] Thus, the stimulus is a key component to what can be considered true agility. The player must perceive an external stimulus and use information from the environment to determine how to formulate the next movement. When this stimulus is removed, the direction change is preplanned and may be understood as change-of-direction (COD) ability. The greatest difference between agility and COD is in the presence of an external stimulus. When the player has to read a signal (e.g., opponent's movements) and respond appropriately based on task goals, the stimulus will dictate the movement solution.

In contrast, COD ability is the *physical capacity* to change direction while decelerating and then reaccelerating, sometimes using a different mode of travel.[2] So, preplanned activities like cutting around cones, redirecting by touching lines on a field, or a wide receiver practicing routes on air are all examples of COD, not agility. In agility, we emphasize how brain comprehension dictates movement solutions, whereas COD focuses primarily on the physical component of movement.

What makes the athlete move with speed in the context of the game? Is it the athlete's ability to change direction in isolation, the athlete's ability to rapidly perceive a situation and make an effective decision, or some combination of both? It appears that, in terms of agility performance in sports like football, it is the ability to perceive and use sport-specific cues from an opponent that distinguishes higher-level athletes from lower-level athletes.

Football coaches spend a great deal of time preparing players to focus on perceptual "keys" that allow them to assess situations and dictate subsequent responses. In this way, what the players are able to perceive and interpret with their brains leads their bodies to respond with movement. This is perceptual-cognitive ability, and it is a major pillar of agility performance. Perceptual-cognitive ability includes visual scanning, anticipation, pattern recognition, knowledge of the situation, decision-making time and accuracy, and reaction time.[2]

In football, all the requisite strength, power, speed, and COD ability can be rendered useless if a player lacks perceptual-cognitive ability. In other words, if a player is unable to properly read the necessary keys and understand how to properly respond to them, he will be ineffective at his position. Compensations may exist, however, whereby a player with high levels of speed can make up for slower cognitive processing or vice versa. But if we can enhance a player's perceptual-cognitive ability while developing his physical movement capabilities, we are taking a more holistic approach to agility development.

SPRINTING VERSUS DECELERATION AND COD

We have seen many players with great acceleration ability struggle to decelerate. They are missing a major component of game performance because football not only requires that players be fast but also capable of stopping fast. Without the ability to decelerate well, effective COD can't happen. A player must always decelerate before redirecting. Lack of deceleration leads to offensive players who can't make defenders miss and defensive players who are left in the dust. Additionally, proper deceleration is crucial for injury reduction. The anterior cruciate ligament (ACL) is at tremendous risk of rupture when deceleration mechanics or deceleration capacity are insufficient. Thus, we believe that deceleration should be just as much of a training priority as acceleration or top speed.

Maneuverability may be considered a subcategory of COD, where the intent of directional change is a slight deviation from the original intended line of travel while maintaining as much velocity as possible, resulting in a curvilinear movement path rather than a jagged COD. A common test of maneuverability used at the NFL combine is the L-drill, also called the 3-cone drill or L-run. The L-drill features sharp, curved running in the final part of the test, as shown in figure 4.1.

Maneuverability also includes the transition from one mode of travel to another, such as sprinting forward and then transitioning into a lateral shuffle. This happens in football when a wide receiver sprints forward and then breaks down to make a stalk block on a defender along the perimeter. Other common maneuverability situations in football would include an edge rusher working along a sharp curvilinear path to bend around an

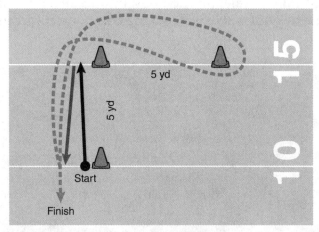

Figure 4.1   The 3-cone drill (L-run) has three stages. First, from a 3-point stance, the athlete sprints 5 yards to the first cone (black arrow). Second, the athlete sprints back to the starting cone (gray arrow). Last, the athlete sprints 5 yards, turns right around the first cone and sprints 5 yards under and around the second cone, sprints 5 yards back to the first cone, then turns left and finishes with a sprint past the starting cone (dashed arrow).

offensive tackle, a running back working up the field on an outside toss play, or a player running down on kickoff coverage and bending his path to track down the returner.

Most decelerations will occur with a forefoot strike, meaning the athlete contacts the ground through the ball of the foot while decelerating. However, very intense decelerations will require the athlete to shift weight more toward the heels and apply pressure across the whole foot. When necessary, this shift should be as brief as possible. In football, being shifted back onto the heels is bad because it makes it very difficult to reaccelerate in a given direction. The forefoot strike allows the athlete to quickly redirect his shin angle to a positive direction across multiple planes to take off in a new direction.

Similar principles occur with a lateral COD in the form of a cut step. A cut step is actually a lateral deceleration to reacceleration maneuver, so it will require positions associated with both deceleration and acceleration. Like any decelerative movement, the center of mass is lowered and the trunk falls forward into a hinge position to increase stability before acceleration. The base of support shifts to outside the center of mass in the opposite direction of the intended path of travel as the player's foot hits the ground near the hips and pushes laterally. For a player to effectively cut to the left, he must plant his right foot under his center of mass and then apply force to the right to allow for a positive lateral line of force application to project his body to the left. Rather than the foot being behind the knee, as seen in linear acceleration, the foot now is pushed laterally outside the knee. But the principle is the same, and the only difference lies in the direction of the force application. Figure 4.2 shows an athlete making an effective cut step.

When changing direction, there will be a plant step that serves as the final action to fully decelerate the body in one direction and reaccelerate it in the next. Thus, there is a braking component (deceleration) and

Figure 4.2   Athlete performing a cut step.

propulsive component (reacceleration) with every change of direction. This leads to significantly longer ground-contact times versus the stance phase in linear sprinting.[3] Table 4.1 compares ground-contact times from top speed sprinting to full deceleration steps. The two major factors that dictate how long the foot stays on the ground during the plant phase are the speed of entry into the deceleration and the angle of direction change. For example, decelerating from a full-speed 20-yard sprint will be much more intense than decelerating from a 5-yard sprint and will require greater braking forces. Likewise, making a 90-degree cut will be much more intense than making a 45-degree cut, as figure 4.3 illustrates.

It is not just the final plant step that is of concern when changing direction but the step prior as well. This step is called the penultimate step or approach step. The approach step is particularly important during more intensive decelerations, such as cutting at an angle of more than 60 degrees. A player who can effectively achieve greater braking forces in the approach step can reduce impact on the knee during the plant step and allow the plant step

Table 4.1   Comparison of Ground-Contact Times in Athletic Actions

Athletic action	Ground-contact time (sec)
Top speed sprinting	≤0.10
Acceleration, first 3 steps	0.16-0.20
First step, 90-degree cut	0.30-0.40
Full deceleration steps	>0.45

Adapted from C. Josse, "A Unilateral to Bilateral Training Progression for Team Sports," SimpliFaster, accessed August 17, 2022, https://simplifaster.com/articles/unilateral-to-bilateral-training-progression/.

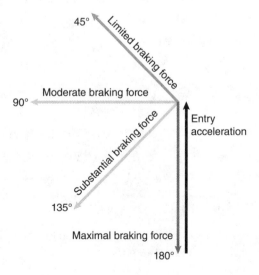

Figure 4.3   Magnitude of braking force associated with cutting angles between 45 degrees and 180 degrees.

to facilitate a faster change of direction.[4] The sharper the angle of direction change, the more important the braking forces of the approach step become. So, it's important for us to coach our players to strategically utilize their steps leading into the plant step to facilitate faster and safer changes of direction in training.

COACHING TO IMPROVE AGILITY AND COD

The primary goal when coaching our players to redirect safely and efficiently is getting them to understand how to reaccelerate out of any COD. Entering the deceleration phase in a poor position or with too much speed may negate the subsequent reacceleration due to a loss of stability and body control. Figure 4.4 shows a theoretical relationship between the deceleration and reacceleration phases of a plant step and how the movement speed for the entry and exit of each COD should be very similar. When a player has more speed than he can control upon entry into the plant step, he will not have an effective transfer of force into the reacceleration phase and will lose the ability to efficiently accelerate out of the plant.

We can help our athletes by coaching the biomechanical principles we discussed previously, like lowering the center of mass and properly placing the base of support. Coaching these positions is easier during closed COD training, like running around cone configurations, since there is no perceptual component. We can use closed activities to help players feel their bodies in different positions, much like we would do in the weight room.

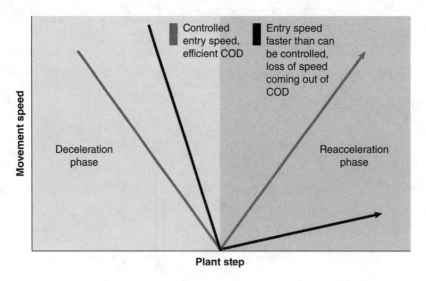

Figure 4.4 Effective versus ineffective change of direction based on the relationship between the phases of deceleration to reacceleration.

With open or reactive activities, coaching is more challenging. Less coaching of body position may be the best approach with these exercises because we don't want our players focusing on their bodies but on external cues. Therefore, coaching the focal points of the perception (e.g., "Keep your eyes on his hips.") is more important when training perceptual-cognitive ability. Subtle movement reminders may be used if the player is failing at an open or reactive task (e.g., "Sink your hips when decelerating so you're more stable when reading your opponent.").

With closed COD activities, we aim to enhance a player's motor potential, which may be understood as the "muscular capacity to produce the greatest quantity of mechanical energy per unit of time" in the game context.[5] In other words, motor potential represents the biomechanical efficiency of movement. Motor potential can be improved with deliberate practice, where we can reinforce the stable components of deceleration and changing direction. Deliberate practice is structured activity with the primary goal being to improve an important aspect of current performance and includes immediate access to feedback from a coach, the opportunity for repetition, and error detection and correction. It requires full attention, maximal effort, and complete concentration.[6]

With open or reactive activities, we aim to solidify a player's technical mastery, which is the player's ability to effectively utilize his motor potential in the game. So, if a running back spends the off-season getting bigger, stronger, and faster but can't incorporate these gains into performing better on the field, then he is struggling to attain technical mastery in football. Due to the complex and chaotic nature of football, a player must be exposed to a variety of gamelike situations in training and encouraged to explore the information available in the environment to seek out opportunities for action. This is called exploratory practice.

Unlike deliberate practice, exploratory practice should be player-centered, not coach-centered. This means that we allow the player to explore and make his own decisions based on what he perceives. After all, this is how it will be on a football field. We can provide clues to the player to help guide his decision-making, but the player must begin to take ownership to retain his developing technical gains. One way to think about technical mastery is that it represents an athlete who is highly adaptable and able to find stable movement solutions in a variety of chaotic situations. Over-coaching and holding a player's hand through these kinds of activities will greatly diminish adaptability and have a negative effect on learning and skill development.

ASSESSING AGILITY AND COD

Testing and monitoring for agility and COD are complicated endeavors, and there is no consensus on how best to test each of these qualities. For example, one of the most commonly used COD assessments in football is the pro agility test, also called the 20-yard shuttle or 5-10-5 test. The general testing protocol is as follows:

1. The player starts with the feet straddling a starting line in a square stance so that the starting line bisects the hips.

2. The player puts one hand down on the ground, indicating which direction he will begin the test, left or right. If the left hand is down, he will start to the left and vice versa.

3. The test begins with his first movement. The player travels 5 yards in the starting direction. Once he gets to the next line 5 yards away, he has to drop his near hand and touch the line with his fingertips.

4. After the line is touched, the player redirects in the opposite direction and travels to a line 10 yards away. Once he gets to the next line 10 yards away, he has to drop his near hand and touch the line with his fingertips.

5. After the second line is touched, the player redirects in the opposite direction and finishes the drill by sprinting back through the starting line, 5 yards away.

So, in this test, the player will cover 20 yards between two changes of direction (5 yd + 10 yd + 5 yd = 20 yd total). On the surface, this assessment seems like a valid measurement of a player's ability to change direction. But the test has been criticized since it has been found that players who have superior acceleration capabilities may be able to compensate for poor cut steps during each COD and still achieve a time considered "good." Therefore, the actual CODs may not be the limiting component to the test. Additionally, the coach monitoring the test does not have any information about how each COD was performed, only the resulting time of how long it took the player to travel 20 yards. So, it can be difficult to say for certain that the pro agility test is an assessment of COD ability.

The same problem arises with other COD tests like the 3-cone drill (or L-run), the T-test, the Illinois Agility Test, and the 5-0-5 test. All these assessments may feature compensations when players have superior acceleration capabilities, and some (like the T-test and Illinois Agility Test) may allow athletes exhibiting high levels of endurance and coordination to compensate and have superior performance.

One form of assessment and monitoring that may be more useful is the COD deficit, which measures the difference in time between a linear sprint and a COD drill of the same total length. For example, the coach could measure the difference in time between a player's 10-yard sprint and having a player sprint 5 yards out, touch the line with one foot, and sprint back 5 yards, covering 10 yards total. In this way, the coach is better able to get an understanding of how much more time the player consumes having to change direction in the latter situation, which can provide insight into that player's COD speed.

Due to the perceptual-cognitive elements associated with agility performance, testing agility is even more difficult than testing COD speed. Some assessments use timing gates, and the player has to move, respond to a generic stimulus (e.g., a light flash or coach pointing in a direction), and finish through a predetermined line, but the primary issue with these tests is that agility in football is based on highly specific information like reading the proper opponent keys and cues to determine the most effective subsequent action. Using generic stimuli will not differentiate high performers in football from low performers because all players will be exposed to the same unfamiliar stimulus. Therefore, it may be best to assess the player's agility in the context of the game when performing sport-specific practice or when assessing game film. This will primarily be the realm of football coaches, but strength coaches may communicate with football coaches to get an understanding of where each player stands and what may be done in training to help develop the right perceptual-cognitive qualities for enhancing in-game agility.

In summary, testing and monitoring COD speed and agility can be quite challenging, but this does not mean that these qualities should not be trained. It's better to monitor something than to monitor nothing, so common tests like the pro agility or L-run may certainly be incorporated due to the vast available normative data from the NFL combine as well as high school combines as to what the desirable standards are in those tests.

EXERCISES AND DRILLS TO DEVELOP COD SPEED

Developing COD speed involves using exercises that challenge the athlete to develop power out of positions that simulate the multidirectional plant-and-cut steps that occur in football games. Additionally, the ability to decelerate and reaccelerate are paramount to COD performance, so various drills may be used to develop these qualities. It's important to note that these exercises should be performed as explosively as possible but with great coordination and body control. In this section, we present some of the COD drills that we incorporate into our training program.

Lateral Low Push

The lateral low push develops the concentric explosive power to reaccelerate from a 90-degree cut step.

Execution

1. Begin the exercise in an athletic ready position with the feet square, a lowered center of mass, and a stance slightly wider than hip-width.

2. Drive off the outside foot explosively in a lateral direction while keeping the center of mass low, aiming to project horizontally as far as possible. Emphasize pushing the ground away.

3. Both feet will leave the ground temporarily before you land on both feet in an athletic ready position.

4. The arms will follow a natural side-to-side swinging motion that resembles that of skating.

5. The goal is to cover as much ground as possible on each horizontal push-off.

45-Degree Low Push Forward

The 45-degree low push forward is used to develop the concentric explosive power to reaccelerate from a 45-degree cut step.

Execution

1. Begin the exercise in an athletic ready position with the feet square, a lowered center of mass, and a stance slightly wider than hip-width.

2. Drive off the outside foot explosively in a 45-degree angle while keeping the center of mass low, aiming to project diagonally as far as possible. Emphasize pushing the ground away.

3. Both feet will leave the ground temporarily before you land on both feet in an athletic ready position. When landing, the hips should return to a forward-facing square position before the next repetition.

4. The arms will follow a natural diagonal swinging motion that resembles a combination of sprinting and skating.

5. The goal is to cover as much ground as possible on each diagonal push-off.

45-Degree Low Push Backward

The 45-degree low push backward is used to develop the push-off power required for a drop step or crossover step when performed backward.

Execution

1. Begin the exercise in an athletic ready position with the feet square, a lowered center of mass, and a stance slightly wider than hip-width.
2. Drive off the outside foot explosively and open the hip in a backward-moving 45-degree angle while keeping the center of mass low, aiming to project diagonally as far as possible. Emphasize pushing the ground away.
3. Both feet will leave the ground temporarily before you land on both feet in an athletic ready position. When landing, the hips should return to a forward-facing square position before the next repetition.
4. The arms will follow a natural diagonal swinging motion that resembles a combination of sprinting and skating.
5. The goal is to cover as much ground as possible on each diagonal push-off.

Half-Kneeling Hip Turn Acceleration

The half-kneeling hip turn acceleration develops the ability to initiate movement laterally with maximal acceleration over a large range of motion.

Execution

1. Begin the exercise in a half-kneeling position, with the inside knee on the ground and the outside foot forward, facing perpendicular to the intended line of travel. Have the inside arm forward and the outside arm back.
2. Drive off the outside foot explosively and open the hip 90 degrees toward the intended line of travel while keeping the center of mass low, aiming to project optimally into a linear acceleration position by the subsequent step.
3. Continue accelerating linearly for the intended distance (e.g., 10 yd).
4. The arms will follow a natural diagonal swinging motion that resembles a combination of sprinting and skating before settling into a linear sprinting rhythm.
5. The goal is to cover an optimal amount of ground that projects the body horizontally but still allows for efficient postures and shin angles into the linear acceleration phase.

Split Stance Vertical Deceleration to Hip Turn Acceleration

The split stance vertical deceleration to hip turn acceleration develops the ability to rapidly drop the center of mass, then quickly and powerfully redirect movement laterally, finishing with a maximal effort acceleration.

Execution

1. Begin the exercise standing upright and facing perpendicular to the intended line of travel. Arms will be at the sides.
2. Lift the arms overhead and allow the body to rise onto the toes. Rapidly drive the arms down as the feet leave the ground and land in a split stance with the outside foot forward.
3. Immediately after attaining the split stance, drive off the outside foot explosively and open the hip 90 degrees toward the intended line of travel while keeping the center of mass low, aiming for a linear acceleration position by the subsequent step.
4. Continue accelerating linearly for the intended distance (e.g., 10 yd).
5. The arms will follow a natural diagonal swinging motion that resembles a combination of sprinting and skating before settling into a linear sprinting rhythm.
6. The goal is to drop low into the split stance and then transfer the momentum of the drop into the hip turn and acceleration, covering an optimal amount of ground that projects the body horizontally but still allows for efficient postures and shin angles into the linear acceleration phase.

Vertical Jump to Single-Leg Landing

The vertical jump to single-leg landing is used to develop the ability to decelerate and stabilize on one leg in a vertical plane.

Execution

1. Begin the exercise standing upright with the arms at the sides.
2. Lift the arms overhead while keeping the feet flat. Rapidly drive the arms down and lower the center of mass, then perform a vertical countermovement jump (see chapter 7) by quickly reversing the arm action upward while extending the hips, knees, and ankles to take off vertically into the air as high as possible.
3. Land from the jump on one leg by absorbing through the ball of the foot first before sinking into a single-leg athletic position with

the center of mass lowered, the hips slightly back, and the spine neutral, bending at the knee and ankle. At the end of the absorption phase, the arms will be in a sprint-ready position, with the lead arm in front with the hand near the chin, and the rear arm back with the hand near the hip.

4. Hold this single-leg athletic position for about 2 seconds to ensure a "stick" landing before resetting for the next repetition. If the stick landing is not attained, add an extra repetition to that leg.

5. The goal is to jump as high as possible and learn to control the impact from the fall on one limb by decelerating and maintaining a stable posture.

Lateral Jump to Single-Leg Landing

The lateral jump to single-leg landing is used to develop the ability to decelerate and stabilize on one leg in a lateral plane.

Execution

1. Begin the exercise standing upright with the arms at the sides.

2. Lift the arms overhead while keeping the feet flat. Rapidly drive the arms down and lower the center of mass, then perform a lateral countermovement jump by quickly reversing the arm action sideways while extending the hips, knees, and ankles to take off laterally and horizontally through the air as far as possible.

3. Land from the jump on the outside leg by absorbing through the ball of the foot first before sinking into a single-leg athletic position with the center of mass lowered, the hips slightly back, and the spine neutral, bending at the knee and ankle. The foot will be outside the knee, and the knee will be outside the hip on initial impact. At the end of the absorption phase, the arms will be in a sprint-ready position, with the inside arm in front with the hand near the chin, and the outside arm back with the hand near the hip.

4. Hold this single-leg athletic position for about 2 seconds to ensure a "stick" landing before resetting for the next repetition. If the stick landing is not attained, add an extra repetition to that leg.

5. The goal is to jump as far as possible in a horizontal direction and to learn to control the impact on one limb by decelerating and maintaining a stable posture.

Transverse Jump to Single-Leg Landing

The transverse jump to single-leg landing is used to develop the ability to decelerate and stabilize on one leg in a rotational plane.

Execution

1. Begin the exercise standing upright with the arms at the sides.
2. Lift the arms overhead while keeping the feet flat. Rapidly drive the arms down and lower the center of mass, then perform a rotational countermovement jump by quickly reversing the arm action sideways while extending the hips, knees, and ankles to take off backward, diagonally, and horizontally through the air as far as possible. The angle of rotation will fall somewhere between 90 and 135 degrees before landing.
3. Land from the jump on the outside leg by absorbing through the ball of the foot first before sinking into a single-leg athletic position with the center of mass lowered, the hips slightly back, and the spine neutral, bending at the knee and ankle. The foot will be slightly outside the knee, and the knee will be slightly outside the hip on initial impact. At the end of the absorption phase, the arms will be in a sprint-ready position, with the inside arm in front with the hand near the chin, and the outside arm in the back with the hand near the hip.
4. Hold this single-leg athletic position for about 2 seconds to ensure a "stick" landing before resetting for the next repetition. If the stick landing is not attained, add an extra repetition to that leg.
5. The goal is to jump as far as possible in a horizontal direction and learn to control the impact on one limb by decelerating and maintaining a stable posture.

Vertical Jump to Lateral Bound

The vertical jump to lateral bound is used to progress the ability to rapidly decelerate and transfer momentum into a directional change across multiple movement planes.

Execution

1. Begin the exercise standing upright with the arms at the sides.
2. Lift the arms overhead while keeping the feet flat. Rapidly drive the arms down and lower the center of mass, then perform a vertical countermovement jump by quickly reversing the arm action upward while extending the hips, knees, and ankles to take off vertically into the air as high as possible (see figures *a-c*).
3. Land from the jump on one leg by absorbing through the ball of the foot first before sinking into a single-leg athletic position with

the center of mass lowered, the hips slightly back, and the spine neutral, bending at the knee and ankle (see figure *d*).

4. Immediately upon absorbing the landing impact, drive off the outside foot explosively and cover as much ground as possible horizontally and laterally while keeping the center of mass low (see figure *e*).

5. Land from the push-off in an athletic ready position with the feet square, a lowered center of mass, and a stance slightly wider than hip-width (see figure *f*).

6. The goal is to jump as high as possible and then transfer the momentum of the subsequent fall into a single-leg lateral push-off as far as possible to develop the ability to decelerate and reaccelerate movement in a vertical-to-horizontal plane transition.

Figure 4.5   Vertical jump to lateral bound.

Single-Leg Vertical Jump to Lateral Bound

The single-leg vertical jump to lateral bound is used to progress the ability to rapidly decelerate and transfer momentum across vertical-to-horizontal movement planes with an added stability challenge because of remaining on one leg for the entire exercise.

Execution

1. Begin the exercise standing upright on the outside leg with the arms at the sides.

2. Lift the arms overhead while keeping the foot flat. Rapidly drive the arms down and lower the center of mass, then perform a single-leg vertical countermovement jump by quickly reversing the arm action upward while extending the hip, knee, and ankle to take off vertically into the air as high as possible.

3. Land from the jump on the same leg by absorbing through the ball of the foot first before sinking into a single-leg athletic position with the center of mass lowered, the hips slightly back, and the spine neutral, bending at the knee and ankle.

4. Immediately upon absorbing the landing impact, drive off the outside foot explosively and cover as much ground as possible horizontally and laterally while keeping the center of mass low.

5. Land from the jump on the same leg by absorbing through the ball of the foot first before sinking into a single-leg athletic position with the center of mass lowered, the hips slightly back, and the spine neutral, bending at the knee and ankle. The foot will be inside the knee and the knee will be inside the hip on initial impact. At the end of the absorption phase, the arms will be in a sprint-ready position, with the inside arm in front with the hand near the chin, and the outside arm back with the hand near the hip.

6. The goal is to jump as high as possible and then transfer the momentum of the subsequent fall into a single-leg lateral push-off as far as possible to develop the ability to decelerate and reaccelerate movement in a vertical-to-horizontal plane transition with the increased stability challenge from being on one leg.

Vertical Jump to Transverse Bound

The vertical jump to transverse bound is used to progress the ability to rapidly decelerate and transfer momentum across vertical-to-horizontal movement planes with rotation.

Execution

1. Begin the exercise standing upright with the arms at the sides.
2. Lift the arms overhead while keeping the feet flat. Rapidly drive the arms down and lower the center of mass, then perform a vertical countermovement jump by quickly reversing the arm action upward while extending the hips, knees, and ankles to take off vertically into the air as high as possible (see figures *a-c*).

Figure 4.6   Vertical jump to transverse bound.

3. Land from the jump on one leg by absorbing through the ball of the foot first before sinking into a single-leg athletic position with the center of mass lowered, the hips slightly back, and the spine neutral, bending at the knee and ankle (see figure *d*).

4. Immediately upon absorbing the landing impact, drive off the outside foot explosively and cover as much ground as possible backward, horizontally, and laterally while keeping the center of mass low. The body will rotate 90-135 degrees while in the air (see figure *e*).

5. Land from the push-off in an athletic ready position with the feet square, a lowered center of mass, and a stance slightly wider than hip-width (see figure *f*).

6. The goal is to jump as high as possible and then transfer the momentum of the subsequent fall into a single-leg rotational push-off covering as much horizontal distance as possible to develop the ability to decelerate and reaccelerate movement in a vertical-to-horizontal plane transition with rotation.

Single-Leg Vertical Jump to Transverse Bound

The single-leg vertical jump to transverse bound is used to progress the ability to rapidly decelerate and transfer momentum across vertical-to-horizontal movement planes with rotation and an added stability challenge due to remaining on one leg for the entire exercise.

Execution

1. Begin the exercise standing upright on the outside leg with the arms at the sides.

2. Lift the arms overhead while keeping the foot flat. Rapidly drive the arms down and lower the center of mass, then perform a single-leg vertical countermovement jump by quickly reversing the arm action upward while extending the hip, knee, and ankle to take off vertically into the air as high as possible.

3. Land from the jump on the same leg by absorbing through the ball of the foot first before sinking into a single-leg athletic position with the center of mass lowered, the hips slightly back, and the spine neutral, bending at the knee and ankle.

4. Immediately upon absorbing the landing impact, drive off the outside foot explosively and cover as much ground as possible backward, horizontally, and laterally while keeping the center of mass low. The body will rotate 90-135 degrees while in the air.

5. Land from the jump on the same leg by absorbing through the ball of the foot first before sinking into a single-leg athletic position with the center of mass lowered, the hips slightly back, and the spine neutral, bending at the knee and ankle. The foot will be inside the knee and the knee will be inside the hip on initial impact. At the end of the absorption phase, the arms will be in a sprint-ready position, with the inside arm in front with the hand near the chin, and the outside arm back with the hand near the hip.

6. The goal is to jump as high as possible and then transfer the momentum of the subsequent fall into a single-leg rotational push-off covering as much horizontal distance as possible to develop the ability to decelerate and reaccelerate movement in a vertical-to-horizontal plane transition with rotation with the increased stability challenge from being on one leg.

Band Partner Lateral Low Push

The band partner lateral low push accentuates the explosive push-off of the outside leg laterally and horizontally by working against increasing resistance as the band lengthens.

Execution

1. Before beginning the exercise, attach two elastic bands by tying them together or using an attachment device. Place one loop around the waist and the other loop around the partner's waist. If a partner is not available, the other loop may be placed around a squat rack or other immovable object.

2. Begin the exercise by facing perpendicular to the partner and walking out far enough to create tension between the bands. Then, stand upright with the arms at the sides.

3. While the partner stays grounded and keeps the band tension steady, lift the arms overhead, then rapidly drive the arms down and lower the center of mass before explosively driving through the outside foot, aiming to project horizontally as far as possible. Emphasize pushing the ground away.

4. Both feet will leave the ground temporarily before the athlete lands on both feet, back in an athletic ready position.

5. The arms will follow a natural side-to-side swinging motion that resembles that of skating.

6. The goal is to cover as much ground as possible on each horizontal push-off.

Band Partner Consecutive Lateral Bounding

The band partner consecutive lateral bounding is used to accentuate the explosive push-off of the outside leg by working against band resistance on the way out and deceleration of the outside leg by absorbing the increased pull from the band tension on the way back in.

Execution

1. Before beginning the exercise, attach two elastic bands by tying them together or using an attachment device. Place one loop around the waist and the other loop around the partner's waist. If a partner is not available, the other loop may be placed around a squat rack or other immovable object.

2. Begin the exercise by facing perpendicular to the partner and walking out far enough to create tension between the bands. Then, stand upright with the arms at the sides.

3. While the partner stays grounded and keeps the band tension steady, lift the arms overhead, then rapidly drive the arms down

and lower the center of mass before explosively driving through the outside foot, aiming to project horizontally as far as possible. Emphasize pushing the ground away.

4. Both feet will leave the ground temporarily before the athlete lands on the other foot and rapidly drives back toward the start. Continue driving off each foot explosively back and forth for the predetermined repetitions or time frame.

5. The arms will follow a natural side-to-side swinging motion that resembles that of skating.

6. The goal is to cover as much ground as possible on each horizontal push-off.

Band Partner-Assisted Single-Leg Deceleration

The band partner-assisted single-leg deceleration is used to accentuate the deceleration capacity of each limb by absorbing the impact and momentum gained by having the assisted tension of a band pull you faster horizontally.

Execution

1. Before beginning the exercise, attach two elastic bands by tying them together or using an attachment device. Place one loop around the waist and the other loop around the partner's waist. If a partner is not available, the other loop may be placed around a squat rack or other immovable object.

2. Begin the exercise by facing the partner and walking out far enough to create tension between the bands. Then, stand upright with the arms at the sides.

3. While the partner stays grounded and keeps the band tension steady, lift the arms overhead, then rapidly drive the arms down and lower the center of mass before explosively jumping forward off both feet, aiming to project as far forward as possible. Emphasize pushing the ground away.

4. Both feet will leave the ground temporarily before the athlete lands on the lead foot and rapidly decelerates momentum by keeping the hips back, lifting the chest up slightly, and bending at the knee and ankle. Hold the "stick" position for 1-2 seconds before walking back to the start position for the next repetition.

5. The arms will follow a natural forward swing like a broad jump (see chapter 7) before falling into a sprint-ready position upon landing, where the lead arm's hand is by the chin and the rear arm's hand is by the hip.

6. The goal is to cover as much ground as possible on each horizontal push-off and still have control and stability upon landing.

Lateral Consecutive Bounding to Acceleration

The lateral consecutive bounding to acceleration exercise is used to emphasize the rapid switching from absorption to propulsion and finishing with a maximal effort acceleration.

Execution

1. Begin the exercise by facing perpendicular to the intended line of travel, standing upright with the arms at the sides.

2. Lift the arms overhead, then rapidly drive the arms down and lower the center of mass before explosively pushing off the outside leg, aiming to project horizontally as far as possible. Emphasize pushing the ground away.

3. Both feet will leave the ground temporarily before the athlete lands on the other foot and rapidly drives back toward the start. Repeat the sequence one more time (out, then back in) and upon bounding back to the starting line, immediately perform a hip turn and accelerate maximally for a predetermined distance (e.g., 10 yd).

4. The arms will follow a natural diagonal swinging motion that resembles a combination of sprinting and skating before settling into a linear sprinting rhythm.

5. The goal is to bound back through the starting line and rapidly redirect the momentum of the bound into the hip turn and acceleration, covering an optimal amount of ground that projects the body horizontally but still allows for efficient postures and shin angles into the linear acceleration phase.

Transverse Consecutive Bounding to Acceleration

The transverse consecutive bounding to acceleration exercise emphasizes the rapid switching from absorption to propulsion and finishing with a maximal effort acceleration.

Execution

1. Begin the exercise by facing away from the intended line of travel, standing upright with the arms at the sides.

2. Lift the arms overhead, then rapidly drive the arms down and lower the center of mass before explosively pushing off the outside leg backward while rotating 90-135 degrees, aiming to project horizontally as far as possible. Emphasize pushing the ground away.

3. Both feet will leave the ground temporarily before the athlete lands on the other foot and rapidly drives back toward the start. Repeat

the sequence one more time (out, then back in) and upon bounding back to the starting line, immediately perform a drop step and accelerate maximally for a predetermined distance (e.g., 10 yd).

4. The arms will follow a natural diagonal swinging motion that resembles a combination of sprinting and skating before settling into a linear sprinting rhythm.

5. The goal is to bound back through the starting line and rapidly redirect the momentum of the bound into the drop step and acceleration, covering an optimal amount of ground that projects the body horizontally but still allows for efficient postures and shin angles into the linear acceleration phase.

Cone Zigzag Run

The cone zigzag run exercise is used to challenge the ability to maintain speed as much as possible while changing direction through a series of 45-degree cuts for a predetermined distance.

Execution

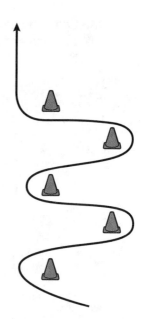

1. Begin the exercise in an athletic ready position with the feet square, a lowered center of mass, and a stance slightly wider than hip-width at the starting cone.

2. Rotate the hips 45 degrees toward the next cone and accelerate to it until past the cone.

3. Make a plant step once past the cone and flip the hips in the opposite direction 45 degrees toward the next cone and accelerate to it.

4. Continue making 45-degree cuts until past the last cone, where a 5-yard maximal linear acceleration is performed to finish the drill.

5. The goal is to make effective plant steps at each cone, preserving as much speed as possible and gaining ground out of each plant toward the next cone.

Figure 4.7 Cone zigzag run.

Cone "N" Drill

The cone "N" drill is used to challenge multiple sharp CODs (e.g., >90 degrees) while maintaining as much speed as possible with a maximal acceleration at the finish.

Execution

1. Begin the exercise by standing in a 2-point stance with the front foot behind and outside the first cone.

2. Maximally accelerate into a linear sprint until past the first cone.

3. Make a plant step once past the cone and flip the hips back downhill at approximately 135 degrees toward the next cone and accelerate past it.

4. Repeat the same plant step once past the next cone before finishing with a maximal linear acceleration through the finish cone.

5. The goal is to challenge sharper angles of COD, and the coach may manipulate the entry speed into the deceleration by spacing the cones closer or farther apart. More distance will lead to greater acceleration, more entry speed, and greater deceleration intensity. Multiple drill stations may be set up beside each other to have players race around the cone configuration and add competition.

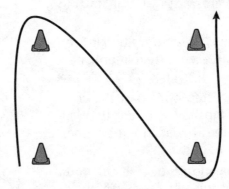

Figure 4.8　Cone "N" drill.

Cone "U" Drill

The cone "U" drill is used to challenge sharp maneuverability with rounded CODs with a maximal acceleration at the finish.

Execution

1. Begin the exercise by standing in a 2-point stance with the front foot behind and inside the first cone.
2. Maximally accelerate into a linear sprint until past the first cone.
3. Make a tightly rounded redirection once past the cone to flip the hips back downhill to face the starting cone and accelerate past it.
4. Make a wider rounded redirection toward the next cone along the intended line of travel and accelerate past it.
5. Maintain a curvilinear path past the next cone and reposition the body to attain a linear sprint posture for a maximal acceleration at the finish.
6. The goal is to challenge maneuverability at various curvilinear paths, and the coach may manipulate the entry speed into the deceleration by spacing the cones closer or farther apart. More distance will lead to greater acceleration, more entry speed, and greater deceleration intensity. Multiple drill stations may be set up beside each other to have players race around the cone configuration and add competition.

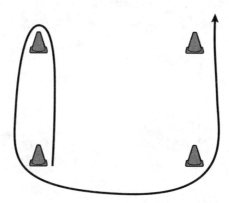

Figure 4.9   Cone "U" drill.

Cone "90-90" Drill

The cone "90-90" drill is used to challenge multiple CODs at approximately 90 degrees while maintaining as much speed as possible with a maximal acceleration at the finish.

Execution

1. Begin the exercise by standing in a 2-point stance with the front foot behind and outside the first cone.
2. Maximally accelerate into a linear sprint until past the first cone.
3. Make a plant step once past the cone and flip the hips laterally at approximately 90 degrees toward the outside edge of the next cone and accelerate past it.
4. Repeat the same plant step once past the next cone before finishing with a maximal linear acceleration through the finish cone.
5. The goal is to challenge a sharp angle of COD, and the coach may manipulate the entry speed into the deceleration by spacing the cones closer or farther apart. More distance will lead to greater acceleration, more entry speed, and greater deceleration intensity. Multiple drill stations may be set up beside each other to have players race around the cone configuration and add competition.

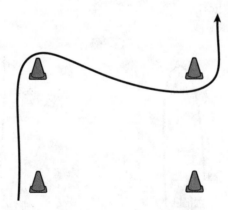

Figure 4.10   Cone "90-90" drill.

10-5-5 Shuttle Run

The 10-5-5 shuttle run exercise is used to challenge multiple CODs at approximately 180 degrees while maintaining as much speed as possible with a maximal acceleration at the finish.

Execution

1. Begin the exercise by standing in a 2-point stance with the front foot behind the starting line.
2. Maximally accelerate into a linear sprint for 10 yards.
3. Make a plant step at the 10-yard line, flip the hips 180 degrees back toward the starting line, and accelerate back 5 yards.
4. Repeat the same plant step at the 5-yard line and flip the hips 180 degrees back toward the finish line.
5. Finish with a 5-yard maximal acceleration through the 10-yard line.
6. The goal is to challenge a very sharp angle of COD, and the coach may decide to manipulate the execution coordination by having players plant with different feet at each plant (e.g., touch the first line with the right foot, touch the second line with the left foot, then finish). Multiple drill stations may be set up beside each other to have players race through the exercise for speed and accuracy to add competition.

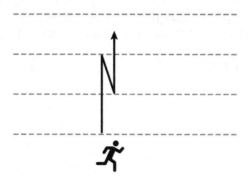

Figure 4.11   10-5-5 shuttle run.

EXERCISES AND DRILLS TO DEVELOP PERCEPTUAL-COGNITIVE ABILITY

Developing perceptual-cognitive ability requires the athlete to use information to guide movement decisions. In this way, the athlete perceives a stimulus and uses cognition to determine what that stimulus means in context. Different perceptual stimuli can be incorporated in training, such as a coach pointing in a given direction, reacting to a tennis ball bouncing off a surface, or flashing light systems where players have to respond to a given color. However, these general examples of cues differ from what the players will experience in a football game.

As an example, one of the most important player-to-player interactions in football is between a ballcarrier and a tackler in the open field. While we can't have players tackling each other in the off-season, we may still design activities that represent this interaction from a specific perceptual standpoint, like implementing open field tag drills where the players have to track the opponent and attempt to close space or create space. This kind of activity can have a positive effect on the players' perceptual-cognitive learning in a context that resembles a football situation. The stimulus used here is another human (the opponent), so each player must read, anticipate, decide, and respond to the actions of the other while abiding by the task goal (e.g., cross the line for a touchdown without getting tagged).

In this section, we have provided some of our most common and simple perceptual-cognitive drills that we incorporate in our training program where the perceptual stimuli are the players themselves. We are able to manipulate the complexity of the drill by changing constraints like the size of the drill area, the number of players involved in each drill, and the specific task (e.g., mirroring, chasing, dodging, etc.).

"X" Box Partner Reaction Drill

The "X" box partner reaction drill is used to get players to read and interpret the movements of an opponent while making accurate movement decisions. One player will assume the role of leader while the other will take on the role of follower. The leader will choose where to move, and the follower must respond accurately based on the leader's movements. The challenge and skill development are skewed toward the follower player to interpret and respond to the movements of the leader player.

Execution

1. Begin the exercise by setting up two drill areas. Create two square "box" spaces, placing cones 5 yards apart from each other. Each player will stand in the center of his own box area, facing each other in an athletic ready position with the feet square, a lowered center of mass, and a stance slightly wider than hip-width.

2. At the start of the drill, the leader player decides to move toward one of the cones at each corner of the box area, planting at the cone before returning back to the center of the box area. The follower player must read and mirror the actions of the leader in opposition. So, if the leader decides to move forward to the front right cone of his box area, the follower must retreat toward the back left cone of his box area. After mirroring the actions of the leader, the follower also returns to the middle of his box area before waiting to react to the leader's next movement.

3. The leader makes three cone movements. To finish the drill, the leader then settles back to the middle of the box and decides when to turn 180 degrees and retreat out of the box with maximal acceleration while the follower must react and chase the leader through the finish.

4. The goal is to challenge the ability to perceive, interpret, and react to an opponent. This drill emphasizes the brain components more than the physical components, challenging the follower's ability to appropriately respond to what is seen from the leader.

Figure 4.12 "X" box partner reaction drill.

Partner Mirror Reaction Drill

The partner mirror reaction drill is used to challenge the ability to perceive and attempt to manipulate an opponent, either from an evasive role or from a mirroring role. The evasive player attempts to create space and separation from the mirroring player while the mirroring player attempts to constrain space and stay close to the evasive player. The challenge and skill development are skewed toward the evasive player to create space.

Execution

1. Begin the exercise by having two players face each other across a starting line between two cones spaced 5 yards apart.

2. The mirroring player offsets to one side of the evasive player with the goal of maintaining that leverage when the drill starts. The mirroring player is instructed to read the near hip (the hip to the leverage side) to perceive the actions of the evasive player.

3. When the drill starts, the evasive player attempts to create lateral space away from the mirroring player either by expanding out away from the mirroring player or by breaking the mirroring player's leverage by going across the mirroring player's body.

4. The mirroring player attempts to constrain space by maintaining leverage and not allowing the evasive player to expand too much laterally.

5. The drill continues for the allotted time, which is typically 5-10 seconds.

6. The goal is to challenge the ability to perceive, interpret, and manipulate an opponent. The best players in football can use their superior skills and perceptual-cognitive abilities to manipulate their opponents in their favor. This drill emphasizes the brain components far more than the physical components, given the small work space.

7. Coaches may increase the spacing of the cones (e.g., 10 yd apart) to give more space to the evasive player and challenge the mirroring player. Coaches may also incorporate Velcro evasion belts where the evasive player attempts to create enough separation to "break the belt" while the mirroring player attempts to prevent separation, which allows for a more objective measure of winning or losing the drill.

Figure 4.13   Partner mirror reaction drill.

Partner Blind Mirror Reaction Drill

The partner blind mirror reaction drill is used to challenge the ability of the mirroring player to perceive and locate the evasive player when sight is obstructed due to the evasive player being behind the mirroring player. The evasive player attempts to create space and separation from the mirroring player while the mirroring player attempts to constrain space and stay close to the evasive player. The challenge and skill development are skewed toward the mirroring player to constrain space.

Execution

1. Begin the exercise by having the mirroring player face away from the evasive player across a starting line between two cones spaced 5 yards apart.

2. The mirroring player offsets to one side of the evasive player with the goal of maintaining that leverage when the drill starts. The mirroring player is instructed to look over his shoulder to locate and perceive the actions of the evasive player.

3. When the drill starts, the evasive player attempts to create lateral space away from the mirroring player either by expanding out away from the mirroring player or by breaking the mirroring player's leverage by going across the mirroring player's body.

4. The mirroring player attempts to constrain space by locating the evasive player behind the body and maintaining leverage and not allowing the evasive player to expand too much laterally.

5. The drill continues for a time decided by the evasive player, which should be 3-6 seconds. After the minimum time, the evasive player decides when to take off into a linear acceleration for 5-10 yards. At this point, the mirroring player must locate and respond to the evasive player by pressing the near hip and closing space through the finish.

6. The goal is to challenge the ability to perceive, interpret, and respond to an opponent when sight is obstructed.

7. Coaches may increase the spacing of the cones (e.g., 10 yd apart) to give more space to the evasive player and challenge the mirroring player. Coaches may also incorporate Velcro evasion belts where the evasive player attempts to create enough separation to "break the belt" while the mirroring player attempts to prevent separation, which allows for a more objective measure of winning or losing the drill.

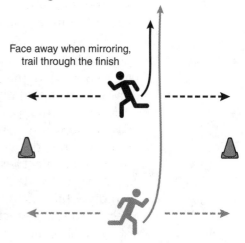

Face away when mirroring, trail through the finish

Figure 4.14 Partner blind mirror reaction drill.

Run to 90-Degree Cut on Reaction

The run to 90-degree cut on reaction exercise challenges the ability to successfully evade an opponent by perceiving a human stimulus and effectively moving in the opposite direction of the opponent by changing direction at approximately 90 degrees and finishing with a maximal acceleration. The challenge and skill development are skewed toward the ability to evade and create space.

Execution

1. Begin the exercise by standing in a 2-point stance with the front foot behind the starting line.
2. Maximally accelerate into a linear sprint for 10 yards toward the opponent, keeping the perception and gaze on the hips of the opponent.
3. The opponent is instructed to shift left or right when the moving person is 2-3 yards away.
4. Accurately perceive and interpret the movement of the opponent without reducing speed—if the opponent moves left, cut to the right and vice versa.
5. Once the movement decision is made, change direction as rapidly as possible toward the next cone set at a 90-degree angle and 5 yards away.
6. Accelerate maximally past the cone and then make a plant step and flip the hips 90 degrees toward the finish line.
7. Finish with a 5-yard maximal acceleration.
8. The goal is to challenge the ability to perceive, interpret, and accurately make a movement decision that results in evading the opponent. The other goal is to expose players to CODs under duress, which is more representative of the CODs that happen in a game due to the chaotic nature and unpredictability of player-to-player interactions.
9. The most important component is to instruct players to accelerate maximally toward the human stimulus. Players may attempt to slow down upon entry to make a more accurate decision, but the training effect lies in the ability to make the decision rapidly while moving fast because this is characteristic of football game dynamics and is necessary to enhance perceptual-cognitive speed.

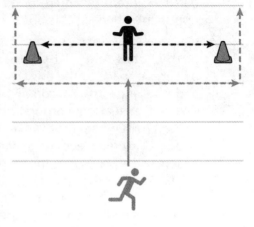

Figure 4.15   Run to 90-degree cut on reaction.

Retreat and React

The retreat and react exercise is used to challenge the ability to rapidly locate, track, and mirror an opponent by closing down space and maintaining coverage through the finish. The challenge and skill development are skewed toward the mirroring player to constrain space.

Execution

1. Begin the exercise by having the evasive player start behind a cone in a 2-point stance. Have the mirroring player face the evasive player in a square stance behind a cone set 2 yards to the side and 5 yards away from the evasive player. A finish set of cones are set 15 yards away from the evasive player, 10 yards apart.

2. At the start of the drill, the evasive player maximally accelerates toward the finish cones while the mirroring player turns 180 degrees and retreats backward 10 yards before flipping the hips back around to locate the evasive player.

3. The evasive player attempts to manipulate the mirroring player by making maneuvers to gain separation through the finish line while the mirroring player attempts to establish leverage and close down space, staying tight to the evasive player through the finish.

4. The goal is to challenge the ability to perceive, interpret, and accurately make a movement decision that results in evading the opponent. The other goal is to expose players to CODs under duress, which is more representative of the CODs that happen in a game due to the chaotic nature and unpredictability of player-to-player interactions.

5. Coaches may make the width of the drill space larger (e.g., 15 yd wide) to give more space to the evasive player and challenge the mirroring player.

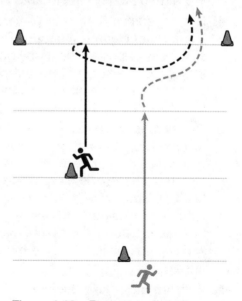

Figure 4.16   Retreat and react.

Open Field Tag

The open field tag exercise is used to replicate an open field tackle situation, challenging the evasive player to create space and make the pursuit player miss before scoring. It challenges the pursuing player to prevent that from happening by closing down space and tagging off on the hip of the evasive player. The challenge and skill development are balanced for both players, but the smaller the space, the more challenge for the evasive player and vice versa for the pursuit player.

Execution

1. Begin by setting up an area that is 10 yards deep and 10 yards wide by making a box of cones. Both players face each other on the same side of the box but at opposite ends, 10 yards apart.

2. At the start of the drill, the evasive player attempts to find a way to get past the pursuit player without being tagged and cross the opposite end of the box to "score." The pursuit player must maintain leverage and close down space to tag off on the hip of the evasive player before sprinting and finishing through the opposite end of the box.

3. The pursuit player must touch the hip of the evasive player with both hands to count as a successful stop and is not allowed to jump, dive, or leave his feet in any way to do so. The pursuit player is encouraged to close down enough space that he is able to get within a forearm's length away from the evasive player rather than leaning and reaching, which would likely result in a missed tackle in live football action.

4. It is imperative that both players move at maximal intensity to simulate a chaotic game situation. The evasive player is instructed to finish across the opposite side of the box at full effort and not halt movement if tagged. Likewise, the pursuit player must pursue until a tag is made or until the evasive player crosses and "scores" before finishing through the other end of the box.

5. The goal is to challenge the ability to perceive, interpret, and effectively manipulate the opponent to achieve a task. The other goal is to expose players to CODs under duress, which is more representative of the CODs that happen in a game due to the chaotic nature and unpredictability of player-to-player interactions.

6. Coaches may make the width of the drill space larger (e.g., 15 yd wide) to give more space to the evasive player and challenge the pursuit player.

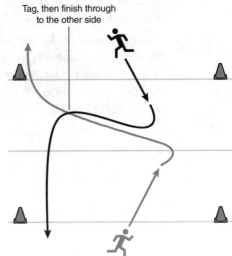

Figure 4.17 Open field tag.

Double-Blind Open Field Tag

The double-blind open field tag exercise is used for the same reasons as the traditional open field tag exercise, with the added complexity of each player not knowing the location of the opponent before the exercise begins. The challenge and skill development are balanced for both players, but the smaller the space, the more challenge for the evasive player and vice versa for the pursuit player.

Execution

1. Begin by setting up an area that is 10 yards deep and 10 yards wide by making a box of cones. Both players face away from each other at opposite ends, 10 yards apart.

2. Before the start of the drill, a coach gives a verbal cue of "Set!" This tells each player to move laterally along his starting line to wherever he wants, unaware of what the other player is doing. After waiting about 3 seconds, the coach yells "Go!" Both players turn around and the drill begins.

3. At the start of the drill, each player locates the other. The evasive player attempts to find a way to get past the pursuit player without being tagged and cross the opposite end of the box to "score." The pursuit player must maintain leverage and close down space to tag off on the hip of the evasive player before sprinting and finishing through the opposite end of the box.

4. The pursuit player must touch the hip of the evasive player with both hands for it to count as a successful stop and is not allowed to jump, dive, or leave his feet in any way to do so. The pursuit player is encouraged to close down enough space that he is able to get within a forearm's length away from the evasive player rather than leaning and reaching, which would likely result in a missed tackle in live football action.

5. It is imperative that both players move at maximal intensity to simulate a chaotic game situation. The evasive player is instructed to finish across the opposite side of the box at full effort and not halt movement if tagged. Likewise, the pursuit player must pursue until a tag is made or until the evasive player crosses and "scores" before finishing through the other end of the box.

6. The goal is to challenge the ability to perceive, interpret, and effectively manipulate the opponent to achieve a task with the added challenge of removing visual interpretation before the exercise starts. The other goal is to expose players to CODs under duress, which is more representative of the CODs that happen in a game due to the chaotic nature and unpredictability of player-to-player interactions. Thus, maximum focus, competitiveness, and intensity are key to the effectiveness of this exercise.

7. Coaches may make the width of the drill space larger (e.g., 15 yd wide) to give more space to the evasive player and challenge the pursuit player.

Cone Tunnel Open Field Tag

The cone tunnel open field tag exercise is used for the same reasons as the traditional open field tag exercise, with the added intensity of a larger field space and added complexity of each player having to sprint through a defined tunnel of cones before interacting with each other. The challenge and skill development are skewed toward the pursuit player, who must perform at high speed under pressure.

Execution

1. Before beginning the exercise, two separate cone configurations are set up across from each other, one for the evasive player and one for the pursuit player. The starting line for each cone configuration should align the players so that they are 15-20 yards away from one another, facing each other. Set up both cone configurations in two columns that serve as tunnels for the players to run through before interacting with each other. Both cone tunnels should be approximately 1-2 yards wide, and the evasive player's tunnel should be about 3 yards long while the pursuit player's tunnel should be about 6 yards long. The pursuit player's longer tunnel is a purposeful disadvantage intended to mimic the pursuit angles and intensity of actions of defensive football players when pursuing a ballcarrier during game plays.

2. The drill starts by having the evasive player initiate movement so that the pursuit player responds. At the start of the exercise, both players must sprint fully through their respective tunnels before the players interact in the open middle space. The evasive player attempts to find a way to get past the pursuit player without being tagged and cross the opposing starting line to "score." The pursuit player must maintain leverage and close down space to tag off on the hip of the evasive player before sprinting and finishing through the opposing starting line.

3. The pursuit player must touch the hip of the evasive player with both hands to count as a successful stop and is not allowed to jump, dive, or leave his feet in any way to do so. The pursuit player is encouraged to close down enough space that he is able to get within a forearm's length away from the evasive player rather than leaning and reaching, which would likely result in a missed tackle in live football action.

4. It is imperative that both players move at maximal intensity to simulate a chaotic game situation. The evasive player is instructed to finish across the opposing starting line at full effort and not halt movement if tagged. Likewise, the pursuit player must pursue until

a tag is made or until the evasive player crosses and "scores" before finishing through the opposing starting line.

5. After completing the drill, the players should switch roles for the subsequent repetition, and continue swapping back and forth for the total allotted repetitions.

6. The goal is to challenge the ability to perceive, interpret, and effectively manipulate the opponent to achieve a task. The other goal is to expose players to CODs under duress, which is more representative of the CODs that happen in a game due to the chaotic nature and unpredictability of player-to-player interactions. Thus, maximum focus, competitiveness, and intensity are key to the effectiveness of this exercise.

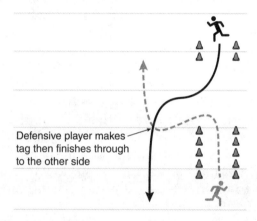

Figure 4.18   Cone tunnel open field tag.

Defensive player makes tag then finishes through to the other side

AGILITY AND COD TRAINING PROGRAM

Developing agility and COD is based on a logical progression of gradual exposure to higher intensities (in the case of COD) and higher complexities (in the case of agility). Some programs follow a progression of closed to open in terms of working all closed COD drills for a period before moving to open or reactive agility drills. We believe there are benefits to keeping open or reactive drills in the program throughout the off-season training period, not just isolated to the final phases. However, we still shift the overall emphasis from closed to open as the program unfolds. In this way, the open activities used early will be simple and low intensity from a physical standpoint, utilized primarily to activate perceptual-cognitive engagement.

At the onset of the off-season, COD development can start with exercises geared toward enforcing multidirectional force application and absorption. This would include low pushes, single-leg landing variations, and multidirectional accelerations. From here, the COD work can progress to intensifying the plant step at various angles (e.g., 45-135 degrees) and manipulating the angles, the entry speed, and the competitive nature (e.g., having multiple athletes race through a cone configuration).

As we build the capacity to handle higher intensities of deceleration and COD, we start to progress the open or reactive activities to visit the same level of intensity and simultaneously develop the associated perceptual-cognitive ability of evading, mirroring, pursuing, and so on. So, after a certain level of COD intensity has been visited with a closed activity, we try to apply that same level of intensity in an open environment. Thus, the COD intensity of the open activities always lags slightly behind the COD intensity of the closed drills. We feel that this allows our players' bodies to adapt to the physical impact of the higher COD intensity so they can better focus on the perceptual aspects of the open activities.

In each off-season, our primary aim is to gradually build exposure to high intensities of COD and complexity of open or reactive activities so we can better bridge the transition into spring football practice or fall training camp. We can summarize this process with a basic four-stage progression as shown in figure 4.19.

At the beginning of off-season training, we can spend 2-3 weeks emphasizing introductory COD mechanics using basic, low-intensity closed drills that expose players to multidirectional positions and movement planes. Next, we can increase the volume and intensity of COD by incorporating drills that emphasize various angles while introducing a small number of open drills to add context and develop basic perceptual-cognitive ability. From here, we continue to intensify the COD efforts while shifting more of the training time toward open or reactive activities and raise their complexity. In the final stage, we aim to maintain COD capacity while

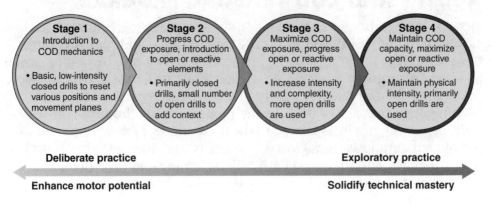

Figure 4.19 Four-stage progression of change-of-direction training.

primarily utilizing open or reactive activities as the final step toward starting preseason football practice.

The progression follows a gradual continuum from emphasizing deliberate practice and enhancing motor potential early on before shifting toward exploratory practice and solidifying technical mastery as we approach the in-season period. In table 4.2, we show a sample agility and COD progression for college football players during the summer off-season leading into fall training camp.

Table 4.2 Sample Progression for COD and Agility Training

Stage and emphasis	Training notes	Sample training sessions for each stage	
Stage 1: *Primary aim:* Introduction to COD mechanics *Secondary aim:* Minimal volume of low-complexity reactive drills	Basic, low-intensity closed drills to introduce various positions and movement planes. Activate perceptual-cognitive processing with low-complexity open drills in small spaces.	**Day 1:** *COD development* Low push series: 2 × 10 yd each: • Lateral (left and right) • 45 degree (forward and backward) Half-kneeling hip turn acceleration: 2 × 10 yd each way *Agility development* Partner mirror reaction drill with 5 yd between cones: 4-6 total repetitions (half of the repetitions as evasive player, half as mirroring player)	**Day 2:** *COD development* Single-leg landing series: 1 × 3 each leg for each variation: • Vertical jump to single-leg landing • Lateral jump to single-leg landing • Transverse jump to single-leg landing Split stance vertical deceleration to hip turn acceleration: 2 × 10 yd each way *Agility development* "X" box partner reaction drill: 4 total repetitions (half as leader, half as follower)

(continued)

Table 4.2 Sample Progression for COD and Agility Training *(continued)*

Stage and emphasis	Training notes	Sample training sessions for each stage	
Stage 2: *Primary aim:* Progress COD intensity and volume *Secondary aim:* Add more open drills for basic agility development	Progress closed drills with combinations of movements, greater entry speeds, and added competition. Increase complexity of open drills and increase the size of the drill spaces.	**Day 1:** *COD development* Band partner lateral low push: 2 × 5 each way Band partner consecutive lateral bounding: 2 × 3 each way (1 repetition = out and back in) Lateral consecutive bounding to acceleration: 2 × 10 yd each way Transverse consecutive bounding to acceleration: 2 × 10 yd each way *Agility development* Partner blind mirror reaction drill: 4-6 total repetitions (half of the repetitions as evasive player, half as mirroring player)	**Day 2:** *COD development* Band partner-assisted single-leg deceleration: 2 × 5 each leg Cone zigzag run: 4 total repetitions (2 each way) Cone "90-90" drill: 4 total repetitions (2 each way) *Agility development* Run to 90-degree cut on reaction: 4-6 total repetitions (half of the repetitions as evasive player, half as opponent)
Stage 3: *Primary aim:* Maximize COD intensity *Secondary aim:* Increase intensity and volume of open drills to progress agility development	Closed drills reach their maximum intensity in terms of movement combinations, entry speeds, and competition. Complexity of open drills starts to match agility demands of football in isolated situations. Various field sizes and shapes are incorporated.	**Day 1:** *COD development* Cone "90-90" drill: 4 total repetitions (2 each way) 10-5-5 shuttle run: 4 total repetitions (2 each way) *Agility development* Retreat and react: 4-6 total repetitions (half of the repetitions as evasive player, half as mirroring player)	**Day 2:** *COD development* Cone "N" drill: 4 total repetitions (2 each way) Cone "U" drill: 4 total repetitions (2 each way) *Agility development* Open field tag: 4-6 total repetitions (half of the repetitions as evasive player, half as pursuit player)

Stage and emphasis	Training notes	Sample training sessions for each stage	
Stage 4: *Primary aim:* Maximize intensity and volume of agility development with primarily open drills *Secondary aim:* Maintain COD capacity with reduced volume of closed drills	Open drills reach their maximum intensity in terms of complexity and matching reactive demands of football situations. Various field sizes and shapes are still incorporated. Closed drills are maintained to prepare for the open drills and to maintain COD capacity.	**Day 1:** *COD development* Cone "90-90" drill: 4 total repetitions (2 each way) *Agility development* Retreat and react: 4-6 total repetitions (half of the repetitions as evasive player, half as mirroring player) Double-blind open field tag: 4-6 total repetitions (half of the repetitions as evasive player, half as pursuit player)	**Day 2:** *COD development* Cone "N" drill: 4 total repetitions (2 each way) *Agility development* Open field tag: 4-6 total repetitions (half of the repetitions as evasive player, half as pursuit player) Cone tunnel open field tag: 4-6 total repetitions (half of the repetitions as evasive player, half as pursuit player)

CONCLUSION

While COD and agility are separate skills and we could make the argument that agility is most important for football, we believe that both are necessary inclusions in a holistic training program. Simply stated, we can use COD exercises to train the body and agility exercises to train the brain and body together. We use COD exercises for overload patterns we know will occur on the field, whereas agility exercises are used to incorporate *situations* we know will occur. The specific movements will vary from repetition to repetition as the player learns to problem solve and accomplish different tasks. Ultimately, being able to operate with speed in situations of COD and agility are the most important forms of game-related speed that any football player can possess. So, it's paramount that we include these parameters in a complete conditioning program for football.

Chapter 5

Strength Training

An individual's strength depends on several factors, including external resistance level, joint angle, joint orientation, movement speed, and movement type. Because of this, discussing the strength of an athlete without specifying the conditions under which the strength is produced is somewhat meaningless. Muscular strength can be defined as a muscle's ability to exert force on an external resistance.[1] Strength is synonymous with force, and the greatest strength efforts are those in which the most force is produced. So, when we refer to *maximum strength training*, we are referring to training the muscles' ability to produce maximum force.

In addition, while performing most exercises and athletic movements, our muscles go through different types of contractions. These contractions can be classified into three groups: eccentric, isometric, and concentric. Each contraction type is its own unique form of strength. For example, eccentric contractions occur when the muscle is being lengthened under load, so eccentric strength refers to the ability to maintain high tension when yielding to high forces. This is commonly seen when a player is lowering the barbell during a squat or bench press, but it also occurs when yielding to the impact from a jump or changing direction or when an offensive lineman takes on a defensive bull rush. When yielding against resistance, the muscles are about 50% stronger than when they overcome resistance.[2]

An isometric muscle action occurs when the muscle length and joint angle remain relatively unchanged as tension is produced. Two simple examples of isometric contractions would be the following:

1. *Pushing against an immoveable object, like trying to push your arms through a brick wall.* This is called an *overcoming isometric*, since you would be trying to overcome the resistance of the wall but would not be capable of it.

2. *Holding a weight in place, like when performing a barbell squat and holding the bottom position, preventing any further movement.* This is called a *yielding isometric*, since you would have first yielded to a load in the eccentric phase (the lowering of the weight) and then tried to prevent movement.

Isometric muscle actions are performed in every dynamic movement that players make on the field. This is because every time a player yields against and overcomes force, there's always a transition point between yielding and overcoming. That transition point is where isometric action occurs because movement will have to stop for at least a moment before being redirected.

Concentric strength is the most commonly understood form of "strength," because a concentric action occurs when muscle strength is sufficient to overcome a load. In other words, this is the "lifting" phase of the exercise, so it's the lockout back to the starting position in a squat or bench press. The muscle lengthens under load during eccentric action, but during concentric action, the muscle shortens as it contracts. This occurs when the force the muscle generates exceeds the load acting on it, so if a player has to overcome a 200-pound load on a bar in addition to the force of gravity and produces greater forces than these through the muscles, then he will be successful in lifting the weight. When a player overcomes his own body weight and the resistance of gravity to launch himself into the air during a jump, this is also a concentric action, as would be an accelerative step when sprinting forward or reaccelerating after a decelerative step while changing direction. Thus, concentric muscle actions are extremely important to football players because strength, speed, and power outputs allow athletes to make plays and perform to the best of their abilities.

Lastly, the magnitude of strength a player requires will depend on several factors, including training age (how long the player has been in a consistent organized training environment), biological age (how old the player is), playing position, time of the year, current health status, football skill, and a great many other factors. It may not be possible to definitively say when a player is "strong enough," but our aim in this chapter is to provide an overview of various strength training practices to help coaches formulate a more holistic picture of what it means to be strong in football.

TRAINING ECCENTRIC, ISOMETRIC, AND CONCENTRIC MUSCLE ACTION

Developing holistic strength starts with the recognition that each muscle contraction type (eccentric, isometric, and concentric) requires special attention throughout the training process. There are various ways to develop each form of muscle action, and we will review some of them here.

Eccentric Training

Several eccentric training modalities can be used in a training program. Two of the most common are *tempo eccentrics* and *supramaximal eccentrics*. Tempo eccentrics refer to when the weight is controlled down for a specific amount of time. For example, in a barbell squat, the player would lower the bar for 5 seconds before coming back up dynamically.

Supramaximal eccentrics refer to using loads that are heavier than what the athlete would be capable of lifting for a 1-repetition maximum (1RM), and eccentric-only repetitions are performed. For example, in a barbell bench press, a player would load a weight between 110% and 130% of his respective bench press 1RM, lower the bar to his chest under control, and have a coach or training partner then assist him with lifting the bar back up to the starting position. This way, the player is only experiencing lowering the weight without the lifting phase, hence the eccentric-only concept.

In our training program, we tend to stay away from supramaximal eccentric loading due to the associated risks of using excessively heavy loads with developing athletes. Instead, we typically incorporate tempo eccentrics when we want to emphasize eccentric loading with weights. We believe the slower tempo helps our players learn to coordinate the primary lifting movements at a faster rate since it allows them to feel each position as they move through the full range of motion.

Several other benefits reported from eccentric training include increased maximal strength, greater nervous system activation, and an increase in the size of type II fast-twitch muscle fibers.[3] In addition, improving the ability to actively produce tension when muscles use lengthening force can have a positive impact on withstanding high forces in athletic movements like changing direction, sprinting, and jumping. This is especially likely in developing high school or college-aged players.

Isometric Training

Isometric training can help train specific weak points in a range of motion to positively influence performance on the field. For example, if a defensive lineman trains isometrically at the joint angles he achieves when coming out of a stance, it can have a positive influence on his ability to get off the ball by building stability into the first step when initiating movement. This has been shown in research where it was found that there is a significant positive relationship between isometric strength and the first 5 yards of a sprint.[4] But, the truth is that isometric muscle actions are performed in just about every dynamic movement. This is because every time a player absorbs and then overcomes force, there's always a transition point, and that transition point is where isometric action occurs. When changing direction, there is always a momentary stop in motion before movement is redirected.

In our training program, we will mostly use yielding isometrics, particularly on the primary lifts like the barbell squat, barbell Romanian deadlift, or barbell bench press. In these examples, we have our players lower the bar, pause for 3 seconds at the bottom, then return to the start. This is similar to the tempo eccentrics, and we believe there is a positive effect in helping players learn to control and apply force in different ways across different segments of a range of motion. We might also incorporate an auxiliary exercise like a long-duration isometric calf raise standing on a platform, where we have the player pause for 20 seconds at the top position with the heel elevated and the calf fully flexed, pause 20 seconds halfway down where the foot is parallel to the ground, and then pause 20 seconds at the bottom stretched position where the heel is below the forefoot.

Concentric Training

Concentric strength is the most measurable form of strength and, traditionally, coaches will prescribe the primary weight training exercises in their conditioning programs based on the percentage of a player's 1RM. The measure of 1RM is typically tested by having a player perform 1 repetition of an exercise for an increasing number of sets separated by a full recovery period (approximately 2-3 min), where load is added for each subsequent set until the player is unable to go heavier. The heaviest load used is then considered the 1RM, which would indicate a player's concentric strength. Using percentages of 1RM will help guide athletes with weight selections to perform the prescribed repetitions and achieve the desired training outcome. Table 5.1 shows the maximum number of achievable repetitions for each given percentage of 1RM between 65% and 100%.

When we refer to "strength" going forward, we will be specifically referring to concentric strength. The magnitude of strength each player needs will depend on several factors, including training age (how long the player has been in a consistent organized training environment), biological age (how old the player is), playing position, time of the year, and so on. Once an athlete develops a good base of strength and movement, more specific strength training will need to be implemented.

Table 5.1 Number of Maximal Repetitions Associated With Percentage of 1-Repetition Maximum

Number of reps	% 1RM
1	100
2	95
3	93
4	90
5	87
6	85
7	83
8	80
9	77
10	75
11	70
12	67
15	65

Reprinted by permission from reference 5. Data from references 6, 7, 8, and 9.

VELOCITY-BASED STRENGTH TRAINING

A common modern practice throughout college football (and increasingly more popular in the high school setting as well) is velocity-based training (VBT), which refers to using technology to track the velocity of the barbell during various primary lifting exercises. There are different forms of technology for this purpose, but the most common devices are linear position transducers, which are essentially cable tethers attached to a computing base that look like a string that hangs from the bar to the floor. As the tether moves within the computing base, a display screen presents the concentric velocity of the barbell, allowing coaches to measure the speed of the bar on each repetition. An example of this technology is the TENDO Unit, which is pictured in figure 5.1.

There is a nearly perfect linear relationship between average concentric bar velocity and percentage of 1RM,[10] so we can assign a velocity range that coincides with a given percent range of 1RM, but the actual weight on the bar will fluctuate based on fluctuations in fitness and freshness from day to day. With younger players, this is less important because they can seemingly improve strength performance in a linear fashion for a long time (e.g., up to a year). However, advanced players will experience diminishing returns, and on a given day a player's 1RM can range up to 18% above or below a previously established 1RM, just based on his cur-

Figure 5.1   TENDO Unit attached to a barbell to measure bar velocity.

rent readiness. This means an athlete who is prescribed a load of 80% of his 1RM may actually be experiencing a lifting effort that is equivalent to between 62% and 98% of his 1RM on a given day.[10] So, some days, a weight might feel very easy to lift, and the next day the same weight might feel extremely heavy. This is what we mean by fluctuations in performance. So, instead of assigning a specific weight, we can assign a velocity range to ensure that we are always operating at, say, 80% of intensity due to the bar speed being achieved, even if the specific weight on the bar changes from session to session.

Using barbell velocity tracking can help coaches target the exact stimulus the athlete needs. Some of the advantages of VBT include the following:

- *Auto-regulation*: Auto-regulation simply means that the training load can be regulated automatically each day based on the current fitness state of the player. As players become more advanced, it becomes more important to monitor daily fitness and freshness as best as possible. VBT is a form of training that can be used to account for the day-to-day fluctuations in performance by adjusting the training load based upon the bar velocity.

- *Immediate objective feedback*: Another important aspect of VBT is the immediate feedback the player receives. Research has shown that athletes who receive the feedback of bar velocity on each repetition can significantly improve performance versus athletes who did not receive this feedback.[10] The velocity can lead to motivation where players try to beat their previous repetitions in terms of bar speed, so the intent of each effort rises. By consistently achieving higher bar speeds and requiring more weight at any given speed, the body will adapt by producing greater improvements in strength.

- *Specificity of training*: Another benefit of VBT is the specificity of training. Specificity is important in training football players because of positional demands. These specific adaptations will depend on the load on the bar and the average bar velocity. Two athletes can be assigned the same exercise with the same sets, reps, and weight on the bar, but if the bar velocity is different, then there will be very different outcomes. If one athlete moves the bar slowly or for more repetitions, the adaptations may result in muscle hypertrophy and increases in muscular strength. If another athlete moves the bar as fast as they can at the same relative intensity, improvements in muscular strength and power will be much greater. Therefore, adjustments in load and velocity can lead to specific training outcomes.

Table 5.2 presents different average bar velocities and their associated ranges of percent 1RM.

Table 5.2 Mean Velocity Ranges Associated With Percentage Ranges of 1-Repetition Maximum

Velocity (m/sec)	% 1RM
<0.5	80%-100%
0.5-0.75	65%-80%
0.75-1.0	45%-65%
1.0-1.3	30%-45%
>1.3	<30%

Adapted from B. Mann, "The Velocity Zones Explained," GymAware, accessed August 17, 2022, https://gymaware.com/velocity_zones/.

PRIMARY EXERCISES TO DEVELOP LOWER-BODY STRENGTH

The primary exercises that we utilize to develop lower-body strength are implemented with a goal of being simple in execution but effective in achieving positive strength adaptations. Specifically, we want exercises that utilize the entire lower body and are capable of producing high levels of force, so we try not to get too fancy when developing maximum strength. The harder the movement may be from a coordination standpoint, the less likely we can develop high levels of force, so we believe that simple and heavy are very effective ways to get the strength stimulus we desire. The following are three of the primary strength exercises that we use to develop lower-body strength.

Barbell Squat

The barbell squat is a compound lower-body movement used primarily to develop lower-body strength.

Execution

1. The barbell will be placed on the middle of the traps, with the hands on the barbell just outside of the shoulders.
2. Unrack the barbell and take two steps back. Set the feet shoulder-width apart, with the feet straight or slightly pointed out (see figure *a*).
3. Inhale, brace the abdominals, and pull the elbows down to engage the lats.
4. To initiate the movement, break at the hips and bend the knees until reaching the prescribed depth (see figure *b*).
5. When squatting, it is important to keep a flat back, with the feet flat and the knees out.

Figure 5.2   Barbell squat.

Hex Bar Deadlift

The hex bar deadlift is a compound lower-body movement performed with a hexagonal-shaped barbell. The hex bar allows for the torso to be more upright compared to a traditional barbell deadlift. This reduces compression forces and stress on the low back.

Execution

1. Stand in the middle of the hex bar with the feet shoulder-width apart and the toes straight.
2. Squat down with a flat back, chest up and eyes straight ahead. When grabbing the handles, engage the abdominals and create tension in the lats before lifting the bar (see figure *a*).
3. Stand up with the bar in the hands and return to the starting position while controlling the eccentric portion, keeping the back flat, chest up, and eyes straight ahead (see figure *b*).

Figure 5.3   Hex bar deadlift.

Hex Bar Deadlift, Concentric Only

The concentric-only hex bar deadlift is the same movement as the hex bar deadlift, the only difference being the bar drops at the top of the movement instead of controlling it down. This movement is great for when athletes are in competition, such as in-season or spring ball. Eliminating the eccentric portion produces less soreness while still getting the stimulus of lifting the weight.

EXERCISES TO DEVELOP POSTERIOR-CHAIN STRENGTH

Posterior-chain strength refers to developing the muscles on the back side of the lower body, primarily the gluteal muscles and the hamstrings. Many strength programs feature primary exercises like the barbell squat but may neglect developing high levels of posterior-chain strength. This muscle group is paramount to having a solid base of strength for movements like sprinting, changing direction, tackling, or blocking an opponent. In addition, balancing posterior-chain strength with the muscles of the front of the body (e.g., the quadriceps muscles) can help athletes develop a better foundation for overall stability at the hip, knee, and ankle joints. In particular, strong gluteal and hamstring muscles can help stabilize the knee joint and protect against potentially damaging inward collapsing (also called *valgus*) of the knee on ground contact. So, having strong posterior-chain muscles at the hip and knee joints will not only improve performance but also can have a protective effect when performing various athletic movements. The following are some of the most important posterior-chain strength exercises we use in our program.

Barbell Romanian Deadlift

The barbell Romanian deadlift (barbell RDL) is a lower-body movement used to develop the posterior chain, specifically the glutes and hamstrings.

Execution

1. Grip the bar just outside the thighs.
2. Unrack the bar, take two steps back, and set the feet hip-width apart, with the toes pointed straight ahead (see figure *a*).
3. Keeping the back flat, chest up, and eyes looking straight ahead, initiate the movement by pushing the hips back (hip hinge) with slight knee flexion.
4. Control the barbell down, keeping it in contact with the legs until the chest is approximately parallel to the floor while maintaining a flat back (see figure *b*).
5. To initiate the concentric movement, pull through the hamstring and glutes while pushing the hips forward, pulling the barbell upward back to the starting position.

Figure 5.4   Barbell Romanian deadlift.

Barbell Hip Thrust

The barbell hip thrust is a lower-body movement that targets the muscles of the posterior chain, specifically the glutes, hamstrings, and low back.

Execution

1. Sit on the floor with the back up against a bench.
2. Roll a loaded barbell over the legs until it rests in the crease of the hips (see figure *a*).
3. With the upper back against the bench, knees bent, feet flat, and toes pointed straight ahead, lift the hips to come into a glute bridge position (see figure *b*).
4. At the top of the movement, the chin should be tucked to the chest with the hips extended, focusing on squeezing the glutes.

Figure 5.5 Barbell hip thrust.

EXERCISES TO DEVELOP SINGLE-LEG STRENGTH

Single-leg strength is another area that can tend to be neglected in strength training programs that are primarily focused on heavy bilateral (double-leg) strength exercises like barbell squats or hex bar deadlifts. However, single-leg movements are coordinated in different ways than bilateral movements and will also feature different muscle firing patterns. For example, the way in which the gluteal muscles are utilized when performing a dumbbell step-up will be different than a barbell squat, even though both are examples of movements featuring deep hip flexion and knee flexion to extension. In the step-up movement, stability is challenged so more stabilizing muscles are brought into the equation, like the small stabilizing glute muscles surrounding the hip joint. While the overall force outputs will be lower than bilateral movements, single-leg strength is an area of strength training that can leave a lot of untapped potential if neglected, but it can help add to more force-producing prowess if included. The following are some of the top single-leg strength exercises that we include in our program.

Barbell Reverse Lunge

The barbell reverse lunge is a single-leg exercise used to primarily develop the quadriceps muscles around the knee, as well as the gluteal (buttocks) muscles of the hip. However, the hamstrings are also involved, especially in the extension of the hip when stepping back to the starting position.

Execution

1. Start standing fully upright while supporting a barbell on the shoulders (see figure *a*).
2. Step back with one leg and descend toward the ground while ensuring that the back hip stays extended, so that the trunk remains in a neutral posture and the front of the hips stay above the front heel. If performed properly, the back leg should experience a significant stretch through the hip flexors, and the trunk should not break at the waist where it falls forward (see figure *b*).
3. Lightly touch the ground with the back knee. There should be a positive shin angle of the front foot, where the front knee is pushing forward toward the front toe with the whole foot remaining on the ground.
4. Drive through the hip of the front leg and the midfoot of the front foot to return to the starting position.

Figure 5.6   Barbell reverse lunge.

Barbell Step-Up

The barbell step-up is a lower-body movement that develops single-leg strength and stability. This movement targets the muscles of the groin, quadriceps, hamstrings, and hips.

Execution

1. Stand upright, supporting a barbell on the shoulders and standing in front of a bench or box that is set to around knee height.
2. Step on the box with a single leg, keeping the leg on the ground extended (see figure *a*).
3. Drive through the foot to raise onto the box (see figure *b*).
4. While performing the movement, maintain a neutral spine and keep the chest up and eyes straight ahead.
5. To finish the movement, step off the box one leg at a time and return to the starting position.

Figure 5.7   Barbell step-up.

EXERCISES TO DEVELOP UPPER-BODY PRESSING STRENGTH

In football, the upper-body muscles are used when making physical contact with an opponent, such as making a block, shedding a block, or making a tackle, all of which are actions that every position has to perform. Even kickers and punters will be asked to shed a block and tackle a ballcarrier from time to time. Being able to properly drive through an opponent with a stable shoulder position or grapple with an opponent to shed a block or make a tackle are vital aspects of the game, so having a strong upper body is a major component of the sport of football. Again, we believe simple and heavy are the best ways to improve our players' abilities to produce high forces through their upper bodies. The following are some of the exercises that we incorporate when developing upper-body pressing strength.

Barbell Bench Press

The barbell bench press is a compound movement that primarily targets the muscles of the chest, shoulders, and triceps.

Execution

1. Lie flat on the bench with the eyes directly under the bar.
2. Keep the 5 points of contact throughout the entire movement: both feet on the ground, glutes on the bench, shoulders flat on the bench, and head flat on the bench.
3. Grab the barbell slightly wider than shoulder-width apart and unrack the bar, letting the bar settle where the wrists are directly over the elbows (see figure *a*).
4. Initiate the eccentric phase by lowering the bar under control to chest level (see figure *b*).
5. To initiate the concentric phase, press the barbell off the chest, back to the starting position.

Figure 5.8   Barbell bench press.

Barbell Incline Bench Press

The barbell incline bench press is a compound movement that primarily targets the muscles of the chest, shoulders, and triceps. The incline will put a greater emphasis on the upper chest and shoulders.

Execution

1. Lie on a bench set to an incline angle of 15-30 degrees with the eyes directly under the bar.
2. Keep the 5 points of contact throughout the entire movement: both feet on the ground, glutes on the bench, shoulders flat on the bench, and head flat on the bench.
3. Grab the barbell slightly wider than shoulder-width apart and unrack the bar, letting the bar settle where the wrists are directly over the elbows (see figure *a*).
4. Initiate the eccentric phase by lowering the bar under control to chest level (see figure *b*).
5. To initiate the concentric phase, press the barbell off the chest, back to the starting position.

Figure 5.9   Barbell incline bench press.

Barbell Close-Grip 2-Board Bench Press

The barbell close-grip 2-board bench press is a compound movement that primarily targets the muscles of the chest, shoulders, and triceps. The close-grip 2-board bench press will put a greater emphasis on the triceps and take the stress off the shoulders because it does not involve a full range of motion.

Execution

1. Lie flat on the bench with the eyes directly under the bar.
2. Keep the 5 points of contact throughout the entire movement: both feet on the ground, glutes on the bench, shoulders flat on the bench, and head flat on the bench.
3. Grab the barbell with the hands shoulder-width apart or slightly inside shoulder-width.
4. Initiate the eccentric phase by lowering the bar under control to the board.
5. Pause on the board so there is no bouncing.
6. To initiate the concentric phase, press the barbell off the board, back to the starting position.

Barbell Bench Press With Chains

The barbell bench press with chains is a compound movement that primarily targets the muscles of the chest, shoulders, and triceps. Chains are used for accommodating resistance. The chains will be the lightest at the bottom of the movement and heaviest at the top of the movement. This will allow a greater resistance through the entire range of motion.

Execution

1. Lie flat on the bench with the eyes directly under the bar.
2. Keep the 5 points of contact throughout the entire movement: both feet on the ground, glutes on the bench, shoulders flat on the bench, and head flat on the bench.
3. Grab the barbell slightly wider than shoulder-width apart, placing the wrist directly over the elbow.
4. Initiate the eccentric phase by lowering the bar under control to chest level.
5. To initiate the concentric phase, press the barbell off the chest, back to the starting position.

Dumbbell Bench Press

The dumbbell bench press is an upper-body movement that targets the muscles of the chest, shoulders, and triceps. The dumbbell bench press is similar to the barbell bench press, but uses dumbbells instead of a barbell. This will allow for a greater range of motion and the shoulder joint to move more freely.

Execution

1. Lie flat on the bench with a dumbbell in each hand.
2. Keep the 5 points of contact throughout the entire movement: both feet on the ground, glutes on the bench, shoulders flat on the bench, and head flat on the bench.
3. Press the dumbbells off the chest and extend the arms to the top of the movement (see figure *a*).
4. Lower the dumbbells under control back to the chest (see figure *b*).

Figure 5.10   Dumbbell bench press.

Dumbbell Incline Bench Press

The dumbbell incline bench press is an upper-body movement that targets the muscles of the chest, shoulders, and triceps. The incline will put a greater emphasis on the upper chest and shoulders. The dumbbell incline bench press is similar to the barbell incline bench press, but uses dumbbells instead of a barbell. This will allow for a greater range of motion and the shoulder joint to move more freely.

Execution

1. Lie on a bench set to an incline angle of 15-30 degrees with a dumbbell in each hand.
2. Keep the 5 points of contact throughout the entire movement: both feet on the ground, glutes on the bench, shoulders flat on the bench, and head flat on the bench.
3. Press the dumbbells off the chest and extend the arms to the top of the movement.
4. Lower the dumbbells under control back to the chest.

Dumbbell Floor Press

The dumbbell floor press is an upper-body movement that targets the muscles of the chest, shoulders, and triceps. Similar to the barbell close-grip 2-board bench press, the dumbbell floor press will put a greater emphasis on the triceps and take stress off the shoulders because it does not involve a full range of motion.

Execution

1. Lie faceup on the floor with a dumbbell in each hand.
2. The triceps will be flat on the floor with the forearms vertical.
3. Extend the arms and press the dumbbells up to the top of the movement (see figure *a*).
4. Return to the starting position by controlling the dumbbells down until the triceps are flat on the floor (see figure *b*).

Figure 5.11   Dumbbell floor press.

Half-Kneeling Landmine One-Arm Press

The half-kneeling landmine one-arm press is a predominantly upper-body movement that primarily targets the shoulder muscles. The landmine press is a middle ground between a horizontal press such as a bench press and a vertical press such as an overhead press.

Execution

1. Start in a half-kneeling position so there is a slight stretch in the hip flexor.
2. Hold the barbell in the hand on the same side the knee is down (see figure *a*).
3. Contract the glute on the leg that is up, brace the core, and maintain a neutral spine throughout the entire movement.
4. Press the barbell straight out and not across the body (see figure *b*).
5. Return to the starting position by controlling the barbell down and perform all of the prescribed repetitions on one arm before repeating on the other arm.

Figure 5.12   Half-kneeling landmine one-arm press.

Dumbbell One-Arm Push Press

The dumbbell one-arm push press is an upper-body movement that primarily targets the shoulder muscles. Performing the movement one arm at a time will also work to improve muscle imbalances and shoulder stability.

Execution

1. Start with a dumbbell racked on the shoulder and the elbow pointed out in front of the body.
2. Set the feet hip-width to shoulder-width apart.
3. Brace the abdominal muscles and perform a slight bend of the knees while maintaining a neutral spine.
4. Extend the hips and knees and press the dumbbell overhead until the elbow is locked out and the legs are straight.
5. Return to the starting position by controlling the dumbbell down back to the shoulder and perform all the prescribed repetitions on one arm before repeating on the other arm.

Dumbbell Two-Arm Push Press

The dumbbell two-arm push press is an upper-body movement that primarily targets the shoulder muscles. It is similar to the dumbbell one-arm push press, but uses two dumbbells at once.

Execution

1. Start with the dumbbells racked on the shoulders and the elbows pointed out in front of the body.
2. Set the feet hip-width to shoulder-width apart.
3. Brace the abdominal muscles and perform a slight bend of the knees while maintaining a neutral spine.
4. Extend the hips and knees and press the dumbbells overhead until the elbows are locked out and the legs are straight.
5. Return to the starting position by controlling the dumbbells down back to the shoulders.

Landmine Push Press

The landmine push press is an upper-body movement that primarily targets the shoulder muscles. Performing the movement one arm at a time will also work to improve muscle imbalances and shoulder stability. It is similar to the half-kneeling landmine one-arm press, but should be done standing, using the legs to help drive the barbell up.

Execution

1. Start with the top of the barbell on the shoulder with the elbow pointed out in front of the body.
2. Set the feet hip-width to shoulder-width apart.
3. Brace the abdominal muscles and perform a slight bend of the knees while maintaining a neutral spine.
4. Extend the hips and knees and press the barbell straight out until the elbow is locked out and the legs are straight.
5. Return to the starting position by controlling the barbell down back to the shoulder.
6. Complete the allotted repetitions on one side before repeating on the other side.

EXERCISES TO DEVELOP UPPER-BODY PULLING STRENGTH

In addition to pressing strength, pulling strength is paramount in football. Having great pressing strength capabilities with poor pulling strength can result in instability at the shoulder joint and leave untapped strength potential for actions like shedding a block or making a tackle. Posterior-chain strength is largely important for both the lower and upper body. Again, there will be a performance-enhancing and protective effect of balancing the upper body's ability to pull with strength against the ability to press with strength. We simply cannot resort to building high levels of pressing strength and neglect properly developing pulling strength as a complement. To build a holistically strong player, we have to strengthen the back muscles of the upper body. The following are some of the exercises that we incorporate for developing upper-body pulling strength in our program.

Neutral Grip Chin-Up

The neutral grip chin-up is a multijoint exercise in which reps are performed with the palms facing one another. This movement builds strength and muscle in the upper back, lats, biceps, and core.

Execution

1. Grab the neutral grip handles so the palms are facing one another and hang from the bar (see figure *a*).
2. Pull up by flexing at the elbows and pulling with the lats until the chin is level or over the bar (see figure *b*).
3. Pause for a second at the top and then control back down until the arms are extended in the starting position.

Figure 5.13 Neutral grip chin-up.

3-Way Chin-Up

The 3-way chin-up is a multijoint exercise in which reps are performed utilizing the neutral grip chin-up, the underhand grip chin-up, and the overhand grip chin-up. This movement builds strength and muscle in the upper back, lats, biceps, and core. Using different handgrips focuses on different muscle groups and facilitates the completion of more reps. Start with the overhand grip chin-up, progress to the neutral grip chin-up, and then finish with the underhand grip chin-up. Progress from highest to lowest level of difficulty so the harder exercise is completed first when the muscles are fresh to perform more reps.

Execution

1. Start with the overhand grip chin-up.
2. Pull up by flexing at the elbow and pulling with the lats until the chin is level or over the bar.
3. Pause for a second at the top and then control back down until the arms are extended in the starting position.
4. After the prescribed reps are performed, progress to the next handgrip.
5. Perform all three handgrips in consecutive fashion.

Suspension Trainer Pull-Up

The suspension trainer pull-up is an upper-body pulling exercise that primarily targets the muscles of the upper back. The movement can be progressed from standing to feet elevated on a bench or box.

Execution

1. Begin with the feet on the ground or elevated on a bench or box and suspension trainer handles in the hands (see figure *a*).
2. The body should remain in a straight line from head to toe.
3. Row up by flexing at the elbows and pulling with the back until the arms reach the chest (see figure *b*).
4. Pause for a second at the top and then control back down until the arms are extended in the starting position.

Figure 5.14 Suspension trainer pull-up.

Machine Seated Row

The machine seated row is an upper-body pulling exercise that primarily targets the muscles of the upper back.

Execution

1. Sit on the machine with the chest against the pad and the hands on the handles (see figure *a*).
2. Keeping the chest on the pad, pull with both arms, flexing at the elbows to bring the handles to the chest (see figure *b*).
3. Pause for a second at the top of the movement and contract the back muscles.
4. Extend the arms under control back to the starting position.

Figure 5.15   Machine seated row.

Machine Alternating Seated Row

The machine alternating seated row is an upper-body pulling exercise that primarily targets the muscles of the upper back. Athletes will perform the movement by alternating arms, one at a time.

Execution

1. Sit on the machine with the chest against the pad and the hands on the handles.
2. Keeping the chest on the pad, pull with one arm, flexing at the elbow to bring the handle to the chest.
3. Pause for a second at the top of the movement and contract the back muscles.
4. Extend the arm under control back to the starting position. Then repeat with the other arm.

Dumbbell Chest-Supported Row

The dumbbell chest-supported row is an upper-body pulling exercise that primarily targets the muscles of the upper back.

Execution

1. Lie facedown on an incline bench set to an incline angle of 15-30 degrees with a dumbbell in each hand (see figure *a*).
2. Keeping the chest on the bench, pull with both arms, flexing at the elbows to bring the dumbbells to chest level (see figure *b*).
3. Pause for a second at the top of the movement and contract the back muscles.
4. Extend the arms under control back to the starting position.

Figure 5.16   Dumbbell chest-supported row.

Dumbbell One-Arm Row

The dumbbell one-arm row is an upper-body pulling exercise that primarily targets the muscles of the upper back.

Execution

1. Start with the feet shoulder-width apart and with a slight bend in the knees.
2. Hinge at the hips so that the chest is parallel to the floor and the back is flat with a dumbbell in one hand (see figure *a*).
3. While maintaining a neutral spine, row the dumbbell toward the ribs by flexing at the elbow and pulling with the lat (see figure *b*).
4. Pause for a second at the top of the movement and contract the back muscles.
5. Extend the arm under control back to the starting position. Perform all the prescribed repetitions on one arm before repeating on the other arm.

Figure 5.17   Dumbbell one-arm row.

Machine Lat Pull-Down

The machine lat pull-down is an upper-body pulling exercise that primarily targets the muscles of the upper back and lats.

Execution

1. Begin seated on the machine with the chest up and the hands on the handles (see figure *a*).
2. Pull the handles down toward the chest, leaning back slightly and keeping the chest up (see figure *b*).
3. Pause for a second at the top of the movement and contract the muscles of the upper back and lats.
4. Extend the arms under control back to the starting position.

Figure 5.18   Machine lat pull-down.

STRENGTH TRAINING PROGRAM

The off-season phase is the primary time to develop high levels of strength. Most teams at the collegiate level will begin off-season training with the winter training period, which typically begins in January and leads into the spring football practice period around April. After the spring period, the next off-season phase is the summer training period, which begins around June and concludes at the beginning of fall training camp in August. The fall training camp period is typically about 4 weeks long and leads into the competitive season, which typically begins in September and progresses through to the end of December or into the beginning of January, depending on bowl or playoff appearances or lack thereof.

Each of these phases requires slightly different approaches to strength training to ensure that the players are getting an adequate stimulus for maintaining muscle strength and size, but not so much of a stimulus that the players are overstressed when football practices or games are of primary importance. A well-developed plan must be put into place so that the right qualities are being trained at the right time of year.

Off-Season Strength Training

Immediately after the last game during the fall or after the cessation of spring practice, players will be given a few weeks away from the facilities to recover from the stresses of practice, a competitive season, or both. This is a time for players to rest and recover, including rehabilitating injuries, while maintaining some level of fitness by staying active when possible. It's important to think of this time as "time away," not "time off," so players will also work to reestablish and increase work capacity during this time in preparation for the off-season training periods. After this 2- to 4-week period, we will begin off-season training. From a strength training perspective, the winter off-season and summer off-season periods can be designed very similarly since the goal is to get as strong as possible in the absence of added football stressors.

As stated previously, one training modality that can be used at the beginning of off-season training is tempo eccentrics. The benefit of eccentric exercise at the beginning of the winter training cycle is to prepare muscles and other connective tissues like ligaments and tendons for more intense work later in the training cycle. They will also help ingrain proper lifting technique and help the players get strong without jumping right into maximal intensity loads. Going too heavy too early can have negative impacts on the players' bodies because they may have experienced some form of detraining (losing fitness levels) during their time off following the in-season period. So, using submaximal loads (e.g., <85% of 1RM) in the first few weeks of winter with tempo eccentrics can get the players back into the groove of training again.

Following a period of eccentric training, yielding isometric training can be used, which is also beneficial in preparing muscles, ligaments, and tendons. From here, we can progress to the final weeks of the off-season training program, when we will remove the tempo eccentrics and yielding isometrics and instead prioritize maximal concentric strength. This will be the time to realize the effects of strength and muscle gains developed in the prior weeks and have a better idea of how strong the players are. It's also important to note that concentric strength is not ignored during the eccentric and isometric development weeks but is present throughout the entire training process, and some exercises will feature a tempo (e.g., 3 sec eccentric) and others will not. A sample training progression template for off-season strength training is provided in table 5.3.

Table 5.3　Sample Off-Season Strength Training Progression

Winter training: weeks 1-2			
Day 1		**Day 2**	
Exercise type	**Exercise**	**Exercise type**	**Exercise**
Primary press	Barbell close-grip 2-board bench press	Primary compound	Barbell squat (3 sec eccentric)
Primary pull	Neutral grip chin-up (3 sec eccentric)	Posterior chain	90-degree back extension
Secondary press	Half-kneeling landmine one-arm press	Single leg	Barbell reverse lunge
Secondary pull	Dumbbell one-arm row	Secondary posterior chain	Stability ball leg curl
Day 3		**Day 4**	
Exercise type	**Exercise**	**Exercise type**	**Exercise**
Primary press	Barbell bench press (3 sec eccentric)	Primary compound	Hex bar deadlift
Primary pull	Machine seated row	Posterior chain	Barbell Romanian deadlift (3 sec eccentric)
Secondary press	Dumbbell one-arm push press	Single leg	Barbell reverse lunge
Secondary pull	Machine lat pull-down	Secondary posterior chain	Partner Nordic hamstring curl

(continued)

Table 5.3 Sample Off-Season Strength Training Progression *(continued)*

Winter training: weeks 3-4			
Day 1		**Day 2**	
Exercise type	**Exercise**	**Exercise type**	**Exercise**
Primary press	Barbell incline bench press	Primary compound	Barbell squat (3 sec isometric)
Primary pull	Neutral grip chin-up (3 sec isometric)	Posterior chain	90-degree back extension
Secondary press	Half-kneeling landmine one-arm press	Single leg	Barbell reverse lunge
Secondary pull	Dumbbell chest-supported row	Secondary posterior chain	Roller leg curl
Day 3		**Day 4**	
Exercise type	**Exercise**	**Exercise type**	**Exercise**
Primary press	Barbell bench press (3 sec isometric)	Primary compound	Hex bar deadlift
Primary pull	Machine seated row	Posterior chain	Barbell Romanian deadlift (3 sec isometric)
Secondary press	Dumbbell two-arm push press	Single leg	Barbell reverse lunge
Secondary pull	Machine lat pull-down	Secondary posterior chain	Partner Nordic hamstring curl
Winter training: weeks 5-8			
Day 1		**Day 2**	
Exercise type	**Exercise**	**Exercise type**	**Exercise**
Primer	Medicine ball chest pass for distance	Primary compound	Barbell squat (0.4-0.6 m/sec)
Primary press	Barbell bench press with chains (0.75-1.0 m/sec)	Posterior chain	Barbell hip thrust
Primary pull	3-way chin-up	Single leg	Dumbbell step-up
Secondary press	Landmine push press (>1.3 m/sec)	Secondary posterior chain	Roller leg curl
Secondary pull	Machine alternating seated row		

Day 3		Day 4	
Exercise type	Exercise	Exercise type	Exercise
Primary press	Low-incline barbell bench press (0.4-0.6 m/sec)	Primer	Band-resisted broad jump
Primary pull	Dumbbell chest-supported row	Primary compound	Hex bar deadlift (>0.75-1.0 m/sec)
Secondary press	Dumbbell bench press	Posterior chain	Barbell Romanian deadlift
Secondary pull	Machine lat pull-down	Single leg	Barbell reverse lunge
		Secondary posterior chain	Partner Nordic hamstring curl

Spring Practice and In-Season Strength Training

During spring football and in-season practices, the players will be partaking in a myriad of activities that involve sprinting, jumping, cutting, blocking, tackling, and various sport-specific skills. They will also be engaged heavily in learning and the mental processing of learning the playbook and game tactics. All these factors place significantly more stress on the body than during off-season training periods when sports practice is not occurring. Therefore, this stress to the body must be accounted for when creating a training plan for players as they enter these practice periods.

In the off-season, the strength and conditioning staff has vast control over the physical stresses being placed on the players, with the exception of some hours each week being used for player-led practices or individual drills with coaches when allowed. But during the in-season period, the football coaches take over, and the players are funneled into position-specific stress accumulation, and we must support them during this time. So, it is important to reduce the overall volume of the strength and conditioning work when athletes begin practice, most of which is accomplished through the reduction or elimination of conditioning elements like speed, power, agility, or endurance training. As strength coaches, we can still emphasize strength during in-season practice and competitive periods since this will be less developed when players are at practice, typically only stimulated when players are engaged with each other in combative ways like blocking, tackling, and disengaging. So, even though practices are being performed and football activities serve as the primary stressor, we can support the players by maintaining their muscle mass and further developing their strength capabilities as practices and the season unfold. A sample training progression template for in-season strength training is provided in table 5.4.

Table 5.4 Sample In-Season Strength Training Template

Spring training			
Day 1		**Day 2**	
Exercise type	**Exercise**	**Exercise type**	**Exercise**
Primary press	Barbell close-grip 2-board bench press	Primary press	Dumbbell incline bench press
Primary pull	Machine seated row	Primary pull	3-way chin-up
Primary compound	Barbell squat	Secondary pull	Dumbbell one-arm row
Posterior chain	Barbell Romanian deadlift		
Day 3			
Exercise type	**Exercise**		
Primary press	Dumbbell floor press		
Primary pull	Suspension trainer pull-up		
Primary compound	Hex bar deadlift		
Posterior chain	90-degree back extension		

CONCLUSION

In conclusion, strength training is multifaceted and should include some aspects of developing eccentric, isometric, and concentric strength. When it comes to improving maximum strength, concentric strength reigns supreme, but neglecting eccentric or isometric muscle action leaves many positive adaptations untapped and reduces the possibility of developing a holistically strong athlete. Likewise, we have to develop a balance of strength across the body, including primary lower-body strength, lower-body posterior-chain strength, upper-body pressing strength, and upper-body pulling strength. When it comes to training for strength, we believe that simple and heavy are the main concepts that lead to consistently strong players. However, the loading that we impart on the players must coexist with all other stressors in the program, so we must be mindful of where we are in the competitive periods of the year, especially spring football practice or the in-season period, when higher volumes of football-related activities are present. Lastly, we may incorporate more advanced forms of monitoring, like velocity-based training, to help us objectively stay on target for the strength qualities we aim to emphasize while also allowing for the natural fluctuations and auto-regulation of loading to take place throughout the year.

Chapter 6

Muscle Hypertrophy Training

Muscle hypertrophy refers to building muscle, so when we are training for hypertrophy, we want to put muscle mass on our players. This increase in muscle mass can be more effective and efficient with proper guidance and motivation by the coaching staff. The increase in the size of a muscle depends on factors like genetic background, age, and gender.[1] However, various training techniques also affect the hypertrophic response and influence muscle size. The goal is to achieve a hormone response in the body that signals for it to start building muscle, which may be accomplished by mechanical tension, muscle damage, and metabolic stress. In this chapter, we will discuss the aspects associated with building muscle hypertrophy and provide sample auxiliary exercises and programming aspects that we incorporate to add muscle size to our players.

MECHANICAL TENSION, MUSCLE DAMAGE, AND METABOLIC STRESS

The muscle damage that occurs during resistance exercise is vital in increasing muscle hypertrophy because of the resulting regeneration that occurs after exercising. Weight training, or any form of resistance training, imposes muscle damage from mechanical tension that is produced by force generation and stretch, which serves as the signal that causes a muscle-building response in the body. Muscle damage often leads to a burning sensation or discomfort associated with muscular fatigue. This sensation is a result of metabolic stress, which actually refers to how the body's natural energy production is disrupted, forcing the body to find a way to maintain a sense of balance to continue performing work.

Changing the parameters of resistance training—such as intensity, volume, and the duration of rest intervals—can all influence metabolic stress. In particular, a high volume of work with short rest intervals leads to greater metabolic stress. Another factor that raises metabolic stress is increased time under tension, which refers to how long the muscle is under tension for the duration of a set. For example, the muscles will be under tension longer if we have our players perform 10 repetitions than if we have them perform 2 repetitions. Additionally, purposefully slowing down the tempo of the exercise, such as performing tempo eccentrics or yielding isometrics as explained in chapter 5, can also lead to more time under tension. By inducing metabolic stress, we can activate an increased muscle fiber recruitment because more units will be called on to provide work as the initial fibers start to fatigue. Therefore, when our goal is a gain in muscle mass, it is imperative for our players to keep training through this state of fatigue.

For us as coaches, this will likely require verbal encouragement because it is human nature to slow down or stop when fatigue becomes great. Fatigue can lead players to prematurely quit on themselves mentally during an exercise set due to high levels of discomfort. To continue performance under fatigue, encouraging discipline and motivation for players is an important factor that can affect performance regardless of physical or physiological state.[2] To build muscle mass, it is crucial that we motivate players to continue through the demanded time under tension or repetitions to get a potent muscle-building response. That being said, it's important that we mention that if exercise technique becomes biomechanically dangerous, the exercise must be stopped. But if the exercise technique is safe and a player is simply experiencing discomfort from fatigue, we can encourage the player to continue straining to get a more potent effect for hypertrophy.

After sessions of high metabolic stress, such as hypertrophy training, the body responds to the damaged muscle by activating an inflammatory response. This is displayed in the redness and swelling that is seen in the muscles post-training. This inflammatory response leads to hormones like growth factors being released, which then promote and induce the enlargement of the contractile muscle fiber components. Therefore, the process of metabolic stress from resistance exercise enables the body to increase levels of circulating anabolic (muscle-building) hormones. This is not referring to anabolic steroids that would be injected into the body, but rather the naturally occurring anabolic hormones the body makes to support various processes like building muscle. These hormones interact with the nervous system and muscle tissue to maximize neuromuscular system adaptations and increase muscle fiber size and recruitment.

ACTIVATING A HORMONE RESPONSE FOR MUSCLE GROWTH

Hormones are nothing more than chemical messengers in the body. They are tasked with traveling throughout the body to tell certain body parts to perform functions. For muscle growth, two of the most potent anabolic hormones are testosterone and growth hormone. A player's training experience, the exercise selection in the training program, the exercise intensity and volume, and the current strength levels of the player will all affect the acute release of testosterone. The most prominent benefit of testosterone is that it increases muscular strength and protein synthesis, the latter of which refers to putting the body in an anabolic state that can lead to muscle growth. Namely, protein synthesis must exceed or balance protein degradation to achieve hypertrophy of skeletal muscle. Also, as high-school-aged children mature from middle school years, the strength and conditioning practitioner must keep in mind that hormones and growth factors improve at a significant rate due to puberty.

Exercises that emphasize a large amount of muscle mass, such as the barbell squat or hex bar deadlift, have been shown to positively influence acute elevations in natural testosterone due to a strong metabolic component associated with performing these movements with high resistive loads.[3] Furthermore, the intensity and volume programmed for these exercises are also influencing factors. Other factors that affect testosterone response postexercise include age and training experience. If two young players are the same age (e.g., 17 years old), the player with more experience in a training environment can have higher levels of naturally circulating testosterone than the other player.

Growth hormone (GH) has direct effects on the hypertrophy of skeletal muscle and most other tissues. GH is predominantly secreted in peaks shortly after the onset of sleep, a few hours after a meal, and during moments of high metabolic stress, with the greatest levels of secretion occurring during sleep. Therefore, sleep is a vital component to healthy and adequate GH levels, which help regenerate and grow muscle. This is why some coaches talk about how it's not always about how you train but about how you recover from how you train.

FACTORS ASSOCIATED WITH MUSCLE HYPERTROPHY

Three of the most important factors associated with inducing muscle hypertrophy include the following:

1. Mechanical tension
2. Muscle damage
3. Metabolic stress

   Mechanical tension is produced by force generation and stretch, which is potent to muscle growth when there is a combination of both. Furthermore, mechanical unloading will result in atrophy (loss of muscle) while mechanical loading leads to hypertrophy. The mechanical tension achieved during lifting weights disturbs the integrity of the skeletal muscle, and localized muscle damage occurs during training in the form of small tearing of the muscle fibers. This muscle damage is important because it serves as the signal that causes a muscle-building response in the body. These tears initiate an inflammatory response that removes the cellular debris caused by the trauma, and the muscle damage releases various growth factors to promote muscle hypertrophy. Lastly, metabolic stress may optimally promote muscular hypertrophy without the need for very high loads. Imposing metabolic stress upon a muscle group can cause a build-up of cellular byproducts, and this process can have a hypertrophic response if the athlete can withstand the "burning" sensation associated with this build-up of byproducts during the set.

   Hypertrophy training based on these factors will have a higher chance of optimally promoting muscle growth. Essentially, the targeted muscles will grow more efficiently if adequately put under positive stress, which means enough to invoke an anabolic response but not cause excessive muscle damage or injury.

TRAINING VARIABLES FOR HYPERTROPHY

The primary training variables that we will discuss for building muscle mass in football players are the following:

1. Exercise intensity
2. Time under tension
3. Exercise volume
4. Muscular fatigue

Exercise Intensity

The intensity of a given training session is said to be the most important exercise variable to promoting muscle growth. It appears that a moderate intensity is most optimal for promoting a hypertrophic response, which equates to using a load that falls between 67% and 85% of 1RM and 6-12 repetitions.[4] However, it's not just about the repetitions but also the time under tension that the muscle experiences. Thus, there's a difference between performing 6 repetitions as fast as possible and performing them with a slow, controlled tempo.

Time Under Tension

Our muscles do not know the number of repetitions that are being performed during a set, and they only respond to time under tension. The recommended repetitions are simply used to target a certain time under tension. An effective set duration producing positive changes in muscle hypertrophy has been shown to be between 30 and 40 seconds, regardless of whether the volume protocol was 3 sets of 12 repetitions or 6 sets of 6 repetitions.[5] In both cases, the cumulative effects of metabolic stress and working muscle fatigue were able to promote enough muscle trauma to elicit a hypertrophic response.

Different tempos that have been shown to have a hypertrophic response are tempo eccentrics (e.g., lowering a barbell for 5-6 sec to the chest during a bench press before pressing), yielding isometrics (e.g., pausing for 3 sec at the bottom of a barbell squat), and controlled concentric training. Eccentric training produces the most significant hypertrophic response due to the lengthening of muscle under tension, which produces more pronounced muscle damage and metabolite accumulation compared to concentric muscle-shortening action. An important consideration is that this typically leads to increased soreness within the next 24-48 hours post-training because of the associated trauma and increased metabolic demand.

It is also imperative to plan rest periods to emphasize time under tension. Rest intervals can be broken down into short (i.e., <30 sec), moderate (i.e., 60-90 sec), or long (i.e., >2 min). Long rest intervals are the least effective for muscle hypertrophy due to interference with the anabolic response and a decrease in metabolic stress. On the other hand, short rest periods may result in decreased strength capacity from set to set, but the metabolic stress is increased. Since it's best to aim for the best of both worlds, we recommend moderate rest periods for optimal gains in muscle size.[4]

Exercise Volume

The load utilized in a set can be defined as the intensity of an exercise, but the total number of sets and repetitions performed during a training session represents the volume. For adding muscle mass, higher volume (e.g., 3-4 sets of 6-12 repetitions) has shown superiority over single-set protocols, but it is not clear if it is because of greater muscle tension, muscle damage, metabolic stress, or the combination of all three.[6] During higher-volume protocols, testosterone and growth hormone levels are elevated on the last set as compared to single-set protocols. This is especially true for training protocols that demand increased metabolic stress.

Muscular Fatigue

Whenever an athlete starts to struggle with lifting a given load, the athlete is experiencing muscular fatigue. If he continues, he will eventually get to the point where he can no longer lift the load, which is called muscle failure. Training close to muscle failure is necessary to maximize hypertrophy. When one trains until muscle failure, it causes the muscle to activate more motor units while fatigued. The elevated number of recruited motor units causes an additional stimulus for a hypertrophic response. Furthermore, a greater elevation in growth hormone occurs when an athlete performs a load until failure rather than a set number of repetitions.

When going near muscle failure, the safety of the exercise is critical. For example, the risk of injury of performing the back squat or bench press until failure is much greater than performing a chest-supported row or chin-ups until failure. The aim for a hypertrophic response is not as important as the player's safety. Training until muscle failure should be used sparingly throughout a program. Using this method excessively may result in resting testosterone levels being blunted and players experiencing psychological burnout. Therefore, training in this way should be followed by a tapering period to allow the muscle tissue to recover.

MUSCLE HYPERTROPHY EXERCISES AND MODALITIES

Principles of developing muscle hypertrophy have been discussed throughout this chapter, and we will share the exercises we implement to promote these principles in this section. The exercises will be broken down into muscle groups classified by upper- and lower-body exercises and the type of movement performed in each exercise. Furthermore, suggested repetition schemes and rest times when programming each exercise will be discussed because some muscle groups respond more effectively to higher repetitions and less rest while others are the opposite.

Hypertrophy Exercises for the Shoulders and Upper Back

In football, the shoulders take on physical trauma through actions associated with blocking and tackling. In addition, players collide with the ground when tackling or being tackled, so having dense musculature surrounding the shoulders is important to protect underlying structures like bones and ligaments from impact trauma. The following are some of the common shoulder and upper back hypertrophy exercises that we use in our program.

Dumbbell Incline Rear Delt Raise

The dumbbell incline rear delt raise is used to develop the muscles of the posterior (back side) shoulder in addition to the muscles around the upper back, such as the rhomboids and trapezius muscles.

Execution

1. Lie facedown on a bench set to an incline angle of 15-30 degrees (see figure *a*).
2. Hold a dumbbell between 5 and 20 pounds in each hand.
3. Keeping the elbows slightly bent, pull the hands apart while keeping the wrists in line with the forearms (see figure *b*).
4. Squeeze the shoulder blades together at the top and pause for a full second before lowering the dumbbells back to the starting position under control.

Recommended volume range for hypertrophy: 2-3 sets of 15-20 repetitions or approximately 35 seconds of time under tension

Figure 6.1   Dumbbell incline rear delt raise.

Dumbbell Bent-Over Rear Delt Raise

The dumbbell bent-over rear delt raise is another exercise used to develop the muscles of the posterior (back side) shoulder in addition to the muscles around the upper back, such as the rhomboids and trapezius muscles.

Execution

1. Start by standing, holding a dumbbell between 5 and 20 pounds in each hand.
2. Bend at the waist, keeping the back flat, until the chest is approximately parallel to the ground (see figure *a*).
3. Keeping the elbows slightly bent, pull the hands apart while keeping the wrists in line with the forearms (see figure *b*).
4. Squeeze the shoulder blades together at the top and pause for a full second before lowering the dumbbells back to the starting position under control.

Recommended volume range for hypertrophy: 2-3 sets of 15-20 repetitions or approximately 35 seconds of time under tension

Figure 6.2   Dumbbell bent-over rear delt raise.

Dumbbell Standing Side Raise

The dumbbell standing side raise is used to develop the muscles of the lateral (side) shoulder in addition to the muscles around the upper back, such as the trapezius muscles.

Execution

1. Start by standing, holding a dumbbell between 5 and 20 pounds in each hand (see figure *a*).
2. Keeping the elbows slightly bent, lift the arms out to the sides until reaching shoulder height, keeping the wrists in line with the forearms (see figure *b*).
3. Hold the arms at shoulder height and pause for a full second before lowering the dumbbells back to the starting position under control.

Recommended volume range for hypertrophy: 2-3 sets of 15-20 repetitions or approximately 35 seconds of time under tension

Figure 6.3   Dumbbell standing side raise.

Plate Standing Front Raise Bus Driver

The plate standing front raise bus driver is used to develop the muscles of the anterior (front) shoulder in addition to the muscles around the upper back, such as the trapezius muscles.

Execution

1. Start by standing, holding a weight plate with both hands (typically 25-45 lb).
2. Lift the plate up in front of the body to the level of the shoulders, keeping the arms straight.
3. Hold the plate at this height and rotate the plate with the arms until one hand is on top of the other vertically, then switch directions.
4. Keep alternating back and forth for the allotted repetitions or time.

Recommended volume range for hypertrophy: 1-2 sets of 30-35 seconds of time under tension

Barbell Shrug

The barbell shrug is used to develop the muscles of the upper back and neck, in particular the trapezius muscles that elevate the shoulders in the shrugging motion. The muscles of the forearm responsible for grip strength are also developed during the time under tension.

Execution

1. Start by standing, holding a barbell in front of the body.
2. Shrug the shoulders as high as possible with the intention of having the shoulders touch the ears, even though this will not be fully possible. This helps to maximize muscle tension.
3. At the highest point, squeeze and hold this position for a full second before lowering the weight back down under control.
4. The weight should be heavy and challenging for the player, but the full range of motion should be attainable.

Recommended volume range for hypertrophy: 1-2 sets of 10-15 repetitions or 30-35 seconds of time under tension

Dumbbell Shrug

The dumbbell shrug is another exercise used to develop the muscles of the upper back and neck, in particular the trapezius muscles that elevate the shoulder in the shrugging motion. The muscles of the forearm responsible for grip strength are also developed during the time under tension.

Execution

1. Start by standing, holding a dumbbell in each hand (see figure *a*).
2. Shrug the shoulders as high as possible with the intention of having the shoulders touch the ears, even though this will not be fully possible. This intention helps to maximize muscle tension (see figure *b*).
3. At the highest point, squeeze and hold this position for a full second before lowering the weight back down under control.
4. The weight should be heavy and challenging for the player, but the full range of motion should be attainable.

Recommended volume range for hypertrophy: 1-2 sets of 10-15 repetitions or 30-35 seconds of time under tension

Figure 6.4   Dumbbell shrug.

Hypertrophy Exercises for the Arms

In football, the arms need to be strong to perform actions like blocking and tackling, and developing hypertrophy in the arms can help provide cushion against impact and collision, particularly for ballcarriers who must deal with defensive players attacking their arms to try to get the ball out. In addition, developing hypertrophy in the arms is a great tool to boost positivity from a psychological perspective. Because part of the game of football includes boosting confidence, developing the muscles of the arms is a simple tool that helps players feel more muscular and confident.

Barbell Curl

The barbell curl is used to develop the biceps muscles in addition to the muscles of the forearms responsible for lifting weight from the level of the waist up to the level of the shoulders.

Execution

1. Hold a barbell in front of the hips, with the arms straight and palms facing forward in an underhand grip (see figure *a*).

2. Bend the arms to curl the bar in front of the body until reaching approximately the level of the shoulders (see figure *b*).

3. Hold and pause at this top position for a full second before controlling the weight back down to the starting position.

Recommended volume range for hypertrophy: 2-3 sets of 8-12 repetitions or 30-35 seconds of time under tension

Figure 6.5　Barbell curl.

Dumbbell Hammer Curl

The dumbbell hammer curl is another exercise used to develop the biceps muscles in addition to the muscles of the forearms responsible for lifting weight from the level of the waist to the level of the shoulders.

Execution

1. Hold a dumbbell in each hand at the hips with the arms straight and palms facing toward each other (see figure *a*).
2. Bend the arms to curl the dumbbells in front of the body until reaching approximately the level of the shoulders (see figure *b*).
3. Hold and pause at this top position for a full second before controlling the weight back down to the starting position.

Recommended volume range for hypertrophy: 2-3 sets of 8-12 repetitions or 30-35 seconds of time under tension

Figure 6.6   Dumbbell hammer curl.

Band Hammer Curl

The band hammer curl is another exercise used to develop the biceps muscles in addition to the muscles of the forearms responsible for lifting the band from the level of the waist up to the level of the shoulders. The band challenges the athlete as the resistance is increased as the band is stretched farther during the curl, providing a different experience than that of holding a barbell or dumbbells.

Execution

1. Stand on top of a resistance band and hold the band in front of the hips in both hands, with the arms straight and palms facing inward toward each other. The thumbs will be hooked under the band and facing forward to allow the "hammer" position to be maintained.
2. Bend the arms to curl the band in front of the body until reaching approximately the level of the shoulders.
3. Hold and pause at this top position for a full second before controlling the band back down to the starting position.

Recommended volume range for hypertrophy: 2-3 sets of 8-12 repetitions or 30-35 seconds of time under tension

Cable Rope Triceps Pushdown

The cable rope triceps pushdown is used to develop the triceps muscles in addition to the muscles of the forearm responsible for extending the arm at the elbow joint.

Execution

1. Start by standing at a cable pulley machine and use a rope attachment, setting the height of the rope to where the hands are approximately at the level of the shoulders and chest when holding the rope.
2. Without rounding the back, keep the chest tall and extend the arms into a fully straightened position.
3. Hold and pause in this extended position for a full second before controlling the weight back up to the starting position.

Recommended volume range for hypertrophy: 2-3 sets of 8-12 repetitions or 30-35 seconds of time under tension

Lying Dumbbell Triceps Extension

The lying dumbbell triceps extension is used to develop the triceps muscles in addition to the muscles of the forearm responsible for extending the arm at the elbow joint.

Execution

1. Start by lying faceup on the floor or on a bench, with the arms extended above the chest. Hold a dumbbell in each hand with the palms facing inward toward each other (see figure *a*).

2. Lower the dumbbells under control toward the ground, aiming for the trajectory of the dumbbells to approach the forehead on either side of the head (see figure *b*).

3. Once the dumbbells are beside the head, extend the arms to return to the starting position to complete 1 repetition.

Recommended volume range for hypertrophy: 2-3 sets of 8-12 repetitions or 30-35 seconds of time under tension

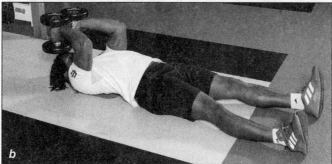

Figure 6.7   Lying dumbbell triceps extension.

Band Triceps Pushdown

The band triceps pushdown is used to develop the triceps muscles in addition to the muscles of the forearm responsible for extending the arm at the elbow joint.

Execution

1. Start standing by a band that has been attached to a lifting rack or pull-up bar above, holding the band to where the hands are approximately at the level of the shoulders and chest (see figure *a*).
2. Without rounding the back, keep the chest tall and extend the arms into a fully straightened position (see figure *b*).
3. Hold and pause in this extended position for a full second before controlling the band back up to the starting position.

Recommended volume range for hypertrophy: 2-3 sets of 8-12 repetitions or 30-35 seconds of time under tension

Figure 6.8   Band triceps pushdown.

Hypertrophy Exercises for the Legs

Building muscle in the legs is a key piece to any complete conditioning program for football. While the arms are largely involved in performing actions like blocking, shedding blocks, tackling, and avoiding tackles (e.g., performing a stiff-arm maneuver), the legs are heavily involved in every football action. From sprinting to cutting, blocking to tackling, jumping to running through contact, the legs must be resilient to handle the stress of playing the game. In addition, with recent developments in tackling techniques aimed at avoiding collision with the head and neck, the legs of ballcarriers are taking on almost all the impact from tackling. Therefore, like the muscles surrounding the shoulders, it's important for the legs to have good muscle bulk to provide protection against intensive collisions. Lastly, the legs are heavier than the arms, so for players who need to gain overall body mass to handle the physical nature of football, developing hypertrophy in the legs is arguably the best first step.

Barbell Forward Lunge

The barbell forward lunge is a single-leg exercise used to primarily develop the quadriceps muscles around the knee, as well as the gluteal (buttocks) muscles of the hip. The backward pushing motion puts more emphasis on the quadriceps when returning back to the starting position.

Execution

1. Start by standing fully upright while supporting a barbell on the shoulder.

2. Step forward with one leg and descend toward the ground while ensuring that the back hip stays extended so that the trunk remains in a neutral posture and the front of the hips stay above the front heel. If performed properly, the back leg should experience a significant stretch through the hip flexors, and the athlete should not break at the waist where the trunk falls forward. The trunk should stay stable because all the movement is performed through the hips and legs.

3. Lightly touch the ground with the back knee. There should be a positive shin angle of the front foot, where the front knee is pushing forward toward the front toe while the whole foot remains on the ground.

4. Drive through the hip of the front leg and the midfoot of the front foot to return to the starting position.

Recommended volume range for hypertrophy: 3-4 sets of 8-10 repetitions on each side

Dumbbell Goblet Lateral Lunge

The dumbbell goblet lateral lunge is a lower-body movement that develops single-leg strength and stability. This movement will also help prepare athletes for lateral movements on the field by strengthening the muscles of the groin, quadriceps, hamstrings, and hips.

Execution

1. Start by standing with the feet hip-width apart and a dumbbell held with both hands in a vertically oriented position under the chin (see figure *a*).
2. Lunge to the side, pushing the hips back and keeping the opposite leg extended (see figure *b*).
3. Keep the chest up, the eyes up, and the toes pointed straight ahead.
4. To stand back up, drive through the foot of the bent leg and stand back up into the starting position.

Recommended volume range for hypertrophy: 3-4 sets of 8-10 repetitions on each side

Figure 6.9   Dumbbell goblet lateral lunge.

Dumbbell Rear-Foot Elevated Split Squat

The dumbbell rear-foot elevated split squat is a single-leg exercise used to primarily develop the quadriceps muscles around the knee, as well as the gluteal (buttocks) muscles of the hip. However, the hamstrings are also involved, especially in the extension of the hip as the athlete presses back to the starting position.

Execution

1. Start by standing upright in front of a bench, box, or specific rear-foot elevated pad with a dumbbell in each hand.
2. Carefully place the back foot on the bench, box, or pad behind the body, where the top of the foot stays in contact with the surface (see figure *a*).
3. Place the front foot a distance away that allows for the hips to stay above the front heel with the torso upright and neutral.
4. Descend under control along a vertical line, being careful not to shift the body forward or backward. This way, a significant stretch is achieved in the back hip while the torso remains upright in neutral alignment and the knee of the front foot is able to press toward the front big toe to attain a positive shin angle. Descend as far as mobility allows (see figure *b*).
5. Press through the front hip and front foot to return to the starting position.

Recommended volume range for hypertrophy: 3-4 sets of 8-10 repetitions on each side

Figure 6.10   Dumbbell rear-foot elevated split squat.

Dumbbell Step-Up

The dumbbell step-up is a lower-body movement that develops single-leg strength and stability. This movement targets the muscles of the groin, quadriceps, hamstrings, and hips.

Execution

1. Hold a dumbbell in each hand at the hips and stand in front of a bench or box that is around knee height.
2. Step on the box with a single leg, keeping the leg on the ground extended.
3. Drive through the foot on the box to raise onto the box or bench.
4. While performing the movement, maintain a neutral spine and keep the chest up and eyes straight ahead.
5. To finish the movement, step off the box one leg at a time and return to the starting position.

Recommended volume range for hypertrophy: 3-4 sets of 8-10 repetitions on each side

90-Degree Back Extension

The 90-degree back extension is a posterior-chain exercise that is used to develop the muscles of the low back, glutes, and hamstrings without loading the spine. This movement is often performed using a glute-ham machine. This movement can be performed using body weight or be progressed by holding weights.

Execution

1. Lie facedown on the glute-ham machine, with the feet anchored into footpads and the thighs on the pads.
2. The machine should be adjusted so the pad sits just below the hip bone, allowing a full range of motion during the exercise.
3. Begin by relaxing the hamstrings, hinging at the waist and allowing the head to travel toward the ground (see figure *a*).
4. Pull with the hamstrings and glute muscles, tucking the chin to the chest as you come up into a horizontal position approximately parallel to the ground (see figure *b*).
5. At the top of the movement, squeeze the hamstrings and glutes to maintain the muscle contraction for 1-2 seconds.
6. To finish the movement, hinge at the hips to bring the body back to the bottom position, maintaining a neutral spine posture.

Recommended volume range for hypertrophy: 2-4 sets of 6-12 repetitions

Figure 6.11 90-degree back extension.

Stability Ball Leg Curl

The stability ball leg curl is a posterior-chain exercise that primarily targets the glutes and hamstrings. This exercise targets the hamstrings as a knee flexor as opposed to a hip extensor in exercises such as a barbell Romanian deadlift or a barbell hip thrust.

Execution

1. Lie faceup on the floor, with the feet on top of a stability ball and the toes pointed straight up.
2. Extend the hips so that the body is in a straight line (see figure *a*).
3. While keeping the hips extended, flex the knees and pull with the hamstrings to bring the feet toward the glutes (see figure *b*).
4. Extend the knees back to the starting position while keeping the hips extended.

Recommended volume range for hypertrophy: 2-4 sets of 6-10 repetitions

Figure 6.12 Stability ball leg curl.

Partner Nordic Hamstring Curl

The partner Nordic hamstring curl is a posterior-chain exercise that targets the hamstrings as a knee flexor. Performing this exercise will strengthen the hamstrings and help reduce the likelihood of a hamstring injury during sprinting.

Execution

1. Begin by kneeling with the knees, hips, and shoulders in line.
2. A partner will anchor the feet to the ground by holding the ankles and driving the feet into the ground (see figure *a*).
3. Slowly lower toward the ground while maintaining a straight line from head to knees (see figure *b*).
4. Keep the chin tucked to the chest and lower as far as possible. If you are unable to control your downward motion, catch yourself with your hands and push yourself back up to the starting position (see figure *c*).

Recommended volume range for hypertrophy: 2-3 sets of 6 repetitions

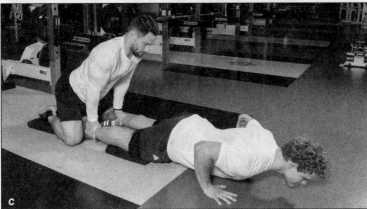

Figure 6.13   Partner Nordic hamstring curl.

PROGRAMMING FOR MUSCLE HYPERTROPHY

Training for hypertrophy must include all previously mentioned principles and have a progressive nature. This means that the intensity or volume of hypertrophy training must be planned over time. However, different training techniques, such as training until failure, should be used sparingly to not increase the likelihood of burnout or injury. Planned exercise selection exposes the athlete's body to different stimuli across different muscle groups to maximize muscle growth.

The following tables show how to integrate hypertrophy work into the weight room with primary strength work. The examples provided are based on an upper-body training session and a lower-body training session. However, integration may be accomplished with full-body training sessions as well. The take-home here is that hypertrophy work is ideally performed after the primary strength work has been completed to avoid excessive fatigue during the primary exercises. Tables 6.1 and 6.2 provide samples for integrating hypertrophy training into the complete conditioning program for the upper body and lower body, respectively.

Table 6.1 Integrating Hypertrophy for Upper Body

Exercise type	Exercise	Exercise prescription
Primary press	Barbell incline bench press	Set 1 = 12 reps Set 2 = 10 reps Set 3 = 8 reps Set 4 = 6 reps
Primary pull	Dumbbell chest-supported row (3 sec eccentric)	3 sets × 8 reps 1 set × max reps
Secondary pull	Dumbbell one-arm row	3 sets × 6 reps
Hypertrophy circuit—2 sets, 30 sec rests between each exercise	Barbell curl	30 sec
	Lying dumbbell triceps extension	30 sec
	Dumbbell incline rear delt raise	30 sec
	Barbell shrug	30 sec

Table 6.2 Integrating Hypertrophy for Lower Body

Exercise type	Exercise	Exercise prescription
Primary lower	Barbell reverse lunge (3 sec eccentric)	4 sets × 6 reps
Posterior chain	Barbell hip thrust	3 sets × 12 reps
Hypertrophy superset—go back and forth with minimal rest	Stability ball leg curl	3 sets × 8 reps
	Dumbbell rear-foot elevated split squat	3 sets × 8 reps

CONCLUSION

Improving muscle hypertrophy is necessary for football players due to the aspects of contact, collision, and sheer physicality of the game. The various principles and methods discussed in this chapter are simple in theory but in practice may be difficult for athletes who are young, deconditioned, or have simply never been pushed beyond discomfort while exercising. Therefore, it is important to educate the athletes on why this type of training is necessary. Furthermore, the athlete should know that the quickest way to achieve results is to work through fatigue and push his body when dealing with discomfort while also exercising in a safe, orthopedically sound manner. The body will become uncomfortable in hypertrophy exercises due to the metabolic stress that ensues, but that is a necessary component to producing the potent muscle-building response we are looking to achieve.

Chapter 7

Power Training

Power is most easily understood as the speed of movement against a given resistance. When we watch a linebacker take on the block of a pulling guard and knock the guard off his feet, we describe the linebacker as being very powerful. This is because he was able to rapidly overcome the resistance of the pulling guard in a split second and send him flying. In the context of performance, power may be thought of as creating as much force as possible in as little time as possible. This ability is paramount for every player in some way.

Power is defined as the product of force and velocity or the product of strength and speed. Thus, the power equation is as follows:

$$\text{Power} = \text{Force} \times \text{Velocity}$$

Another way to think of this equation is this way:

$$Power = Strength \times Speed$$

So, power is different from strength in the sense that strength does not necessarily have a time component to it. When measuring how strong a player is, we are only concerned with the weight that is lifted, not how fast it was lifted. Once we begin the conversation of how quickly strength was generated, we start talking about power. Power is actually about the combination of strength (force) and speed (velocity).

The heaviest strength exercises require the most force, so training a barbell squat with, say, 100% of a 1-repetition maximum (1RM) load will result in very slow movement due to the substantial weight on the bar. Contrast this with an unloaded vertical jump, where the athlete has to jump as high as possible against only his own body weight. In that case, velocity will be very high compared to the heavy squat because the load is only that of the athlete's body. It's important to recognize that power is the *product* of force and velocity, so if we look at the power equation, we realize that the same output of power can be achieved with various contributions of force and velocity. An exercise where the player moves a considerable amount of weight at relatively slower speeds can have the same power output as another exercise where the weight is minimal but the speed of movement is high.

A force–velocity continuum exists where certain exercises will be force-dominant and others will be velocity-dominant based on the load utilized and their nature of execution. For example, a barbell squat with a heavy load (e.g., >80% of 1RM) would be a force-dominant exercise, while, in comparison, a light-resisted sprint (e.g., a sled load equivalent to 10% of body weight) would fall much farther down the continuum toward the "velocity" end. By measuring bar speed in our weight room, we have found that a barbell squat performed for a 1RM may result in an average barbell speed of <0.40 meters per second (m/sec), but a light-resisted sprint with a sled load that is 10% of body weight can easily result in an average velocity of >3.50 meters per second (m/sec) within the first 5 yards. A 5-yard light-resisted sprint is about nine times faster than a maximal effort barbell squat, so each exercise will have a far different experience for the athlete and far different training adaptations. Figure 7.1 shows where different power-based activities might fall along the force–velocity continuum.

Thus, when determining which forms of training to incorporate into a power development program for football players, we need to consider the nature of the position and what qualities are important. For example, we know that down linemen will have to come off the ball quickly and then collide with an opponent of great stature—sometimes someone well over 300 pounds of body weight at the college and professional level. Therefore, it's important that linemen train for power using exercises that feature

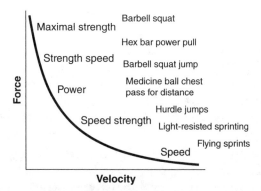

Figure 7.1   Force–velocity characteristics of various common power-based exercises.

higher loads, like different variations of the Olympic clean or heavy-loaded jumps and throws. On the other hand, wide receivers and defensive backs will need the ability to explode into the air and play the ball, so jumping is very much part of their skill repertoires. They should train for power, using exercises that teach them to project their bodies into space, both vertically and horizontally.

It's important to point out that these comparisons do not mean that the linemen should avoid jump training or that backs and receivers should not do loaded power training. Instead, we should understand the emphasis of training based on player position, where frontline players will spend most of the time closer to the force end of the continuum and the perimeter players closer to the velocity end.

COACHING POWER

As we noted in chapter 3 when reviewing acceleration and top speed sprinting, force can be put into the ground horizontally or vertically. For sprinting, athletes need to be proficient in both horizontal and vertical force application to develop acceleration and top speed, respectively. The same holds true for explosive power training. Most of the actions that happen on the football field are performed in a horizontal plane (e.g., accelerating, changing direction to the side, or charging forward and colliding with an opponent), so it makes sense that training horizontal power is important. Exercises like broad jump variations, medicine ball throws for distance, or explosive skipping or bounding for distance are examples of training horizontal power. In addition, exercises like these may have a positive influence over the first one to three steps of acceleration due to their similarity in execution and horizontal direction.

Training for vertical power is most common, as seen in Olympic weight-lifting movements, loaded explosive pulls or jumps, vertical jump training, medicine ball throws, and plyometrics (e.g., depth jumps, hurdle jumps, or explosive skipping or bounding for height). While the horizontal plane may be more specific in terms of actions found on the field for most positions, the vertical plane provides the unique opportunity to train against higher loads since the movements are generally simpler in coordination than horizontal-based movements. So, from a more general standpoint, using vertical plane exercises to develop the body's ability to adapt the nervous system, muscles, and other connective tissues to coordinate explosive action against high loads is valuable. Taking the players out of the horizontal plane also introduces variability to their bodies, reducing the potential for overuse trauma versus when they are kept only in the horizontal plane.

In addition to considering the vertical and horizontal planes, we also consider the discrepancy between explosive and reactive jumping. In our opinion, the latter exists in a class of its own, and improvements in explosive jumping may have little to no influence on improvements in reactive jumping. Explosive jumping has been described as "long response," which essentially refers to the time spent on the ground, where "long" would indicate a ground-contact time that is greater than 250 milliseconds (0.25 sec). Reactive jumping, on the other hand, has been described as "short response," because these exercises are characteristic of ground-contact times that are shorter than 250 milliseconds.

The stretch-shortening cycle (SSC) is the basis of explosive exercises and is a natural muscle function in which a muscle is stretched immediately before contraction. This eccentric to concentric muscular contraction produces a more powerful output than purely concentric action. This is why most athletes will not jump as high when performing a squat jump, in which an athlete lowers the center of mass, pauses for 3 seconds at the bottom position, and then explodes back up, as they do in a typical countermovement jump, in which there is no pause at the bottom.[1] Not all jump training methods are created equal, and an athlete's reactive ability describes the ability to rapidly change from an eccentric to concentric contraction, producing high forces in a minimal amount of time.

With explosive jumping, the longer time spent on the ground allows more time to activate muscle fibers to contribute to the work. Typically, longer ground-contact times are also associated with larger ranges of motion at the various leg joints, so if a player is jumping vertically, the takeoff is usually preceded by a deep squat before the body is launched into the air. The vertical jump test at the NFL combine is a great example of explosive jumping, where the height is the only thing that matters so the participants can spend as much time on the ground as they want before jumping.

Reactive jumping, on the other hand, is based on jumping as high or as far as possible with minimal time spent on the ground. This is on display when a wide receiver is running a deep "go" route at high speeds and must time his jump appropriately to go up and catch the ball over the defensive back while taking off on one foot. There is a time constraint associated with this situation because the ball will not wait for the receiver. The receiver simply has to meet the ball in the air and will not have any time to waste on the ground before going to get it.

The term *reactive* refers to the fact that these jumps will call upon the careful coordination of the muscles with other connective tissues like the tendons to allow the hips, knees, and ankles to quickly stabilize and produce power in a very short time frame. As a result, the movement is more of a "bounce" than an explosive "push." In addition, while many people often assume that the term *plyometrics* encompasses all jumping exercises, it actually only refers to short-response, reactive jumping. The long-response jumping is simply *jump training*. All plyometrics are a form of jumping, but not all forms of jumping are plyometrics.

While most football strength programs feature explosive movements, including explosive jumping exercises, we believe many are missing the important component of reactive jumping (plyometrics). While it's arguable whether down linemen require high levels of reactive power since much of their movements are done with longer ground contacts, the skill positions certainly do. All ballcarriers will be faced with situations in which they have to quickly explode or redirect themselves in response to what is happening in the game. Likewise, defensive players will have to quickly react and respond to what offensive players are doing. Without a sufficient base of reactive ability, skill players may find themselves losing at the point of attack or dealing with a noncontact soft-tissue injury. In the case of injury, it may be theorized that the player was unable to stabilize the joints quickly enough to withstand the forces of the ground contact, which will have surpassed the joint's structural capacity.

TESTING AND MEASURING POWER

The most common tests for measuring explosive power in football are the vertical jump and the broad jump. These tests can measure a player's maximum explosive capability in two different planes of movement: The vertical jump assesses power in the vertical plane, and the broad jump does so in the horizontal plane. However, of the two tests, the broad jump is the most practical in terms of setup, requiring only a tape measure and a yardstick to accurately gauge where the player's back heel lands upon ground contact.

The vertical jump, on the other hand, typically requires more expensive equipment like a Vertec, where a metal pole is adjusted relative to the player's reach length when the arm is extended overhead. The player then jumps and reaches to hit a series of plastic vanes along the pole that indicate how high the player jumped. This form of vertical jump testing is currently utilized at the NFL combine. Other expensive options include various forms of jump mats or force plates that can calculate when the athlete is on the ground and in the air, among several other metrics.

However, inexpensive software applications now exist that may be downloaded onto a phone or tablet and allow coaches to film players performing a jumping action, and the software can calculate data like that from a jump mat or force plate. Although requiring an initial learning curve to operate the software and long periods of time to compile the data for each player measured, a lot of valid and usable information can be gained from implementation, such as ground-contact times and flight times. You can build a vertical jump profile by monitoring the interaction of force and velocity for each player.

While advanced forms of technology provide a deeper dive into various metrics associated with power, typically the most commonly understood and monitored metrics are jump height and jump distance for the vertical jump and the broad jump, respectively. Simply stated, if a player is able to jump higher and farther than before, his power output is improving. So, as long as coaches can find a way to measure vertical or broad jump results, or both, power monitoring can be done consistently.

Testing and measuring reactive power is far more difficult and will typically require a jump mat or force plate to get an accurate assessment. Since the player's contact with the ground is such a critical component to measuring reactive ability, these devices can give information about how the player is rebounding with each takeoff. The most common assessment with these devices is the reactive strength index (RSI), which is measured by performing a series of two or three depth jumps (or drop jumps) at gradually increasing box heights, typically starting at 12 inches and progressing up to 30 inches. In our program, we perform two jumps each at box heights of 12, 18, and 24 inches, progressively. The jump mat or force plate is able to assess ground-contact time, and the RSI value is calculated by dividing jump height by the ground-contact time. If measuring jump height in inches, the value must be converted to meters to get an accurate RSI value, which can be done by using the following conversion:

1 inch = 0.0254 meters

Here is how to calculate RSI with a jump height of 20 inches and a ground-contact time of 0.23 seconds:

20 inches = 0.51 meters

0.51 meters (jump height) / 0.23 seconds (ground-contact time) = 2.22 (RSI value)

Using this formula for RSI, strength coach and sport science practitioner Eamonn Flanagan has presented value thresholds to indicate an athlete's reactive strength ability:

- <1.5—Low reactive strength ability: Need strength development and low-level plyometric activities
- 1.5-2.0—Moderate reactive strength ability: Continue to enhance reactive ability
- 2.0-2.5—Well-established reactive strength ability: High-intensity plyometrics are appropriate for training
- 2.5-3.0—High reactive strength ability: Analyze whether greater reactive strength ability will improve performance
- >3.0—World-class reactive strength ability: Limited capacity to continue improving reactive strength ability

Adapted from E. Flanagan, "The Reactive Strength Index Revisited: Part 2," Push, last modified April 19, 2016, www.trainwithpush.com/blog/reactive-strength-index-revisited-2.

Again, the devices commonly used to assess RSI values are very expensive and not always accessible. But some of the same software programs that can measure jump height through video analysis can also measure RSI. So, there are certainly many options when it comes to testing and measuring power, and we encourage coaches to find the best available option for their teams.

POWER EXERCISES AND DRILLS

This section is divided into exercises and drills devoted to developing explosive power and is followed by those that develop reactive power. Again, not all jumping is the same, and it is critical to understand the desired training effect. Reactive power should be seen as its own motor ability and exists separately from explosive power. This means that exercises for explosive power may not have a positive effect on reactive exercises, and vice versa. Thus, this distinction is vital for preparing complete power-producing capabilities in football players. We believe it's important to give each player a variety of exercises and drills to develop each quality, so we have provided our list of the ones we most commonly use in our program.

Explosive Power Exercises and Drills

Explosive power exercises and drills are activities that emphasize speed of execution in the concentric phase of the movement but feature a long response in terms of the body's interaction with the ground, with ground-contact times that are relatively long (i.e., >0.25 sec) in comparison to reactive activities. In these activities, maximal concentric power is the primary goal, and ground-contact time is not a primary focus. Thus, the aim is to simply jump as high or as far as possible, throw an implement as high or as far as possible, or move heavier resistances at consistent speeds in the case of loaded jumps or Olympic lifting variations. This section will outline the explosive power exercises and drills that we commonly feature in our program.

Countermovement Jump

The countermovement jump is used to develop explosive power by incorporating a countermovement, allowing energy to be stored in the legs that then adds power to the jump.

Execution

1. Begin the exercise standing upright with the arms at the sides.
2. Lift the arms overhead while keeping the feet flat. Rapidly drive the arms down and lower the center of mass, then perform a vertical countermovement jump by quickly reversing the arm action upward while extending the hips, knees, and ankles to take off vertically into the air as high as possible.
3. Land from the jump by absorbing through the ball of the foot first before sinking into a balanced athletic position with the center of mass lowered, the hips slightly back, and the spine neutral, bending at the knees and ankles. At the end of the absorption phase, the arms will be in a ready position, with both arms back near the hips.
4. Reset in the upright position before initiating the next repetition.
5. The goal is to jump as high as possible while taking advantage of countermovement assistance to emphasize vertical explosive power.

Dumbbell Countermovement Jump

The dumbbell countermovement jump is used to develop explosive power against resistance by incorporating a countermovement, allowing energy to be stored in the legs that then adds power to the jump.

Execution

1. Begin the exercise standing upright with the arms at the sides of the hips, holding a dumbbell in each hand.
2. While keeping the arms still, rapidly lower the center of mass, then perform a vertical countermovement jump by quickly driving the ground away and extending the hips, knees, and ankles to take off vertically into the air as high as possible.
3. Land from the jump by absorbing through the ball of the foot first before sinking into a balanced athletic position with the center of mass lowered, the hips slightly back, and the spine neutral, bending at the knees and ankles.
4. Reset in the upright position before initiating the next repetition.
5. The goal is to jump as high as possible while taking advantage of countermovement assistance to emphasize vertical explosive power.

Box Countermovement Jump

The box countermovement jump is used to develop explosive power while minimizing the impact stress of landing, so the jump takeoff is emphasized. The countermovement refers to dipping down through the hips and legs before reversing the motion and extending into the takeoff, which allows energy to be stored in the legs that then adds power to the jump.

Execution

1. Begin the exercise about 6-12 inches away from the box to allow for clearance of the legs on takeoff, standing upright with the arms at the sides. The height of the box is typically set between 18-30 inches, but may be set higher or lower depending on the player's jump capability.

2. Lift the arms overhead while keeping the feet flat. Rapidly drive the arms down and lower the center of mass, then perform a vertical countermovement jump by quickly reversing the arm action upward while extending the hips, knees, and ankles to take off vertically into the air as high as possible (see figures *a-b*).

3. Land from the jump on the box by absorbing through the ball of the foot first before sinking into a balanced athletic position with the center of mass lowered, the hips slightly back, and the spine neutral, bending at the knees and ankles. At the end of the absorption phase, the arms will be in a ready position, with both arms back near the hips (see figure *c*).

4. The player will then step down from the box, not jump down, before initiating the next repetition.

5. The goal is to jump as high as possible regardless of the set box height.

Figure 7.2 Box countermovement jump.

Squat Jump

The squat jump is used to develop explosive power without the added benefit of a countermovement, so the jump emphasizes power from a dead-stop position. To eliminate the countermovement, the player pauses at the bottom position for 3 seconds before rapidly exploding into the air.

Execution

1. Begin the exercise standing upright with the arms at the sides.
2. Lift the arms overhead while keeping the feet flat. Rapidly drive the arms down and lower the center of mass, then pause in the bottom position for 3 seconds. After 3 seconds, quickly reverse the arm action upward while extending the hips, knees, and ankles to take off vertically into the air as high as possible (see figures *a-c*).
3. Land from the jump by absorbing through the ball of the foot first before sinking into a balanced athletic position with the center of mass lowered, the hips slightly back, and the spine neutral, bending at the knees and ankles. At the end of the absorption phase, the arms will be in a ready position, with both arms back near the hips.
4. Reset in the upright position before initiating the next repetition.
5. The goal is to jump as high as possible while minimizing any countermovement assistance to emphasize vertical explosive power from a dead-stop position.

Figure 7.3 Squat jump.

Dumbbell Squat Jump

The dumbbell squat jump is used to develop explosive power against resistance without the added benefit of a countermovement, so the jump emphasizes power from a dead-stop position. To eliminate the counter-movement, the player pauses at the bottom position for 3 seconds before rapidly exploding into the air.

Execution

1. Begin the exercise standing upright with the arms at the sides of the hips, holding a dumbbell in each hand.

2. While keeping the arms still, rapidly lower the center of mass, then pause in the bottom position for 3 seconds. After 3 seconds, quickly drive the ground away while extending the hips, knees, and ankles to take off vertically into the air as high as possible.

3. Land from the jump through the ball of the foot first before sinking into a balanced athletic position with the center of mass lowered, the hips slightly back, and the spine neutral, bending at the knees and ankles.

4. Reset in the upright position before initiating the next repetition.

5. The goal is to jump as high as possible while minimizing any coun-termovement assistance to emphasize vertical explosive power from a dead-stop position.

Barbell Squat Jump

The barbell squat jump is used to develop explosive power against heavy resistance without the added benefit of a countermovement, so the jump emphasizes power from a dead-stop position. To eliminate the counter-movement, the player pauses at the bottom position for 3 seconds before rapidly exploding into the air.

Execution

1. Begin the exercise standing upright with a loaded barbell on the shoulders.
2. While holding the bar tight to the upper back, rapidly lower the center of mass, then pause in the bottom position for 3 seconds. After 3 seconds, quickly drive the ground away while extending the hips, knees, and ankles to take off vertically into the air as high as possible (see figures *a-b*).
3. Land from the jump through the ball of the foot first before sinking into a balanced athletic position with the center of mass lowered, the hips slightly back, and the spine neutral, bending at the knees and ankles (see figure *c*).
4. Reset in the upright position before initiating the next repetition.
5. The goal is to jump as high as possible while minimizing any coun-termovement assistance to emphasize vertical explosive power from a dead-stop position.

Figure 7.4 Barbell squat jump.

Barbell Countermovement Jump

The barbell countermovement jump is used to develop explosive power against heavy resistance by incorporating a countermovement, allowing energy to be stored in the legs that then adds power to the jump.

Execution

1. Begin the exercise standing upright with a loaded barbell on the shoulders.
2. While holding the bar tight to the upper back, rapidly lower the center of mass, then perform a vertical countermovement jump by quickly driving the ground away and extending the hips, knees, and ankles to take off vertically into the air as high as possible.
3. Land from the jump by absorbing through the ball of the foot first before sinking into a balanced athletic position with the center of mass lowered, the hips slightly back, and the spine neutral, bending at the knees and ankles.
4. Reset in the upright position before initiating the next repetition.
5. The goal is to jump as high as possible while taking advantage of countermovement assistance to emphasize vertical explosive power.

Hex Bar Squat Jump

The hex bar squat jump is another variation of an explosive power exercise against heavy resistance without the added benefit of a countermovement, so the jump emphasizes power from a dead-stop position. To eliminate the countermovement, the player pauses at the bottom position for 3 seconds before rapidly exploding into the air.

Execution

1. Begin the exercise standing upright with the arms at the sides of the hips, holding the hex bar.
2. While keeping the arms still, rapidly lower the center of mass, then pause in the bottom position for 3 seconds. After 3 seconds, quickly drive the ground away while extending the hips, knees, and ankles to take off vertically into the air as high as possible.
3. Land from the jump through the ball of the foot first before sinking into a balanced athletic position with the center of mass lowered, the hips slightly back, and the spine neutral, bending at the knees and ankles.
4. Reset in the upright position before initiating the next repetition.
5. The goal is to jump as high as possible while minimizing any countermovement assistance to emphasize vertical explosive power from a dead-stop position.

Hex Bar Countermovement Jump

The hex bar countermovement jump is another variation of an explosive power exercise against heavy resistance that incorporates a countermovement, allowing energy to be stored in the legs that then adds power to the jump.

Execution

1. Begin the exercise standing upright with the arms at the sides of the hips, holding the hex bar.

2. While keeping the arms still, rapidly lower the center of mass, then perform a vertical countermovement jump by quickly driving the ground away and extending the hips, knees, and ankles to take off vertically into the air as high as possible.

3. Land from the jump through the ball of the foot first before sinking into a balanced athletic position with the center of mass lowered, the hips slightly back, and the spine neutral, bending at the knees and ankles.

4. Reset in the upright position before initiating the next repetition.

5. The goal is to jump as high as possible while taking advantage of countermovement assistance to emphasize vertical explosive power.

Band-Resisted Barbell Squat Jump

The band-resisted barbell squat jump is another variation of an explosive power exercise against heavy resistance without the added benefit of a countermovement, so the jump emphasizes power from a dead-stop position. To eliminate the countermovement, the player pauses at the bottom position for 3 seconds before rapidly exploding into the air. The resistance of the band is unique, however, because it adds greater tension as it stretches, so the higher the athlete jumps, the more he is pulled down with increasing tension. This adds a greater impact load and requires the athlete to stabilize faster upon landing.

Execution

1. Before beginning the exercise, place one end of an elastic band around the end of a barbell just inside where the weight plates would be loaded on each side of the bar. Attach the other end of both bands to the bottom of the power rack by using a special rack attachment or looping each band around one of the bottom rails. From here, plates are loaded outside of the band on the end of the barbell if additional weight is desired.

2. Begin the exercise by standing upright with the barbell on the shoulders.

3. While holding the bar tight to the upper back, rapidly lower the center of mass, then pause in the bottom position for 3 seconds.

After 3 seconds, quickly drive the ground away while extending the hips, knees, and ankles to take off vertically into the air as high as possible.

4. Land from the jump through the ball of the foot first before sinking into a balanced athletic position with the center of mass lowered, the hips slightly back, and the spine neutral, bending at the knees and ankles.

5. Reset in the upright position before initiating the next repetition.

6. The goal is to jump as high as possible while minimizing any countermovement assistance to emphasize vertical explosive power from a dead-stop position.

Band-Resisted Barbell Countermovement Jump

The band-resisted barbell countermovement jump is another variation of an explosive power exercise against heavy resistance that incorporates a countermovement, allowing energy to be stored in the legs that then adds power to the jump. The resistance of the band is unique, however, because it adds greater tension as it stretches, so the higher the athlete jumps, the more he is pulled down with increasing tension. This adds a greater impact load and requires the athlete to stabilize faster upon landing. Also, the pull of the band is felt during the countermovement itself, so it will naturally increase the speed requirement for reversing the barbell back up into the takeoff.

Execution

1. Before beginning the exercise, place one end of an elastic band around the end of a barbell just inside where the weight plates would be loaded on each side of the bar. Attach the other end of both bands to the bottom of the power rack by using a special rack attachment or looping each band around one of the bottom rails. From here, plates are loaded outside of the band on the end of the barbell if additional weight is desired.

2. Begin the exercise standing upright with the barbell on the shoulders.

3. While holding the bar tight to the upper back, rapidly lower the center of mass, then perform a vertical countermovement jump by quickly driving the ground away and extending the hips, knees, and ankles to take off vertically into the air as high as possible.

4. Land from the jump through the ball of the foot first before sinking into a balanced athletic position with the center of mass lowered, the hips slightly back, and the spine neutral, bending at the knees and ankles.

5. Reset in the upright position before initiating the next repetition.

6. The goal is to jump as high as possible while taking advantage of countermovement assistance to emphasize vertical explosive power.

Barbell Hang Power Clean

We use the barbell hang power clean sparingly and like to incorporate it primarily with our offensive and defensive linemen to allow them to learn to receive load in an athletic position during the catch phase of the lift. Of course, a ton of benefit is occurring from the pull itself, such as the development of hip power against very high loads upward of 300 pounds, at times. The technique is absolutely crucial in this exercise, so we are careful to ensure that we do not progress the load if the technique is faulty. But, for exploding through heavy weight and then absorbing the same weight in the front of the body on the shoulders, it is a very potent exercise for these position groups.

Execution

1. Begin the exercise standing upright with the arms about shoulder-width apart. Hold the barbell so that the bar is resting against the midthigh (see figure *a*).

2. Initiate the hang clean movement by pushing the hips backward, performing a hinge where the torso moves forward with the back in a neutral alignment. Keeping a slight knee bend, lower the bar while keeping contact with the thighs until the bar is just above the knees (see figure *b*).

3. Bring the bar back up by pressing the hips forward toward the bar and keep the bar in contact with the thighs so that the knees move under the bar.

4. Once the bar approaches the midthigh position, rapidly extend the hips, knees, and ankles in succession so that the heels stay in contact with the floor for as long as possible before the power is transmitted through the ball of the foot. The arms are used to keep the bar close to the body during this process, with shoulders over the bar and arms remaining straight for as long as possible to maximize the vertical projection of the bar.

5. Once the hips fully collide into the bar and extensions at the hips, knees, and ankles are attained, rapidly shrug and begin flexing the elbows to pull the body under the bar (see figure *c*).

6. From here, the arms rotate around and under the bar while lowering into an athletic position with a rigid torso, hips back, and knees bent to about a quarter-squat position.

7. The bar is then "caught," and the weight is accepted through racking the bar across the shoulders with an upright torso, the elbows forward and high so that the upper arms are parallel to the ground. The feet are flat so that the weight is distributed evenly across the base of support (see figure *d*).

8. From here, stand up fully through the hips and knees to achieve one completed repetition.

Figure 7.5 Barbell hang power clean.

Hex Bar Power Pull

The hex bar power pull is one of our favorite exercises to develop power against high resistance, much like the barbell hang power clean. The difference with this exercise versus the barbell hang power clean is that we feel the learning curve for performing this exercise is significantly lower. The barbell hang power clean has multiple stages and components to ensure proper technique. The hex bar power pull, in contrast, is about creating tension before the pull and then exploding with as much power as possible, as vertically as possible, with enough load to ensure the feet do not leave the ground. In this exercise, the key is the initiation of power, specifically the initial rate of force development against heavy weight. This is beneficial for any position.

Execution

1. Begin the exercise with the feet placed between hip- and shoulder-width apart. Squat down toward the hex bar so that the hips are much lower than the shoulders and the torso is relatively upright, much like the bottom position of a squat.

2. Grab the handles of the hex bar and create tension by pressing slightly into the ground with a rigid torso and neutral spine alignment (see figure *a*).

3. Maintain this tension before rapidly pressing through the floor to extend the hips and knees, projecting the bar vertically into the air.

4. Keep the feet flat as long as possible to allow for power to transmit through the hips and knees before pressing through the balls of the feet. It should feel like jumping into the air without fully leaving the floor.

5. The momentum of the bar is carried vertically as the shoulders are shrugged and the arms bend slightly to follow through with the vertical projection of the lower body, but the bar should not be pulled too high. The primary goal is to emphasize the power through the lower body (see figure *b*).

6. After achieving maximum extension, drop quickly with the bar back to the floor without losing grip of the handles. This is more of a "controlled fall," where minimal work should be done to decelerate the bar, but enough control is maintained with the arms to follow a vertically descending bar path.

Figure 7.6 Hex bar power pull.

Long-Response Hurdle Jumps

Long-response hurdle jumps simply refer to performing jumps over hurdles with a longer ground-contact time, making the exercise more explosive. Given the nature of the exercise, higher hurdles (e.g., 18-24 in.) can be used since we are intentionally using longer ground-contact times. We also perform these consecutively, so one jump flows into the next until all the hurdles are cleared.

Execution

1. Begin the exercise standing in front of a set of hurdles (typically 3-5 in total) between 18 and 24 inches high, with an upright posture and arms at the sides of the hips.

2. Lift the arms overhead while keeping the feet flat. Rapidly drive the arms down and lower the center of mass, then perform a vertical countermovement jump by quickly reversing the arm action upward while extending the hips, knees, and ankles to take off vertically and forward into the air to clear the hurdle (see figure *a*).

3. Land from the jump by absorbing through the ball of the foot first before sinking into a quarter- to half-squat position with the center of mass lowered, the hips slightly back, and the spine neutral, bending at the knees and ankles. At the end of the absorption phase, the arms will be in a ready position, with both arms back near the hips (see figure *b*).

4. Once at the lowest point of the squat, reverse the momentum back upward into another consecutive takeoff over the next hurdle and continue in this consecutive fashion until all the hurdles have been cleared (see figure *c*).

5. After clearing the last hurdle, land from the jump by absorbing through the ball of the foot first before sinking into a balanced athletic position with the center of mass lowered, the hips slightly back, and the spine neutral, bending at the knees and ankles to "stick" the landing.

Figure 7.7   Long-response hurdle jumps.

Depth Jump

The depth jump is used to add velocity to a long-coupling, explosive jump by stepping off a box that's moderately high (e.g., 12-24 in.) and free-falling to the ground, where the player quickly generates force and uses the kinetic energy of the fall to transfer into a powerful reflexive reversal that propels the body into the air, if performed effectively. The fall from the box requires the muscles to generate force faster because the feet are not able to create tension on the ground since they are not in contact with the ground. This is one of the greatest exercises for explosive power, but it can be intense, so it's important to start with a shorter box (i.e., 12 in. box) and gradually progress to a 24-inch box.

Execution

1. Begin by standing on a box set between 12 and 24 inches high with the feet between hip- and shoulder-width apart and the toes near the edge of the box (see figure *a*).

2. Step off the box while being careful not to step *down* from the box—the latter will turn a 24-inch box into an 18-inch box in terms of how far the body will fall before contacting the ground.

3. Upon landing, rapidly throw the arms back before immediately reversing them and jumping as high as possible, aiming for minimal horizontal displacement and maximal vertical projection (see figures *b-c*).

Figure 7.8 Depth jump.

Alternating Box Split Jumps

Alternating box split jumps are used to emphasize concentric explosive power of a single leg at a time by placing the front foot on a box and driving through that leg and foot with great explosive power to propel the body vertically into the air. This emphasizes the ability to produce power over a large range of motion primarily on one leg, which can have a positive influence on first-step acceleration, tackling power, and engaging with an opponent.

Execution

1. Start by facing a box (12-18 in. high) with one foot on top of the box and the other foot on the ground. The whole foot should be on the box's surface, with the heel close to the near edge.

2. Lift the arms overhead while keeping the feet flat. Rapidly drive the arms down and shift the center of mass forward toward the lead foot on the box, then quickly reverse the arm action upward while extending the hips, knees, and ankles to take off vertically into the air as high as possible.

3. While in the air, allow the legs to switch places so that the back leg now becomes the lead leg and the landing occurs with the opposite foot on the box. Now the next repetition is initiated with the opposite foot on the box as the lead foot.

Single-Leg Box Jumps From Half-Kneeling Position

Single-leg box jumps from half-kneeling position are the next step to challenge single-leg explosive power progressing from alternating box split jumps. Rather than just working the powerful extension by itself, as the alternating box split jumps do, the kneeling position requires the player to rapidly extend the hip with enough power to launch into the air, after which the same leg has to rapidly drive the knee forward to land on the box with the proper timing. This exercise works the rapid extension-to-flexion mechanism that is seen during accelerative sprinting, so there can be a positive influence on the first few steps of acceleration. This exercise does a tremendous job of training both powerful hip extension and powerful hip flexion on a single leg.

Execution

1. Begin by facing a box (12-24 in. high) in a half-kneeling position, with the back knee on the ground and the weight shifted forward so that the lead knee is pressed toward the toe of the lead foot. Arms are set with the lead hand up by the chin and the back hand by the hip of the lead leg.
2. Rapidly shift the center of mass forward toward the lead leg and extend the hip, knee, and ankle to press the ground away and launch the body forward and upward into the air toward the surface of the box.
3. After the lead leg is fully extended and the body is in the air, the same leg then rapidly swings forward to land on the same foot that was used to take off. There should be a quick, scissor-like action between the lead and back legs to properly time this action.
4. Stick the landing on the box before stepping back down to reset for the next repetition. Perform all the prescribed repetitions on one leg before repeating on the other leg.

Band-Assisted Countermovement Jump

The band-assisted countermovement jump is another exercise variation used to challenge a player's ability to generate as much force as possible in a short time. The band assists with pulling the player into the air through elastic tension, thereby adding much more acceleration to the takeoff than would be possible without the band. Because the takeoff speed will be much faster than under unassisted conditions, the player is challenged to put as much force into the ground as possible during the shortened concentric (upward) phase of the movement. In theory, this can help a player learn to activate and fire muscle fibers faster, which can have a positive effect on explosive performance.

Execution

1. Attach an elastic band with moderate tension to a power rack or pull-up bar so that the band hangs down from above.
2. Pull the band down and place each end in an armpit so that there is some tension in the band even when standing upright. Move back slightly from the anchor point of the band above to minimize any risk of colliding with a rack or bar when taking off into the air.
3. Start upright and then rapidly drop the hips into a countermovement jump so that the band tension increases on the way down and then forcefully retracts in the opposite direction to add significant speed to the takeoff.
4. Jump as high as possible, working with the band and ensuring that the lower body does all the work. The arms should not pull on the band when in the air and should only be used to maintain a firm grip on the band.
5. Land softly, reset into the upright position, and repeat for the designated repetitions.

Power Skips

Power skips are one of the most potent ways to teach players to project their bodies into space through a single-leg takeoff, with the added benefits of requiring no equipment and relatively simplistic execution. As long as sufficient space is available, explosive skipping for height can help reinforce coordination, rhythm, and power in a way that largely resembles the single-leg takeoff actions seen in football (i.e., jumping up to receive or intercept a pass). As one leg extends, the other leg is brought up with a powerful knee drive to where it is bent at approximately 90 degrees and the thigh is at the level of the hip, much resembling the interaction of the thighs during sprinting. In this way, the powerful "push-off" action at the hip is developed for various athletic maneuvers. The interaction with the ground can be emphasized more vertically or more horizontally by instructing players to either skip for height or skip for distance, respectively.

Execution

1. Start behind a line in a split stance where one foot is in front of the other and the body weight is balanced between both feet.
2. Rapidly drive through the front leg and swing the back leg forward, contacting the ground with the whole foot. Project into the air by pressing through the ground. If height is the emphasis, project more vertically, and project more horizontally when emphasizing distance.
3. Land on the same foot used for the takeoff, rapidly drive the opposite leg forward, and repeat the same takeoff and landing pattern on the other side.
4. Continue in this fashion for the designated takeoffs or distance.

Medicine Ball Chest Pass for Distance

Explosive medicine ball throws are another category of drills to help players learn to transmit force, not just through the ground but also into an object. Explosive throws teach athletes how to capitalize on the ground reaction force of pressing into the ground and carrying it into an object like a medicine ball to launch the ball as high or as far as possible. In the medicine ball chest pass for distance, the goal is to launch the medicine ball (typically 10-20 lb) as far as possible by holding it at the level of the chest, sinking through the hips and legs, and then rapidly extending the lower body, followed by the upper body, and throwing the ball forward.

Execution

1. Begin in an upright position with the medicine ball held at chest level.
2. Rapidly drop the hips and bend the legs to begin a countermovement motion. The center of mass is rolled forward at the same time, much like the setup for a takeoff in a broad jump (see figure *a*).
3. Powerfully extend the hips, knees, and ankles to project the body forward at an approximately 45-degree angle to maximize the horizontal jumping distance.
4. Follow through from the lower-body push-off by extending the arms and launching the medicine ball forward along the same angle. At this point, the entire body should be fully extended for a moment (see figure *b*).
5. Once the ball has left the hands, quickly drive both legs forward under the hips to prepare for landing. The landing will resemble the landing pattern from performing a broad jump (see figure *c*).
6. Land softly on both feet and observe the distance achieved by the throw (see figure *d*).

Figure 7.9   Medicine ball chest pass for distance.

Medicine Ball Overhead Backward Throw for Distance

The medicine ball overhead backward throw for distance changes the launch of the ball by facing away from the starting line, holding the medicine ball (typically 10-20 lb) at the hips with the arms straight, sinking through the hips and legs, and rapidly extending the lower body. The arms are extended the whole time, and the goal is to find the optimal release point to launch the ball up and backward as far as possible.

Execution

1. Begin in an upright position with the medicine ball held at the level of the hips with the arms extended.

2. Rapidly drop the hips and bend the legs to begin a countermovement motion. The center of mass shifts slightly backward at the same time, ready to push the ground away in a down-and-forward action (see figure *a*).

3. Powerfully extend the hips, knees, and ankles to project the body backward at an angle to maximize the up-and-back jumping action. Aim for an angle as close to 45 degrees as possible without falling backward and losing balance (see figure *b*).

4. Follow through from the lower-body push-off by raising the extended arms up into the air and timing the release in such a way that the medicine ball is launched as high and as far backward as possible. At this point, the entire body should be fully extended for a moment (see figure *c*).

5. Once the ball has left the hands, quickly shift the center of mass forward to maintain balance while slightly airborne. The actual height of the jump will not be very high because most of the force should have been transmitted into launching the medicine ball.

6. Once upright, turn around and observe the distance achieved by the throw.

Figure 7.10   Medicine ball overhead backward throw for distance.

Medicine Ball Scoop Throw for Distance

The medicine ball scoop throw for distance is similar to the medicine ball chest pass for distance in that the athlete is facing forward and launching the ball forward, but this time the ball (typically 10-20 lb) will be held at the hips with the arms straight. The arms are extended the whole time, and the goal is to find the optimal release point to launch the ball up and forward as far as possible.

Execution

1. Begin in an upright position with the medicine ball held at the level of the hips with the arms extended.
2. Rapidly drop the hips and bend the legs to begin a countermovement motion. The center of mass is rolled forward at the same time, much like the setup for a takeoff in a broad jump (see figure *a*).
3. Powerfully extend the hips, knees, and ankles to project the body forward at an approximately 45-degree angle to maximize the horizontal jumping distance.
4. Follow through from the lower-body push-off by raising the extended arms and launching the medicine ball forward along the same angle. At this point, the entire body should be fully extended for a moment (see figure *b*).
5. Once the ball has left the hands, quickly drive both legs forward under the hips to prepare for landing. The landing will resemble the landing pattern from performing a broad jump (see figure *c*).
6. Land softly on both feet and observe the distance achieved by the throw.

Figure 7.11 Medicine ball scoop throw for distance.

Band-Resisted Broad Jump

While the broad jump is a common assessment of horizontal explosive power, it is also a useful training exercise. However, performing intense broad jumps repeatedly can be very stressful to the leg joints when they absorb ground impact, especially the knees. So, performing the exercise with an elastic band around the waist can help provide resistance at the takeoff and reduce the impact of the landing since the band resistance will help cushion the impact. The band-resisted broad jump is a great exercise for training takeoff power with reduced impact stress, thereby allowing for more training volume to be implemented safely.

Execution

1. Tie an elastic band with moderate tension around a power rack or other columnar object and place the band around the hips at the waistline. If no column is available, a partner can stand behind the athlete and place the same band around the waistline behind the body or hold it in the hands.

2. Begin in an upright position with the arms raised overhead (see figure *a*).

3. Rapidly throw the arms down while dropping the hips and bending the legs to begin a countermovement motion. The center of mass is rolled forward at the same time to maximize the combination between vertical and horizontal propulsion (see figure *b*).

4. Powerfully extend the hips, knees, and ankles to project the body forward at an approximately 45-degree angle to maximize the horizontal jumping distance. The goal is to overcome the tension of the band as powerfully as possible.

5. Follow through by raising the extended arms. At this point, the entire body should be fully extended for a moment (see figure *c*).

6. Once the push into the jump has been achieved, quickly drive both legs forward under the hips to prepare for landing.

7. Land softly on both feet and walk back to the starting position to initiate the next repetition (see figure *d*).

Figure 7.12 Band-resisted broad jump.

Single-Leg Broad Jump, Land on Two

Another important aspect of explosive horizontal power is being able to project forward on one leg with minimal benefit from added momentum. Performing a single-leg broad jump is a great way to develop the ability to rapidly develop force and overcome substantial resistance (i.e., body weight, inertia) to launch the body through the air on a horizontal path through one limb. Landing on two legs helps reduce the overall impact load when ground contact is made after the jump. However, if increased deceleration intensity is desired, this exercise can certainly be performed by jumping off one leg and then landing solely on that same leg.

Execution

1. Begin in an upright position, standing on one leg with the arms raised overhead.

2. Rapidly throw the arms down while dropping the hips and bending the stance leg to begin a countermovement motion. The center of mass is rolled forward at the same time to maximize the combination between vertical and horizontal propulsion.

3. Powerfully extend the hip, knee, and ankle to project the body forward at an approximately 45-degree angle to maximize the horizontal jumping distance.

4. Follow through by raising the extended arms. At this point, the entire body should be fully extended for a moment.

5. Once the push into the jump has been achieved, quickly drive both legs forward under the hips to prepare for landing.

6. Land softly on both feet and walk back to the starting position to initiate the next repetition. Perform all the prescribed repetitions on one leg before repeating on the other leg.

Exercises and Drills to Develop Reactive Power

As we have stated throughout this chapter, reactive power exists in a class of its own due to the unique combination of high-power output performed with minimal ground-contact time. Thus, these exercises feature a movement display that would be better described as a "bounce" rather than a "jump." Like a basketball hitting pavement and recoiling back into the air, it's imperative that athletes attempt to bounce off the ground with minimal dissipation of force or power. The exercises and drills listed here are some of the most commonly incorporated reactive activities in our program.

Plyometric Depth Jump

The plyometric depth jump is used to add intensity to a reactive jump by stepping off a box that's moderately high (e.g., 12-24 in.) and free-falling down to the ground where the player quickly generates force and uses the kinetic energy of the fall to transfer into a powerful reflexive reversal that propels the player into the air. Just like the depth jump, the fall from the box requires the muscles to generate force faster because the feet are not able to create tension on the ground since they are not in contact with the ground. The difference is that the execution of the jump requires as brief of a ground-contact time as possible, ensuring that reactive components are developed instead of just explosive aspects. Thus, it's important to start with a shorter box, like a 12-inch box, and gradually progress to a 24-inch box over time to ensure minimal ground-contact time.

Execution

1. Begin by standing on a box set between 12 and 24 inches high with the feet between hip- and shoulder-width apart and the toes near the edge of the box.

2. Step off the box while being careful not to step *down* from the box—the latter will turn a 24-inch box into an 18-inch box in terms of how far the body will fall before contacting the ground.

3. Upon landing, rapidly throw the arms back before immediately reversing them and jumping as high as possible, aiming for minimal horizontal displacement and maximal vertical projection.

4. The time on the ground should be as minimal as possible, emphasizing the reactive component of the exercise.

Plyometric Hurdle Jumps

Plyometric hurdle jumps are performed in almost exactly the same way as the long-response hurdle jumps with the exception of the time on the ground. What makes these jumps plyometric is the reactive component and enforcing a brief ground-contact time. Lower hurdles should be used first, somewhere between 12 and 18 inches, and the height can be progressed up to 24 inches as long as players are demonstrating the proper interaction with the ground. If the ground-contact time becomes excessive, these will become long-coupling jumps, which will develop explosive power but not reactive power.

Execution

1. Begin the exercise standing in front of a set of hurdles (typically 3-5 in total) between 12 and 24 inches high, with an upright posture and the arms at the sides of the hips.

2. Lift the arms overhead while keeping the feet flat. Rapidly drive the arms down and lower the center of mass, then perform a vertical countermovement jump by quickly reversing the arm action upward while extending the hips, knees, and ankles to take off vertically and forward into the air to clear the hurdle (see figure *a*).

3. Land from the jump by absorbing through the ball of the foot first and attempt to minimize the bending at the hip and knee as much as possible so that the ankle and foot take the brunt of the impact and the legs are able to maintain spring-like stiffness to effectively "bounce" off the ground and over the next hurdle. Ground contact should be as brief as possible (see figure *b*).

4. Continue in this way over the next hurdle and consecutively until all the hurdles have been cleared (see figure *c*).

5. After clearing the last hurdle, land from the jump through the ball of the foot first before sinking into a balanced athletic position with the center of mass lowered, the hips slightly back, and the spine neutral, bending at the knees and ankles to "stick" the landing.

Figure 7.13 Plyometric hurdle jumps.

Single-Leg Hurdle Hop to Box Jump (1-1-2)

The single-leg hurdle hop to box jump (1-1-2) is a way to emphasize a reactive takeoff on one leg before landing softly with both feet on a box. The purpose of the hurdle is to launch the body up into the air so that the next ground contact made carries the momentum of the fall into the subsequent takeoff onto the box, training the body to create proper tensioning strategies to maximize the second takeoff. This is a simple way to get a potent reactive training effect on one leg while minimizing ground impact.

Execution

1. Begin the exercise standing on one leg in front of a hurdle between 6 and 12 inches high, with an upright posture and the arms at the sides of the hips.

2. Lift the arms overhead while keeping the stance foot flat. Rapidly drive the arms down and lower the center of mass, then perform a vertical countermovement jump by quickly reversing the arm action upward while extending the hip, knee, and ankle to take off vertically and forward into the air to clear the hurdle.

3. Land from the jump by absorbing through the ball of the foot first and attempt to minimize the bending at the hip and knee as much as possible so that the ankle and foot take the brunt of the impact and the legs are able to maintain spring-like stiffness to effectively "bounce" off the ground and up onto a box set between 12 and 24 inches high, depending on the athlete's capability. Ground contact should be as brief as possible.

4. Land on the box with both feet through the ball of the foot first before sinking into a balanced athletic position with the center of mass lowered, the hips slightly back, and the spine neutral, bending at the knees and ankles to "stick" the landing.

5. Step down from the box and return to behind the hurdle to initiate the next repetition. Perform all the prescribed repetitions on one leg before repeating on the other leg.

Pogo Jumps

Pogo jumps are one of the simplest, most effective ways to start building reactive ability with athletes. The emphasis is on contacting the ground primarily through the ball of the foot and bouncing off the ground. The goal is to spend as little time as possible on the ground but maximize the time in the air. The motion is very similar to what is seen commonly with jumping rope, but the height of each jump should be much higher, and the arms may help add speed to the takeoff. Pogo jumps can be performed in place or while projecting the body horizontally, but they are best used when emphasizing vertical height rather than trying to go for too much distance where ground contacts become excessive.

Execution

1. Begin in an upright position with the arms bent at approximately 90 degrees in front of the body. The elbows are near the ribs, and the thumbs are just in front of the nose.

2. Maintain the upright position and rapidly throw the arms back and perform a slight countermovement motion where the hip and knee bends are as minimal as possible to initiate the jump at the ankle and foot. The jump can either be entirely vertical or slightly horizontal if the goal is to cover a given distance.

3. When taking off, quickly throw the arms forward before pulling them back to prepare for the next ground contact (see figure *a*).

4. Contact the ground almost exclusively through the ball of the foot and immediately reverse the arm action and take off into the next jump, aiming for a "pop" off the ground where the ground-contact time is as brief as possible but the feet are still attacking the ground to project into the air with power on each consecutive takeoff (see figures *b-c*).

5. Continue in this fashion for the designated takeoffs or distance.

Figure 7.14   Pogo jumps.

Tuck Jumps

Tuck jumps are very similar to pogo jumps except that once the athlete is airborne, the knees are actively driven up toward the hips and then extend back to almost full extension before ground contact. The active knee drive adds speed to the limbs while in the air, making the ground contact more intense than is seen in pogo jumps.

Execution

1. Start behind a line in an upright position with the arms bent at approximately 90 degrees in front of the body. The elbows are near the ribs, and the thumbs are just in front of the nose.

2. Maintain the upright position and rapidly throw the arms back and perform a slight countermovement motion where the hip and knee bends are kept as minimal as possible to initiate the jump at the ankle and foot. The jump can either be entirely vertical or slightly horizontal if the goal is to cover a given distance (see figure *a*).

3. When in the air, rapidly drive the knees up toward the level of the hips and throw the arms forward before quickly pulling them back and extending the legs to prepare for the next ground contact (see figure *b*).

4. Contact the ground almost exclusively through the ball of the foot and immediately reverse the arm action and take off into the next jump, aiming for a "pop" off the ground where the ground-contact time is as brief as possible but the feet are still attacking the ground to project into the air with power on each consecutive takeoff.

5. Continue in this fashion for the designated takeoffs or distance.

Figure 7.15   Tuck jumps.

Extensive A-Skip

The extensive A-skip drill is used to develop a base of reactive ability that we aim to capitalize on as we start incorporating high-speed sprinting. Due to the highly reactive nature of sprinting at high speed, having a solid foundation of reactive power is vital. The coordination in terms of the interaction between the thighs, the postures attained, and the way the foot contacts the ground during the A-skip are all very similar to high-speed sprinting, but it is a power-based drill since the athlete will not actually be running. Thus, it is plyometric in nature but relatively low impact in terms of ground reaction force sustained, so we like to incorporate this drill in a continuous, extensive fashion for longer distances, typically between 30 and 40 yards.

Execution

1. Begin behind a starting line in an upright position with the arms extended by the sides.
2. Initiate the drill by performing a very quick, low-level pogo jump. The arms should remain at the sides for this jump.
3. Upon landing from the pogo action, the next takeoff involves a rapid separation of the thighs where one knee drives up toward the hip to achieve a 90-degree knee bend while the opposite leg is extended into the ground in a way that resembles a single-leg pogo action.
4. The arms should separate from front to back in an opposite and reciprocal manner to the legs, so if the left knee drives forward and the right leg drives back into the ground, then the right arm drives forward as the left arm is swung back behind the body.
5. After this action, the next brief takeoff goes back to a low-level pogo jump with the arms at the sides before initiating the rapid arm and leg separation in the subsequent takeoff. Thus, there is a rhythmical pattern of 2-1-2-1 in terms of how many feet are contacting the ground on subsequent ground contacts.
6. Continue in this manner until the designated distance has been covered.

Extensive High-Knee Running

The extensive high-knee running drill is used with the same goal as the extensive A-skip but with the understanding that the ground reaction force will be higher and more intense. This is because the movement more so resembles sprinting, so the angular speed of the legs will be faster leading into each ground contact and more repetitions of ground contact will be collected over the same distance. So, both intensity and volume of reactive ground contacts will increase when progressing to this drill over the extensive A-skip. Again, we will typically set the distance of each repetition to between 30 and 40 yards.

Execution

1. Begin behind a starting line in an upright position with the arms extended by the sides.

2. Initiate the drill by driving one knee up toward the hip and extending through the stance leg. The arm action should follow in an opposite and reciprocal manner to the legs, so if the left knee drives forward and up, then the right arm follows suit while the left arm extends back behind the body with the right stance leg.

3. Rapidly switch the thighs by pressing through the stance leg and whipping the swing leg back into the ground, contacting the ground almost exclusively through the ball of the foot and keeping ground contact very brief before switching the legs back again. Continue switching the legs and traveling down the field in this manner.

4. It's important to maintain a good range of motion between the legs where one leg is always able to bend up in front of the body at the level of the hip while the other leg is fully extended when making ground contact. The hips also should not drop with each step, and hip height should be maintained on a consistent path throughout the drill.

5. Continue in this manner until the designated distance has been covered.

Alternating Pogo Hops

Alternating pogo hops are used to emphasize the ground contact at the ankle and foot without as much assistance from driving the leg down (as seen in bounding, A-skips, high-knee running, etc.). Instead, because the legs will stay primarily extended with the exception of a slight knee bend, the athlete is forced to bounce down the field by maximizing recoil in a very short time frame, enhancing the activation of and cooperation between the muscles and tissues around the ankle and foot (like the Achilles tendon).

Execution

1. Begin in an upright position with the arms at the sides.
2. Maintain the upright position and initiate the drill by reaching one foot out in front of the body and pressing through the ground to project the body into the air with the hip and knee bends kept as minimal as possible to initiate the jump at the ankle and foot. The jump can either be entirely vertical or slightly horizontal if the goal is to cover a given distance.
3. When in the air, bring the opposite foot out in front of the body to prepare for the next ground contact. Contact the ground almost exclusively through the ball of the foot and immediately take off into the next jump, aiming for a "pop" off the ground where the ground-contact time is as brief as possible but the feet are still attacking the ground to project into the air with power on each consecutive takeoff.
4. Alternate back and forth between each foot and continue in this fashion for the designated takeoffs or distance.

Alternating Bounding

Alternating bounding is one of the most fundamental forms of plyometric training for reactive power. The athlete must be able to properly displace the body through the air to maximize the combination between vertical and horizontal projection to cover ground with each takeoff but do so with minimal ground contact. The scissor action of the thighs requires proper timing as the leg whips down from the hip toward the ground and is just about fully extended upon impact, with the whole foot in contact with the ground as the athlete bounces into the next bound. This drill may be performed for a designated number of takeoffs (e.g., 10 total takeoffs) or based on distance covered (e.g., 20 yd). It is a great drill for developing single-leg reactive power and coordination and may have positive carryover to actions like a single-leg takeoff when a football player goes up to catch a ball.

Execution

1. Start behind a line in a split stance where one foot is in front of the other and the body weight is balanced between both feet.

2. Rapidly drive through the front leg and swing the back leg forward, contacting the ground with the whole foot, and project into the air by pressing through the ground. Emphasize covering good distance by finding an optimal combination of vertical and horizontal force application into the ground. Ground contact should be powerful but brief to allow for reactivity. Spending too much time on the ground will throw off the rhythm and not allow for reactive power development (see figure *a*).

3. As one leg extends, the opposite leg should be driven forward to the level of the hip with the knee bent at approximately 90 degrees. While in the air, rapidly switch the thighs so that the next ground contact is made on the opposite foot (see figures *b-d*).

4. Continue in this fashion until achieving the designated number of takeoffs or distance.

Figure 7.16   Alternating bounding.

Single-Leg Bounding

Single-leg bounding is performed in the same way as alternating bounding but with a greater coordinative challenge, as only one leg contacts the ground in one work series. For example, if the number of takeoffs prescribed is 10 takeoffs on the right leg, every takeoff would be done on the right leg rather than alternating between legs. Then, on the next set, all the takeoffs would be done on the left leg. By bounding on one leg continuously, the athlete has to transmit enough force and power into the ground to continue propelling the body forward with minimal ground-contact time, and coordinate the limbs such that the thighs are able to "scissor" back and forth with the proper timing to get the same foot back under the body with each contact. So, it's a great drill to reinforce limb speed in addition to reactive power.

Execution

1. Start behind a line in a split stance where one foot is in front of the other and the body weight is balanced between both feet.

2. Rapidly drive through the front leg and swing the back leg forward, contacting the ground with the whole foot, and project into the air by pressing through the ground. Emphasize covering good distance by finding an optimal combination of vertical and horizontal force application into the ground. Ground contact should be powerful but brief to allow for reactivity. Spending too much time on the ground will throw off the rhythm and not allow for reactive power development.

3. As one leg extends, the opposite leg should be driven forward to the level of the hip with the knee bent at approximately 90 degrees. While in the air, rapidly switch the thighs and then switch them again so that the next ground contact is made on the same foot that was used to take off. This requires rapid alternating leg speed to properly time both switches before falling back to the ground.

4. Continue in this fashion until achieving the designated number of takeoffs or distance. Perform all the prescribed repetitions on one leg before repeating on the other leg.

Scissor Bounding

Scissor bounding has a similar training effect as alternating pogo hops in that the ankle and foot contact are a major emphasis, but with an added emphasis of attacking the ground with the hamstrings by keeping the legs straight over a greater range of motion. Basically, the trajectory of the legs is the same as in alternating pogo hops, but with scissor bounding, the leg is lifted up toward the hip in front of the body before swinging back down into the ground. Therefore, the athlete has to propel down the field by primarily using the glutes, hamstrings, and muscles around the feet and ankles to improve reactive power in these muscle groups.

Execution

1. Begin in an upright position with the arms at the sides.
2. Maintain the upright position and initiate the drill by reaching one leg out in front of the body and pulling through the ground to project the body forward with the hip and knee bends kept as minimal as possible to emphasize a straight-leg hip extension.
3. As the stance leg extends, swing the opposite leg out in front of the body, keeping it as straight as possible, and raise it near the level of the hip (see figure *a*).
4. When in the air, whip the front leg down and back to prepare for the next ground contact. Contact the ground almost exclusively through the ball of the foot and immediately pull the body through into the next takeoff, aiming for a "pop" off the ground where the ground-contact time is as brief as possible. The force application will be predominantly horizontal where the aim is to attack downfield by moving forward with brief contact times (see figure *b*).
5. Alternate back and forth between each leg and continue in this fashion for the designated takeoffs or distance.

Figure 7.17   Scissor bounding.

POWER TRAINING PROGRAM

Due to the large continuum of power development exercises, we believe it is best to capitalize on power exercises on the same days that we emphasize maximum lower-body strength and acceleration. The days that feature the most power training are classified as nervous-system-intensive days because we couple this work with acceleration efforts and maximum strength work.

So, all the work done on these days will be devoted to promoting a lot of muscle fiber recruitment and nervous system activation. Typically, we want to keep the number of jumps or takeoffs per set within 4-5 repetitions for explosive power training and within 20 yards for plyometrics. The exception to this is reactive power endurance work (which we will cover shortly). That can extend up to 40 yards for skill players, but it is much less intensive by nature. In terms of sets, we will aim for anywhere between 1 and 4 total sets, where the exercises that feature only 1 set are used simply to touch on the coordination and skill components of covering multiple planes of movement, multiple forces and speeds, and explosion against various resisted loads.

In terms of how we might lay out the week, table 7.1 provides an example of power training across a 4-day workout week where Tuesday and Friday are the designated "high nervous-system-intensive" days, and Monday and Thursday are less intensive and might feature more running volume and upper-body hypertrophy work.

Table 7.1 Power Training Distribution Across Week of Training

Monday	Tuesday	Wednesday	Thursday	Friday
Reactive power endurance	Horizontal and vertical explosive power Horizontal and vertical plyometrics Loaded power		Reactive power endurance	Horizontal and vertical explosive power Horizontal and vertical plyometrics Explosive power endurance

Explosive Power Endurance Program

In football, players will be required to perform explosive movements repeatedly over the course of a drive, quarter, and game. Depending on the team's playbook, some players may need to play for over 80 snaps by the end of the game. The players who can continue to perform high-level explosive actions with minimal impact from fatigue are those that have an advantage when entering the fourth quarter. Having a high capacity for the work associated with playing football is a requisite skill for all players at their respective positions.

There are specific forms of field-based conditioning that may be utilized to condition a player for the running demands of the game. However, we see the weight room as another setting to develop conditioning as it relates to the capacity to sustain powerful efforts. One of the ways we do this is through power capacity circuits that combine anywhere from two to four different explosive exercises. We perform them in a sequential circuit. Typically, we will follow a protocol similar to the French contrast method, which has the following sequence:[1]

1. Heavy strength exercise
2. Unloaded jump
3. Loaded jump
4. Plyometric jump or accelerated jump

We will perform 3-4 total sets of this sequence, with each exercise consisting of 1-3 repetitions per set. The players are encouraged to quickly transition from one exercise to the next, and we will time the rest with a stopwatch to communicate to them when to start the next set. We aim for a time of 3 minutes between the start of each set, so once the players finish the first heavy strength exercise, the rest time starts as they transition to the other exercises. Once those are complete, they rest and begin the next set after the 3-minute mark. An example of a sequence that we have used is the following:

1. Barbell squats—3 repetitions
2. Plyometric hurdle jumps (4 hurdles)—4 jumps (one over each hurdle)
3. Hex bar countermovement jumps (95 lb)—3 jumps
4. Plyometric depth jumps (12- to 18-in. box)—3 jumps

The contrasting effect of moving between heavier and lighter loads, with the overall effect of everything shifting more toward higher velocity as the sequence unfolds, allows the athletes to experience a wide range of the force–velocity spectrum in training vertical power. Training with power capacity circuits not only helps players develop the underlying fitness to sustain power against variable loads but also teaches them to properly coordinate their bodies to execute effectively when moving from a force-dominant situation to a velocity-dominant one.

Reactive Power Endurance Program

One of the unique abilities we aim to develop with our players is that of reactive power endurance. To put it simply, this is the ability for a player to maintain a "bounce" for extended repetitions of effort, which is important for players who have to operate at high speeds, like wide receivers, running backs, and defensive backs. Remember that high-speed sprinting is essentially a bound from foot to foot executed rapidly. When a running back breaks a big run (e.g., >20 yards) and propels his body toward the end zone, he will eventually get to where he is upright and running at high speed. If he loses his ability to stay reactive in this moment, he will start to rely on pushing through his muscles more, rather than having help from his tendons and other connective tissues to support the bounce on each step. This can result in excessive fatigue and spending more time on the ground, significantly slowing down, and risking being caught by a chasing defender or forcing his leg muscles to work harder than they can handle and possibly straining a hamstring, quadricep, groin, or hip flexor muscle.

Therefore, the ability to establish and maintain reactive muscle action is hugely beneficial for players who have to cover longer distances. This isn't just beneficial at high speeds, either. Watch a high-level safety move around in the defensive backfield, and you will quickly notice that this player seems to just float across the ground when jogging and striding. Using elasticity when moving on the field helps keep motion efficient, so the muscles don't have to work as hard. There's a clear benefit to reducing fatigue as well as moving gracefully from one area to the next.

In track and field, it's common practice for sprinters and jumpers to perform various circuits of low-level jumps, hops, skips, or bounds to build this base of reactive power endurance. We borrow from this approach and have our skill players perform various reactive power exercises for anywhere from 30-40 yards per repetition. One example would be performing a series of pogo jumps over 30 yards, where the goal is not to jump as high as possible on each takeoff, but rather to get more volume of the foot contacting the ground with a quick "pop" off the ground with each jump. The most potent part of this type of training is developing integrity at the foot and ankle, thereby teaching the lower leg how to properly contact and accept the ground on impact.

Spending too much time on the ground will move the exercise away from being reactive, so ground contact must be as brief as possible. The force application will be primarily vertical to ensure short contact time and that more repetitions occur over the given distance. A common rule is that the player should project forward at approximately the same pace as someone casually walking beside them. We can incorporate other drills that resemble the sprinting action, such as the A-skip or high-knee running, but program them with the intention of building reactive power endurance so we can incorporate them into our power training. When doing this type of work, we will form the players into lines that are two or three players deep so that when the first player finishes his first repetition, he rests while the next one or two lines go. We are not as concerned with full recovery since we are training a form of endurance here. We will typically perform 2 sets of each exercise, which can be done by going through the whole sequence and then starting over or by doing 2 sets of one exercise before moving on to the next. An example reactive power endurance circuit that we have used with our wide receivers and defensive backs is the following:

1. Pogo jumps: 2 × 40 yards
2. Extensive A-skips: 2 × 40 yards
3. Extensive high-knee running: 2 × 40 yards

It should be noted that this type of work can also be used with offensive and defensive linemen; however, it is not as crucial to their positions, and they also carry much larger body masses than the skill players. This can put them at potential risk for ankle and foot issues like stress fractures if done in a way that is excessive. So, when performing reactive power endurance work with linemen, it's likely best to not exceed 20 yards of distance per repetition.

CONCLUSION

Power training is a complex endeavor, in that any form of strength with respect to speed is going to be an expression of power. So, as we have covered here, there is a wide continuum of power-producing capabilities: those that feature high forces at low speeds, those that feature low forces at high speeds, and everything in between. Additionally, there is a major difference in the training effects of executing power exercises, namely differentiating between explosive, or long-coupling power exercises, and reactive, or short-coupling power exercises. It's imperative to know the difference because improvements in explosive power may not have any effect on reactive power and vice versa. To make things even more complicated, we also have to consider the plane of movement when performing power exercises, so we must respect both the vertical and horizontal planes. Overall, to build players with explosive and reactive power, it takes a lot of attention to multiple components, all of which can help us get a little closer to leaving no stone left unturned in our training program.

Chapter 8

Aerobic and Anaerobic Conditioning

The game of football involves short bursts of high-intensity effort that usually last 3-6 seconds, followed by short, incomplete recovery periods lasting 20-40 seconds. These time frames may be used as a blueprint to help develop football players by ensuring they are properly conditioned to operate effectively for the duration of a game. In general, the body uses two broad energy systems: the anaerobic system and the aerobic system. The anaerobic system provides fast energy to the body during the short bursts of activity after each snap of the football, and the aerobic system ensures that energy is sustained throughout longer periods of time like a drive, quarter, half, or the entire game.

The aerobic system helps replenish the energy fuel sources needed for anaerobic activity, and this occurs in between bouts of activity. So, the aerobic system is vital for sustaining high-effort outputs throughout the course of a football game. The higher the density of plays in a game, the more important the aerobic system becomes. When a defense has to play against an up-tempo offense, the aerobic system of each player has to be developed enough to defend against the fast-moving opponent. Thus, the conditioning requirements of football players will depend on their current levels of fitness, their playing positions, and their team's tactics (e.g., up-tempo offense). An overview of the work-to-rest variables in football are presented in table 8.1.

Table 8.1 Average Work-to-Rest Ratios in Football

Average plays per game	50-80
Average series per game	10-12
Average plays per series	4-8
Average time per play	3-6 sec
Average rest time between plays (no timeouts)	20-35 sec
Average time between offensive and defensive series	6-7 min

Adapted by permission from F. Connolly and C. Josse, *The Process, Level I: The Methodology, Philosophy & Principles of Coaching Winning Teams* (Muskegon, MI: Ultimate Athlete Concepts, 2019), 168.

While all 11 players on one side of the field are playing the same sport, the demands placed on each position are quite different. There are several factors to consider when training and preparing these athletes to play their positions optimally. The factors to be considered when training each position include the distance covered, direction of movement, velocity, duration, resistance encountered, number of efforts, and rest between each effort.

- Offensive and defensive linemen begin each play in a deep knee bend either in a 2-point or 3-point stance. Once the ball is snapped, they are then tasked with physically engaging with an opponent who is as large or larger than themselves. They will be required to run, sprint, and push forward, backward, and laterally. Offensive and defensive linemen will typically cover 0-10 yards a play for 3-6 seconds.

- Running backs and linebackers will begin each play in a quarter-squat position. Tight ends will start in a 2-point or 3-point stance (depending on tactics). These positions will be required to sprint, backpedal, move laterally, change direction, and run routes. These big-skill positions will cover 0-40 yards depending on the play and at higher velocities than the offensive and defensive linemen.

- Wide receivers and defensive backs begin each play in more of an upright position and play farther away from the ball. They will be required to sprint, backpedal, jump, make hard cuts, and change direction. These skill positions will cover the most distance, up to 20-40 yards per play, at the highest velocities.
- Mobile quarterbacks will also need to sprint, jump, make hard cuts, and change direction. They will cover similar distances and velocities as skill players. Traditional pocket-passer quarterbacks will need to be able to run, move laterally, and change direction. A pocket-passer will cover less distance than a mobile quarterback and at lower velocities.

Offensive attacks are generally considered pass heavy, run heavy, or balanced. Offenses that are run dominant and huddle between plays should be trained differently than no-huddle offenses that throw the ball more often than they run it. The run-heavy team will typically cover shorter distances and have longer rest periods between each play. Therefore, they will rely more on the anaerobic system than the aerobic system. In contrast, the team that uses a spread formation and runs a hurry-up offense will cover more distance during each play and have shorter rest periods. This team will rely more on the aerobic system because there is less time to recover between each play.

Defensive tactics are in large part dictated by the offense to be stopped. While teams' general philosophies might emphasize a more conservative containment approach or an aggressive blitzing attack, both of these will be needed at times, so players must be trained both anaerobically and aerobically.

ANAEROBIC POWER AND CAPACITY

Anaerobic power development is a foundational component of football training. Before developing anaerobic capacity (the ability to repeat short, explosive bursts of high-intensity effort with incomplete rest), an athlete must first develop the requisite strength and power. If a wide receiver doesn't have the speed or power to run effective routes and beat defenders, or if a defensive lineman doesn't have enough strength, power, and speed to battle against an offensive lineman, it doesn't matter how conditioned they are or how many times they are able to repeat that effort. These athletes must first develop high levels of strength, power, and speed, and then develop the ability to repeat these high-level outputs with short rest (anaerobic capacity). To develop anaerobic power, athletes will perform high-intensity and short-duration exercises such as a sprints, jumps, or throws, separated by complete recoveries, such as a maximal intensity sprint lasting 3-5 seconds followed by a complete recovery. A general rule for recovery when performing maximal intensity sprints is to rest 30 seconds for every 10 yards sprinted. If an athlete performs a 30-yard sprint, they should rest for a minimum of 90 seconds to ensure that the training stays anaerobic.

Once athletes have developed the ability to produce high-level outputs of anaerobic power, they then must be able to repeat these high-level outputs with incomplete recoveries. During the anaerobic power phase, athletes performed high-intensity exercises and their competition maneuvers with complete rest. Now in the anaerobic capacity phase, they must be able to explosively perform these maneuvers with incomplete recovery throughout an entire game. When training to develop anaerobic capacity, it is important to consider the tactics and scheme of the offense as well as the scheme that the defense will face most often. An offense that runs a hurry-up offense will have shorter recovery times between plays than a team that controls the clock and huddles between each play. The development of anaerobic capacity can be general or more specific to the game of football. In terms of general development, anaerobic capacity can be developed by using exercise bikes, medicine balls, battle ropes, and treadmills.

The development of anaerobic capacity can also be more specific to the movements performed in the game of football. One of the best ways to develop anaerobic capacity for football is to perform series of "plays" to develop the specific movements each position needs with specific work-to-rest ratios. The goal of these drills is to mimic the game demands from both a positional and conditioning standpoint. Volume of these drills will begin with the athletes performing 4-5 reps or "plays" of the drills, for 3-4 series or "drives," which corresponds to 12-20 efforts. This will progress as the athletes become more conditioned to 5-10 reps of the drills, for 10-12 series, mimicking both the number of plays the athletes will perform in a game as well as the physical and conditioning needs. Athletes will rest 20-40 seconds between each rep of the drills and 2-3 minutes between each series. The movements used should be position-specific route running, shuffles, backpedals, heavy-resisted sprints, and so on.

Offensive and Defensive Line

Offensive and defensive linemen must have strength, power, and speed to be successful on the football field. These athletes must be able to drive into opponents, sprint, bend, move laterally, and pass set. They must also perform these movements repeatedly throughout the game. To develop the ability to do this, athletes will perform an anaerobic capacity series. For offensive linemen, the movements used will be sprints initiated from a positionally relevant starting position (e.g., 3-point stance), performing a pass-blocking set for several steps before accelerating out, throwing medicine balls for height or distance, pushing weighted sleds, performing reactive drills (e.g., mirroring a partner's actions), or variations of grappling movements to work on combative skills (see table 8.2). For the defensive line, movements performed will be positional sprints, pass rush moves, medicine ball throws, heavy-resisted sprints, reactive drills, and grappling movements (see table 8.3).

Offensive Line

Series 1: Heavy-resisted sprint—The linemen will push or sprint with a loaded sled linearly downfield.

Series 2: Pass set to 5-yard sprint—The linemen will start in their position-specific stances, pass set, and then, on command or when a ball is thrown, they will sprint 5 yards downfield.

Series 3: Medicine ball throw to sprint—The linemen will explosively throw a medicine ball from their stances (or other throw variations) and then sprint 5-10 yards. The linemen can also pass set, explosively throw the medicine ball, and then sprint 5-10 yards downfield.

Series 4: Mirror drill—Cones are placed 5 yards apart on a yard line. There will be a player on either side of the yard line. One player will run and move back and forth in between the cones. The other player (offensive lineman) will have to move his feet, shuffle, and practice staying in position and staying in front the defensive player.

Series 5: Crawls, grapples, hand fighting—Bear crawls, hand fighting, partner lifts, and body locks teach linemen proper body positions and leverage and prepare the body for contact.

Table 8.2 Offensive Line

Series	Exercise	Drill time	Rest	Reps	Rest between series
1	Heavy-resisted sprint	3-6 sec	20-40 sec	4-10	2-3 min
2	Pass set to 5-yard sprint	3-6 sec	20-40 sec	4-10	2-3 min
3	Medicine ball throw to sprint	3-6 sec	20-40 sec	4-10	2-3 min
4	Mirror drill	3-6 sec	20-40 sec	4-10	2-3 min
5	Contact prep	6-10 sec	20-40 sec	4-10	2-3 min

Defensive Line

Series 1: Heavy-resisted sprint—The linemen will push or sprint with a loaded sled linearly downfield.

Series 2: Pass rush to pursuit—The linemen will perform a pass rush move and rush past the line of scrimmage. Then, on command or in reaction to an offensive player, they will pursue the ballcarrier or run to a cone 10-15 yards downfield.

Series 3: Medicine ball throw to sprint—The linemen will explosively throw a medicine ball from their stances (or other throw variations) and then sprint 5-10 yards.

Series 4: Mirror drill—Cones are placed 5 yards apart on a yard line. There will be a player on either side of the yard line. One player will run and move back and forth in between the cones. The other player (defensive player) will shuffle, crossover run, and run to stay on the other athlete's hip, as he would when tracking a player to make a tackle.

Series 5: Crawls, grapple, hand fighting—Bear crawls, hand fighting, partner lifts, and body locks will teach linemen proper body positions and leverage and prepare the body for contact.

Table 8.3　Defensive Line

Series	Exercise	Drill time	Rest	Reps	Rest between series
1	Heavy-resisted sprint	3-6 sec	20-40 sec	4-10	2-3 min
2	Pass rush to pursuit	3-6 sec	20-40 sec	4-10	2-3 min
3	Medicine ball throw to sprint	3-6 sec	20-40 sec	4-10	2-3 min
4	Mirror drill	3-6 sec	20-40 sec	4-10	2-3 min
5	Contact prep	6-10 sec	20-40 sec	4-10	2-3 min

Running Backs, Tight Ends, and Linebackers

Running backs, tight ends, and linebackers also require strength, speed, and power to be successful at their positions. Running backs and tight ends need to be able to run routes, evade defenders, and block and pass protect. For running backs and tight ends, movements used will be positional start sprints, route running, sprints to jump cuts, heavy-resisted sprints, and medicine ball throws (see table 8.4). Linebackers must be able to tackle, drop into pass coverage, pass rush, and engage with opponents. Movements used for linebackers will be positional start sprints, 45-degree drops, backpedal to sprints, mirror drills, heavy-resisted sprints, and medicine ball throws (see table 8.5).

Running Backs and Tight Ends

Series 1: Positional start sprint—Players will begin in their position-specific stances (2-point or 3-point stance). On command, players will sprint a specified distance (5-20 yd).

Series 2: Position-specific route running—Players will run a specified route at full speed and jog back to the line of scrimmage.

Series 3: Sprint, jump cut, sprint—Players will sprint for a specified distance (5-20 yd), perform a planned or reaction-based jump cut, and then sprint for a specified distance (5-10 yd).

Series 4: Heavy-resisted sprint—Players will push a loaded sled and sprint for 10 yards.

Series 5: Medicine ball throw to sprint—Players will perform an explosive medicine ball throw and sprint for a specified distance (5-20 yd).

Table 8.4 Running Backs and Tight Ends

Series	Exercise	Drill time	Rest	Reps	Rest between series
1	Positional start sprint	3-6 sec	20-40 sec	4-10	2-3 min
2	Position-specific route running	3-6 sec	20-40 sec	4-10	2-3 min
3	Sprint, jump cut, sprint	3-6 sec	20-40 sec	4-10	2-3 min
4	Heavy-resisted sprint	3-6 sec	20-40 sec	4-10	2-3 min
5	Medicine ball throw to sprint	3-6 sec	20-40 sec	4-10	2-3 min

Linebackers

Series 1: Positional start sprint—Linebackers will begin in their position-specific stances. On command, players will sprint a specified distance (5-20 yd).

Series 2: 45-degree drop, pass coverage drop to sprint—Linebackers will drop at a 45-degree angle or to a specific coverage. On command or in reaction to a pass, they will sprint 10-15 yards upfield.

Series 3: Mirror drill—Cones are placed 5 yards apart on a yard line. There will be a player on either side of the yard line. One player will run and move back and forth in between the cones. The other player (defensive player) will shuffle, crossover run, and run to stay on the other player's hip, as he would when tracking a player to make a tackle.

Series 4: Heavy-resisted sprint—Players will push a loaded sled and sprint for 10 yards.

Series 5: Medicine ball throw to sprint—Players will perform an explosive medicine ball throw and sprint for a specified distance (5-20 yd).

Table 8.5 Linebackers

Series	Exercise	Drill time	Rest	Reps	Rest between series
1	Positional start sprint	3-6 sec	20-40 sec	4-10	2-3 min
2	45-degree drop, pass coverage drop to sprint	3-6 sec	20-40 sec	4-10	2-3 min
3	Mirror drill	3-6 sec	20-40 sec	4-10	2-3 min
4	Heavy-resisted sprint	3-6 sec	20-40 sec	4-10	2-3 min
5	Medicine ball throw to sprint	3-6 sec	20-40 sec	4-10	2-3 min

Wide Receivers and Defensive Backs

Wide receivers and defensive backs will cover the most distance and require the highest velocities. Wide receivers need to be able to sprint, jump, cut, and change direction. Movements used for wide receivers will be positional starts to sprints, route running, and repeated jumps (see table 8.6). Defensive backs will need to be able to sprint, backpedal, jump, cut, and change direction. Movements used for defensive backs will be positional start sprints, backpedal to sprints, backpedal to crossover runs, backpedal to hip turns, and repeated jumps (see table 8.7).

Wide Receivers

Series 1: Positional start release and sprint—Wide receivers will perform a release from the line of scrimmage and perform a linear sprint for a specified distance (10-20 yd).

Series 2: Corner route—Wide receivers will perform a full-speed corner route and jog back to the line of scrimmage.

Series 3: Post route—Wide receivers will perform a full-speed post route and jog back to the line of scrimmage.

Series 4: Dig route—Wide receivers will perform a full-speed dig route and jog back to the line of scrimmage.

Series 5: Vertical jump to band-resisted broad jump—Wide receivers will perform a vertical jump directly into a band-resisted broad jump.

Table 8.6   Wide Receivers

Series	Exercise	Drill time	Rest	Reps	Rest between series
1	Positional start release and sprint	3-6 sec	20-40 sec	4-10	2-3 min
2	Corner route	3-6 sec	20-40 sec	4-10	2-3 min
3	Post route	3-6 sec	20-40 sec	4-10	2-3 min
4	Dig route	3-6 sec	20-40 sec	4-10	2-3 min
5	Vertical jump to band-resisted broad jump	3-6 sec	20-40 sec	4-10	2-3 min

Defensive Backs

Series 1: Positional start turn and sprint—Defensive backs will begin in a position-specific stance and, on command, turn and sprint a specified distance (5-20 yd).

Series 2: Backpedal to sprint—Defensive backs will backpedal on command and then sprint downhill on command or in reaction to a pass.

Series 3: Backpedal, crossover run to sprint—On command, defensive backs will backpedal, transition into a crossover run, and then sprint downfield to the line of scrimmage.

Series 4: Backpedal, hip turn to sprint—On command, defensive backs will backpedal and then hip turn and transition back to a backpedal on command. Then in reaction to a pass or on command, they will sprint downfield to the line of scrimmage.

Series 5: Vertical jump to band-resisted broad jump—Defensive backs will perform a vertical jump directly into a band-resisted broad jump.

Table 8.7   Defensive Backs

Series	Exercise	Drill time	Rest	Reps	Rest between series
1	Positional start turn and sprint	3-6 sec	20-40 sec	4-10	2-3 min
2	Backpedal to sprint	3-6 sec	20-40 sec	4-10	2-3 min
3	Backpedal, crossover run to sprint	3-6 sec	20-40 sec	4-10	2-3 min
4	Backpedal, hip turn to sprint	3-6 sec	20-40 sec	4-10	2-3 min
5	Vertical jump to band-resisted broad jump	3-6 sec	20-40 sec	4-10	2-3 min

Quarterbacks

A quarterback's physical demands will be determined by the system they are in. Dual-threat quarterbacks will require more running, cutting, and change-of-direction work. Pocket-passer quarterbacks will require less running but will still need the ability to move in the pocket. Movements used for quarterbacks will be resisted drops, drops with lateral movement, drops with vertical escape, roll out to sprints, and zone reads (see table 8.8).

Series 1: Resisted drops—Using a band or resistance cord, quarterbacks will perform 3-5 step drops against resistance.

Series 2: Step drops with movement—Quarterbacks will perform 3-5 step drops and perform lateral, forward, and backward movements on command.

Series 3: Step drops with vertical escape—Quarterbacks will perform 3-5 step drops, step up in the pocket, and vertically escape and sprint upfield for a specified distance (5-20 yd).

Series 4: Rollout to sprint—Quarterbacks will roll out of the pocket and sprint upfield for a specified distance (10-20 yd).

Series 5: Zone read to sprint—Quarterbacks will perform a zone read and then sprint for a specified distance (10-20 yd).

Table 8.8   Quarterbacks

Series	Exercise	Drill time	Rest	Reps	Rest between series
1	Resisted drops	3-6 sec	20-40 sec	4-10	2-3 min
2	Step drops with movement	3-6 sec	20-40 sec	4-10	2-3 min
3	Step drops with vertical escape	3-6 sec	20-40 sec	4-10	2-3 min
4	Rollout to sprint	3-6 sec	20-40 sec	4-10	2-3 min
5	Zone read to sprint	3-6 sec	20-40 sec	4-10	2-3 min

Specialists

Kickers, punters, and long snappers will not require the conditioning that the other positions require. These positions will require general work capacity and the ability to repeat their positional requirements (kicking, punting, and snapping) throughout the week of practice and multiple times per game.

AEROBIC TRAINING AND CAPACITY

Aerobic capacity is extremely important in player recovery between plays, series, quarters, and games. Aerobic capacity also importantly supports the volume of running athletes accumulate over the course of a week, as well as the continuous straining and battling offensive and defensive linemen must endure throughout a game. While a play may only last 3-6 seconds, a typical game will last three and a half hours. If an athlete plays 75 plays during a game, each lasting an average of 4 seconds, a player will only be playing for 5 minutes. All the other time is spent recovering from these high-intensity outputs that occur over these 5 minutes throughout the game. Thus, the more developed the aerobic system, the more efficient the players will be at sustaining their explosive abilities throughout the game.

The way in which aerobic work is performed is also important. Aerobic work can be general to start but must become more specific to meet the competition demands of each football position. Performing positional movements that take place during a game at an aerobic pace will ensure that the oxidative developments occur in the relevant muscles and the relevant motions as they relate to competition demands. Methods of developing aerobic capacity in football include linear tempo runs, medicine ball tempos, extensive medicine ball throws (e.g., players throw a medicine ball for distance, run after it, then perform another throw for allotted repetitions, distance, or time), extended warm-ups (e.g., going through a general dynamic warm-up routine for multiple sets), extensive abdominal exercise circuits, and general strength circuits (e.g., performing a circuit of various auxiliary, remedial, or body weight exercises for allotted repetitions, sets, or time).

Linear Tempo Runs

Linear tempo runs help improve aerobic fitness, work capacity, running mechanics, and foot, ankle, and calf strength. Tempo runs consist of running at a moderate intensity for 10-20 seconds, followed by a rest period of 30-90 seconds. Over the course of a week in both practices and in the game, skill and big-skill players accumulate a large amount of running volume. Skill and big-skill athletes (WRs, DBs, LBs, TEs, and RBs) can cover between 3,000 and 8,000 yards during a game, depending on position and tactics. Tempo runs will help prepare these athletes for the volume of running as well as develop the aerobic system.

The intensity of linear tempo runs should be moderate to ensure recovery between intensive workouts while still developing the aerobic system. There are several ways to monitor the intensity of the tempo runs and to make sure they stay aerobic. The first way to monitor intensity is to track the time and the velocity at which each run is completed. Runs should be completed at 60%-75% of the athlete's best time or velocity. If an athlete runs 100 yards in 12 seconds, he should complete the tempo runs in 16-20 seconds. A 100-yard time can be estimated by an athlete's 40-yard time. If an athlete runs a 4.7-second 40-yard sprint, that can be extrapolated out to an estimated 12-second 100-yard time. If velocity tracking is available, another way to monitor intensity is through monitoring velocity. Velocity should also be kept between 60% and 75% to make sure that the tempo runs remain aerobic to facilitate recovery. If an athlete has a top speed of 20 mph, velocity should remain between 12 and 15 mph.

Medicine Ball Tempos

Medicine ball tempos are similar to the tempo runs discussed earlier. However, instead of just linear or positional tempo movements, athletes will throw and chase a medicine ball for a prescribed distance. This is most often used with offensive and defensive linemen because of the use of explosive throws that mimic movements that are required for their positions.

Extensive Medicine Ball Throws

Extensive medicine ball throws can develop aerobic capacity and local muscular endurance. This is also a great tool for offensive and defensive linemen as well as athletes who are injured or returning from injury who are not yet able to handle large running volumes. While aerobic capacity is important for linemen, how they achieve aerobic development is also important. Offensive and defensive linemen are typically more than 300 pounds, and performing large volumes of running could lead to wear and tear on muscles, ligaments, and joints. Linemen also require much less running than skill and big-skill athletes. To perform extensive medicine ball throws, athletes will stand about 3-6 feet from a wall and perform rhythmic throws with a short range of motion using a ball that bounces back with recoil. The ground may also be used for certain variations where the ball bounces back off the ground. This method can be called "oscillatory," where the muscles responsible for movement are tensed and then relaxed quickly.[1] The weight of the medicine ball should be between 6 and 12 pounds, and the execution of each throw should be for higher repetitions or time intervals, typically 25-50 repetitions or 20-30 seconds of work per variation.

Extensive Chest Pass Throw Into Wall

Face a wall and stand back about 3-6 feet from it. Holding a medicine ball at chest level, rapidly extend the arms so that the ball is thrown horizontally into the wall in a chest pass motion. As the ball bounces back, immediately catch it, absorb the impact, and rapidly throw it back into the wall. Maintain a steady rhythm for the allotted repetitions or time.

Extensive Rotational Throw Into Wall

Stand with your side toward a wall, about 3-6 feet from it. Holding a medicine ball at the level of the hips and slightly shifted toward the outside hip, keep the arms mostly straight (see figure *a*) and rapidly drive through the outside leg, rotating at the hips and following through with the torso so that the ball is thrown horizontally into the wall in a rotational motion (see figure *b*). As the ball bounces back, immediately catch it, absorb the impact, and rapidly throw it back into the wall. Maintain a steady rhythm for the allotted repetitions or time before repeating on the other side of the body.

Figure 8.1 Extensive rotational throw into wall.

Extensive Overhead Throw Into Wall

Stand facing a wall, about 3-6 feet from it. Holding a medicine ball at the level of the rib cage, rapidly perform a slight squatting motion (see figure *a*) before driving through the hips and following through by extending the arms so that the ball is thrown vertically into the wall in an overhead pressing motion (see figure *b*). Keep your eyes on the ball so that the ball can be located on the rebound to avoid any collision with the head. As the ball bounces back, immediately catch it, absorb the impact, and rapidly throw it back into the wall. Maintain a steady rhythm for the allotted repetitions or time.

Figure 8.2 Extensive overhead throw into wall.

Extensive Slam Into the Ground

Stand on a surface that is hard enough to allow recoil of the medicine ball. Lift the medicine ball overhead, rising onto the toes to get as tall as possible (see figure *a*). Keeping the arms mostly straight, rapidly throw the arms down and follow through by dropping at the hips to throw the ball into the ground with a slamming motion (see figure *b*). As the ball bounces back, catch it, raise it back overhead, and rapidly throw it back into the ground. Maintain a steady rhythm for the allotted repetitions or time.

Figure 8.3 Extensive slam into the ground.

Extensive Abdominal Circuits

Extensive abdominal training is another tool to help develop aerobic fitness, work capacity, and endurance. Abdominal strength endurance is important to develop the muscles that stabilize the torso. This stabilization is needed in sprinting, jumping, cutting, and battling with opponents on the field. Extensive abdominal training is accomplished by using exercises of relatively smaller ranges of motion for higher repetitions or time intervals, typically 15-25 repetitions or 20-30 seconds of work per variation.

McGill Curl-Up

Lie on the ground faceup and place the hands and wrists behind the body in the curve of the lower back. Bend one leg while keeping the other straight and lie flat (see figure *a*). Perform a curl-up motion by driving the nose toward the ceiling and bracing at the abdominals (see figure *b*). With the hands behind the back, the range of motion will be restricted, but it's still important to fight for maximum tension at the top of the movement. Maintain a steady rhythm for the allotted repetitions or time and then switch the legs for the next set.

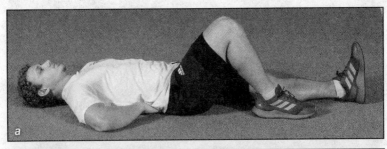

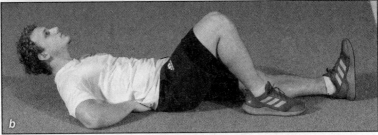

Figure 8.4   McGill curl-up.

Toe Touches

Lie on the ground faceup with the legs off the ground fully extended (see figure *a*). Ideally, the legs are at an angle where the feet are in front of the hips to maximize abdominal tension. Keeping the legs off the ground the entire time, flex at the trunk in an attempt to touch the shoelaces with the fingertips (see figure *b*). Even if it's not quite possible to contact the shoes, this should be the intent to maximize tension in the abdominals. Maintain a steady rhythm for the allotted repetitions or time.

Figure 8.5   Toe touches.

Russian Twist

Sit on the ground with the legs bent and the heels on the ground. Lean back through the torso with the goal of having a torso angle of approximately 45 degrees off the ground to maximize abdominal tension. Keeping the hands together and trunk extended, rotate the torso from left to right as far as possible without bending forward at the spine (see figures *a-b*). Maintain a steady rhythm for the allotted repetitions or time.

Figure 8.6   Russian twist.

V-Sits

Sit on the ground with the legs extended in front of the body, the feet off the ground, and the hands on the ground alongside the body (see figure *a*). Keeping the feet and shoulders off the ground the entire time, fold the body in by bringing the knees and torso toward each other until the legs are bent at approximately 90 degrees (see figure *b*). Extend the legs and lean back the torso to straighten out the whole body back to the starting position. Maintain a steady rhythm for the allotted repetitions or time.

Figure 8.7   V-sits.

PROGRAMMING FOR CONDITIONING

The off-season will be when most conditioning development takes place. In-season conditioning needs will be taken care of through the demands of practices and games. The off-season period will vary based on level, but most teams at the collegiate level will begin off-season training in January and conclude before camp in August. Off-season training can be broken down into distinct phases: winter training, which will go from January to March; spring training, which will go from April to May; and summer training, which will go from June to July. In August, preseason camp will begin, and the conditioning requirements will be met from practicing most days of the week. For players who are still lacking some fitness, extra conditioning may be performed around practice. A well-developed plan must be put into place so that the right conditioning is being trained at the right time of year. This means that more general forms of conditioning may be used when training farther out from the competitive period, and more specific forms must be incorporated as the in-season period approaches. With this in mind, the most specific form of conditioning is football practice itself, which is why the conditioning imparted by the strength and conditioning staff is drastically reduced if not completely eliminated by the time preseason camp begins.

Winter Training (January-March)

Immediately postseason, athletes will have time to recover from the season, rehab injuries, perform general strength training, and develop work capacity in preparation for winter training. Once athletes have had 2-3 weeks postseason, winter training will begin. This will be the optimal time to develop high levels of strength, power, and speed. Winter training will be the farthest athletes will be from practice and games. Therefore, athletes will not need to be in playing condition. However, it's still important to include some conditioning, especially as the players get closer to the spring training phase of the year, when they will be participating in football practices. The following progression outlines 2 days devoted to conditioning that exist with all the other forms of training taking place in the complete program (see tables 8.9-8.14).

Table 8.9 Sample Winter Conditioning Progression, Weeks 1-4: Wide Receivers and Defensive Backs

Conditioning day 1	Week 1	Week 2	Week 3	Week 4
1. Linear tempo	8 reps × 100 yd	10 reps × 100 yd	2 sets × 6 reps × 100 yd	2 sets × 7 reps × 100 yd
2. Extensive medicine ball throws	3-4 variations for 25-50 reps each	3-4 variations for 25-50 reps each	3-4 variations for 25-50 reps each	3-4 variations for 25-50 reps each
Conditioning day 2	Week 1	Week 2	Week 3	Week 4
1. Linear tempo	8 reps × 100 yd	10 reps × 100 yd	2 sets × 6 reps × 100 yd	2 sets × 7 reps × 100 yd
2. Extensive abdominals	3-4 variations for 15-25 reps each	3-4 variations for 15-25 reps each	3-4 variations for 15-25 reps each	3-4 variations for 15-25 reps each

Table 8.10 Sample Winter Conditioning Progression, Weeks 1-4: Tight Ends, Running Backs, Quarterbacks, Linebackers

Conditioning day 1	Week 1	Week 2	Week 3	Week 4
1. Linear tempo	8 reps × 80 yd	10 reps × 80 yd	2 sets × 6 reps × 80 yd	2 sets × 7 reps × 80 yd
2. Extensive medicine ball throws	3-4 variations for 25-50 reps each	3-4 variations for 25-50 reps each	3-4 variations for 25-50 reps each	3-4 variations for 25-50 reps each
Conditioning day 2	Week 1	Week 2	Week 3	Week 4
1. Linear tempo	8 reps × 80 yd	10 reps × 80 yd	2 sets × 6 reps × 80 yd	2 sets × 7 reps × 80 yd
2. Extensive abdominals	3-4 variations for 15-25 reps each	3-4 variations for 15-25 reps each	3-4 variations for 15-25 reps each	3-4 variations for 15-25 reps each

Table 8.11 Sample Winter Conditioning Progression, Weeks 1-4: Offensive Line and Defensive Line

Conditioning day 1	Week 1	Week 2	Week 3	Week 4
1. Positional tempo	Heavy-resisted sprint 6 × 25 yd	Heavy-resisted sprint 8 × 25 yd	Extensive grappling 6 × 20 sec Heavy-resisted sprint 6 × 25 yd	Extensive grappling 8 × 20 sec Heavy-resisted sprint 8 × 25 yd
2. Extensive medicine ball throws	3-4 variations for 25-50 reps each	3-4 variations for 25-50 reps each	3-4 variations for 25-50 reps each	3-4 variations for 25-50 reps each
Conditioning day 2	**Week 1**	**Week 2**	**Week 3**	**Week 4**
1. Linear tempo	8 reps × 60 yd	10 reps × 60 yd	2 sets × 6 reps × 60 yd	2 sets × 7 reps × 60 yd
2. Extensive abdominals	3-4 variations for 15-25 reps each	3-4 variations for 15-25 reps each	3-4 variations for 15-25 reps each	3-4 variations for 15-25 reps each

Table 8.12 Sample Winter Conditioning Progression, Weeks 5-8: Wide Receivers and Defensive Backs

Conditioning day 1	Week 5	Week 6	Week 7	Week 8
1. Linear tempo	8 reps × 100 yd	10 reps × 100 yd	2 sets × 6 reps × 100 yd	2 sets × 7 reps × 100 yd
2. Extensive medicine ball throws or abdominals (alternate each week)	3-4 variations for 25-50 reps each or 15-25 reps each	3-4 variations for 25-50 reps each or 15-25 reps each	3-4 variations for 25-50 reps each or 15-25 reps each	3-4 variations for 25-50 reps each or 15-25 reps each
Conditioning day 2	**Week 5**	**Week 6**	**Week 7**	**Week 8**
Positional drives: Full-speed movements with full recovery between each play and 1-2 min between series	WRs: 15 plays (3 × 5 reps) Full-speed routes, positional release to sprints, release and react	WRs: 20 plays (4 × 5 reps) Full-speed routes, positional release to sprints, release and react	WRs: 25 plays (5 × 5 reps) Full-speed routes, positional release to sprints, release and react	WRs: 30 plays (6 × 5 reps) Full-speed routes, positional release to sprints, release and react
	DBs: 15 plays (3 × 5 reps) Positional drop to sprints, hip turns, crossover runs, run reactions	DBs: 20 plays (4 × 5 reps) Positional drop to sprints, hip turns, crossover runs, run reactions	DBs: 25 plays (5 × 5 reps) Positional drop to sprints, hip turns, crossover runs, run reactions	DBs: 30 plays (6 × 5 reps) Positional drop to sprints, hip turns, crossover runs, run reactions

Table 8.13 Sample Winter Conditioning Progression, Weeks 5-8: Tight Ends, Running Backs, Quarterbacks, Linebackers

Conditioning day 1	Week 5	Week 6	Week 7	Week 8
1. Linear tempo	8 reps × 80 yd	10 reps × 80 yd	2 sets × 6 reps × 80 yd	2 sets × 7 reps × 80 yd
2. Extensive medicine ball throws or abdominals (alternate each week)	3-4 variations for 25-50 reps each or 15-25 reps each	3-4 variations for 25-50 reps each or 15-25 reps each	3-4 variations for 25-50 reps each or 15-25 reps each	3-4 variations for 25-50 reps each or 15-25 reps each
Conditioning day 2	**Week 5**	**Week 6**	**Week 7**	**Week 8**
Positional drives: Full-speed movements with full recovery between each play and 1-2 min between series	TEs: 15 plays Full-speed routes, positional release to sprints, release and react, heavy-resisted sprints	TEs: 20 plays Full-speed routes, positional release to sprints, release and react, heavy-resisted sprints	TEs: 25 plays Full-speed routes, positional release to sprints, release and react, heavy-resisted sprints	TEs: 30 plays Full-speed routes, positional release to sprints, release and react, heavy-resisted sprints
	RBs: 15 plays Full-speed run plays, full-speed routes, sprint-jump cut-sprint, sprint to react, heavy-resisted sprints	RBs: 20 plays Full-speed run plays, full-speed routes, sprint-jump cut-sprint, sprint to react, heavy-resisted sprints	RBs: 25 plays Full-speed run plays, full-speed routes, sprint-jump cut-sprint, sprint to react, heavy-resisted sprints	RBs: 30 plays Full-speed run plays, full-speed routes, sprint-jump cut-sprint, sprint to react, heavy-resisted sprints
	QBs: 15 plays Resisted drops, step drops to lateral and vertical escapes, boots, zone reads	QBs: 20 plays Resisted drops, step drops to lateral and vertical escapes, boots, zone reads	QBs: 25 plays Resisted drops, step drops to lateral and vertical escapes, boots, zone reads	QBs: 30 plays Resisted drops, step drops to lateral and vertical escapes, boots, zone reads
	LBs: 15 plays Pass coverage to sprints, shuffle reaction, shuffle to sprints, heavy-resisted sprints	LBs: 20 plays Pass coverage to sprints, shuffle reaction, shuffle to sprints, heavy-resisted sprints	LBs: 25 plays Pass coverage to sprints, shuffle reaction, shuffle to sprints, heavy-resisted sprints	LBs: 30 plays Pass coverage to sprints, shuffle reaction, shuffle to sprints, heavy-resisted sprints

Table 8.14 Sample Winter Conditioning Progression, Weeks 5-8: Offensive Line and Defensive Line

Conditioning day 1	Week 5	Week 6	Week 7	Week 8
1. Positional tempo	Prowler push 4 × 25 yd Backward or lateral sled drags 5 × 25 yd	Prowler push 5 × 25 yd Backward or lateral sled drags 5 × 25 yd	Medicine ball tempo 4 × 25 yd Backward or lateral sled drags 5 × 25 yd	Medicine ball tempo 5 × 25 yd Backward or lateral sled drags 5 × 25 yd
2. Extensive medicine ball throws or abdominals (alternate each week)	3-4 variations for 25-50 reps each or 15-25 reps each	3-4 variations for 25-50 reps each or 15-25 reps each	3-4 variations for 25-50 reps each or 15-25 reps each	3-4 variations for 25-50 reps each or 15-25 reps each
Conditioning day 2	**Week 5**	**Week 6**	**Week 7**	**Week 8**
Positional drives: Full-speed movements with full recovery between each play and 1-2 min between series	OL: 15 plays Heavy-resisted sprints, pass set to sprints, medicine ball throw to sprints, mirror drill, grapple or hand fighting	OL: 20 plays Heavy-resisted sprints, pass set to sprints, medicine ball throw to sprints, mirror drill, grapple or hand fighting	OL: 25 plays Heavy-resisted sprints, pass set to sprints, medicine ball throw to sprints, mirror drill, grapple or hand fighting	OL: 30 plays Heavy-resisted sprints, pass set to sprints, medicine ball throw to sprints, mirror drill, grapple or hand fighting
	DL: 15 plays Heavy-resisted sprints, pass rush to pursuit, medicine ball throw to sprints, mirror drill, grapple or hand fighting	DL: 20 plays Heavy-resisted sprints, pass rush to pursuit, medicine ball throw to sprints, mirror drill, grapple or hand fighting	DL: 25 plays Heavy-resisted sprints, pass rush to pursuit, medicine ball throw to sprints, mirror drill, grapple or hand fighting	DL: 30 plays Heavy-resisted sprints, pass rush to pursuit, medicine ball throw to sprints, mirror drill, grapple or hand fighting

Spring Training (April-May)

At the collegiate level, spring football practices typically take place in the months of April and May. Practices involve sprinting, jumping, cutting, and tackling, which place stress on the body. This stress on the body must be accounted for when creating a training plan. It is important to reduce intensity or volume, or both, when athletes begin practice. Thus, the specific emphasis on conditioning is achieved in sports practice itself, and more general forms of conditioning like linear tempo runs may be used for players who are still lacking the requisite conditioning to make it through practice successfully.

Summer Training (June-July)

The summer training period will be the most intensive conditioning period of the off-season because it is the closest training phase to the start of the football season. This block is typically around 8 weeks long and must prepare the athletes for the demands of training camp, practices, and games. The first 4 weeks of the block feature 2 days of conditioning work while the last 4 weeks feature 4 days of conditioning to prepare the players for 4 primary days of practice each week during the in-season period. The following progression outlines days devoted to conditioning that exist with all the other forms of training taking place in the complete program (see tables 8.15-8.20).

Table 8.15 Sample Summer Conditioning Progression, Weeks 1-4: Wide Receivers and Defensive Backs

Conditioning day 1	Week 1	Week 2	Week 3	Week 4
1. Extensive medicine ball throws	3-4 variations for 25-50 reps each	3-4 variations for 25-50 reps each	3-4 variations for 25-50 reps each	3-4 variations for 25-50 reps each
2. Linear tempo	8 reps × 100 yd	10 reps × 100 yd	2 sets × 6 reps × 100 yd	2 sets × 7 reps × 100 yd
3. Extensive abdominals	3-4 variations for 15-25 reps each	3-4 variations for 15-25 reps each	3-4 variations for 15-25 reps each	3-4 variations for 15-25 reps each
Conditioning day 2	**Week 1**	**Week 2**	**Week 3**	**Week 4**
1. Change of direction	Shuttle, zigzag, or cone reactions drills × 4	Shuttle, zigzag, or cone reactions drills × 4	Reactive positional drill × 8-10 reps	Reactive positional drill × 8-10 reps
2. Positional tempo	2 sets × 5 reps × 50 yd	2 sets × 6 reps × 50 yd	3 sets × 5 reps × 50 yd	3 sets × 5 reps × 50 yd
3. Extensive abdominals	3-4 variations for 15-25 reps each	3-4 variations for 15-25 reps each	3-4 variations for 15-25 reps each	3-4 variations for 15-25 reps each

Table 8.16   Sample Summer Conditioning Progression, Weeks 1-4: Tight Ends, Running Backs, Quarterbacks, Linebackers

Conditioning day 1	Week 1	Week 2	Week 3	Week 4
1. Extensive medicine ball throws	3-4 variations for 25-50 reps each	3-4 variations for 25-50 reps each	3-4 variations for 25-50 reps each	3-4 variations for 25-50 reps each
2. Linear tempo	8 reps × 80 yd	10 reps × 80 yd	2 sets × 6 reps × 80 yd	2 sets × 7 reps × 80 yd
3. Extensive abdominals	3-4 variations for 15-25 reps each	3-4 variations for 15-25 reps each	3-4 variations for 15-25 reps each	3-4 variations for 15-25 reps each
Conditioning day 2	**Week 1**	**Week 2**	**Week 3**	**Week 4**
1. Change of direction	Shuttle, zigzag, or cone reactions drills × 4	Shuttle, zigzag, or cone reactions drills × 4	Reactive positional drill × 8-10 reps	Reactive positional drill × 8-10 reps
2. Positional tempo	2 sets × 5 reps × 40 yd	2 sets × 6 reps × 40 yd	3 sets × 5 reps × 40 yd	3 sets × 5 reps × 40 yd
3. Extensive abdominals	3-4 variations for 15-25 reps each	3-4 variations for 15-25 reps each	3-4 variations for 15-25 reps each	3-4 variations for 15-25 reps each

Table 8.17   Sample Summer Conditioning Progression, Weeks 1-4: Offensive Line and Defensive Line

Conditioning day 1	Week 1	Week 2	Week 3	Week 4
1. Extensive medicine ball throws	3-4 variations for 25-50 reps each	3-4 variations for 25-50 reps each	3-4 variations for 25-50 reps each	3-4 variations for 25-50 reps each
2. Positional tempo	Heavy-resisted sprint 8 reps × 10 yd	Heavy-resisted sprint 10 reps × 10 yd	Heavy-resisted sprint 2 sets × 6 reps × 10 yd	Heavy-resisted sprint 2 sets × 7 reps × 10 yd
3. Extensive abdominals	3-4 variations for 15-25 reps each	3-4 variations for 15-25 reps each	3-4 variations for 15-25 reps each	3-4 variations for 15-25 reps each
Conditioning day 2	**Week 1**	**Week 2**	**Week 3**	**Week 4**
1. Change of direction	Shuttle, zigzag, or cone reactions drills × 4	Shuttle, zigzag, or cone reactions drills × 4	Reactive positional drill × 8-10 reps	Reactive positional drill × 8-10 reps
2. Positional tempo	2 sets × 4 reps × 20 yd	2 sets × 5 reps × 20 yd	3 sets × 4 reps × 25 yd	3 sets × 4 reps × 25 yd
3. Extensive abdominals	3-4 variations for 15-25 reps each	3-4 variations for 15-25 reps each	3-4 variations for 15-25 reps each	3-4 variations for 15-25 reps each

Table 8.18 Sample Summer Conditioning Progression, Weeks 5-8: Wide Receivers and Defensive Backs

Conditioning day 1	Week 5	Week 6	Week 7	Week 8
Linear tempo	8 reps × 100 yd	10 reps × 100 yd	2 sets × 6 reps × 80 yd	2 sets × 7 reps × 80 yd

Conditioning day 2	Week 5	Week 6	Week 7	Week 8
Positional drives: Anaerobic capacity plays with incomplete recovery	WRs: 18 plays (3 × 6 reps)	WRs: 24 plays (3 × 8 reps)	WRs: 32 plays (4 × 8 reps)	WRs: 32 plays (4 × 8 reps)
3- to 5-sec plays with 25-35 sec of rest and 2-3 min between series	DBs: 18 plays (3 × 6 reps)	DBs: 24 plays (3 × 8 reps)	DBs: 32 plays (4 × 8 reps)	DBs: 32 plays (4 × 8 reps)

Conditioning day 3	Week 5	Week 6	Week 7	Week 8
Linear tempo	8 reps × 100 yd	10 reps × 100 yd	2 sets × 6 reps × 100 yd	2 sets × 7 reps × 100 yd

Conditioning day 4	Week 5	Week 6	Week 7	Week 8
Positional drives: Anaerobic capacity plays with incomplete recovery	WRs: 18 plays (3 × 6 reps)	WRs: 24 plays (3 × 8 reps)	WRs: 32 plays (4 × 8 reps)	WRs: 40 plays (5 × 8 reps)
3- to 5-sec plays with 25-35 sec of rest and 2-3 min between series	DBs: 18 plays (3 × 6 reps)	DBs: 24 plays (3 × 8 reps)	DBs: 32 plays (4 × 8 reps)	DBs: 40 plays (5 × 8 reps)

Table 8.19 Sample Summer Conditioning Progression, Weeks 5-8: Tight Ends, Running Backs, Quarterbacks, Linebackers

Conditioning day 1	Week 5	Week 6	Week 7	Week 8
Linear tempo	8 reps × 80 yd	10 reps × 80 yd	2 sets × 6 reps × 80 yd	2 sets × 7 reps × 80 yd

Conditioning day 2	Week 5	Week 6	Week 7	Week 8
Positional drives: Anaerobic capacity plays with incomplete recovery 3- to 5-sec plays with 25-35 sec of rest and 2-3 min between series	TEs: 18 plays (3 × 6 reps)	TEs: 24 plays (3 × 8 reps)	TEs: 32 plays (4 × 8 reps)	TEs: 32 plays (4 × 8 reps)
	RBs: 18 plays (3 × 6 reps)	RBs: 24 plays (3 × 8 reps)	RBs: 32 plays (4 × 8 reps)	RBs: 32 plays (4 × 8 reps)
	QBs: 18 plays (3 × 6 reps)	QBs: 24 plays (3 × 8 reps)	QBs: 32 plays (4 × 8 reps)	QBs: 32 plays (4 × 8 reps)
	LBs: 18 plays (3 × 6 reps)	LBs: 24 plays (3 × 8 reps)	LBs: 32 plays (4 × 8 reps)	LBs: 32 plays (4 × 8 reps)

Conditioning day 3	Week 5	Week 6	Week 7	Week 8
Linear tempo	8 reps × 100 yd	10 reps × 100 yd	2 sets × 6 reps × 100 yd	2 sets × 7 reps × 100 yd

Conditioning day 4	Week 5	Week 6	Week 7	Week 8
Positional drives: Anaerobic capacity plays with incomplete recovery 3- to 5-sec plays with 25-35 sec of rest and 2-3 min between series	TEs: 18 plays (3 × 6 reps)	TEs: 24 plays (3 × 8 reps)	TEs: 32 plays (4 × 8 reps)	TEs: 32 plays (4 × 8 reps)
	RBs: 18 plays (3 × 6 reps)	RBs: 24 plays (3 × 8 reps)	RBs: 32 plays (4 × 8 reps)	RBs: 32 plays (4 × 8 reps)
	QBs: 18 plays (3 × 6 reps)	QBs: 24 plays (3 × 8 reps)	QBs: 32 plays (4 × 8 reps)	QBs: 32 plays (4 × 8 reps)
	LBs: 18 plays (3 × 6 reps)	LBs: 24 plays (3 × 8 reps)	LBs: 32 plays (4 × 8 reps)	LBs: 32 plays (4 × 8 reps)

Table 8.20 Sample Summer Conditioning Progression, Weeks 5-8: Offensive Line and Defensive Line

Conditioning day 1	Week 5	Week 6	Week 7	Week 8
Positional tempo	3 sets × 5 reps × 20 yd	3 sets × 6 reps × 20 yd	4 sets × 5 reps × 25 yd	4 sets × 5 reps × 25 yd
Conditioning day 2	**Week 5**	**Week 6**	**Week 7**	**Week 8**
Positional drives: Anaerobic capacity plays with incomplete recovery	OL: 18 plays (3 × 6 reps)	OL: 24 plays (3 × 8 reps)	OL: 32 plays (4 × 8 reps)	OL: 32 plays (4 × 8 reps)
3- to 5-sec plays with 25-35 sec of rest and 2-3 min between series	DL: 18 plays (3 × 6 reps)	DL: 24 plays (3 × 8 reps)	DL: 32 plays (4 × 8 reps)	DL: 32 plays (4 × 8 reps)
Conditioning day 3	**Week 5**	**Week 6**	**Week 7**	**Week 8**
Positional tempo	3 sets × 5 reps × 20 yd	3 sets × 6 reps × 20 yd	4 sets × 5 reps × 25 yd	4 sets × 5 reps × 25 yd
Conditioning day 4	**Week 5**	**Week 6**	**Week 7**	**Week 8**
Positional drives: Anaerobic capacity plays with incomplete recovery	OL: 18 plays (3 × 6 reps)	OL: 24 plays (3 × 8 reps)	OL: 32 plays (4 × 8 reps)	OL: 32 plays (4 × 8 reps)
3- to 5-sec plays with 25-35 sec of rest and 2-3 min between series	DL: 18 plays (3 × 6 reps)	DL: 24 plays (3 × 8 reps)	DL: 32 plays (4 × 8 reps)	DL: 32 plays (4 × 8 reps)

CONCLUSION

Improving the parameters of anaerobic and aerobic conditioning is essential for football players to reduce the negative impact of rising fatigue and to have the capacity to perform at a high level throughout each game across the entire season. This chapter presented one perspective on how a conditioning training program for football can be designed, but each coach must tailor the endurance components of the training program to match the required physical demands for players based on the team's tactical approach to the game. This will ultimately determine the proper balance between anaerobic and aerobic emphases. The activities and programs presented here should provide the information needed to customize a conditioning plan that best serves your players and program.

Chapter 9

Nutrition and Recovery

Understanding the fueling habits that optimize recovery, improve health, and ultimately drive performance is essential to long-term success. The goal is to consume the appropriate foods and fluids, in the appropriate amounts, at the appropriate times. Most athletes understand the role proper nutrition and hydration play in sport performance and recovery. It's important that we help educate our players on how to provide the body with the nutrients needed to fuel the demands of practice, competition, and training, as well as enhance recovery.

FUELING FOR PERFORMANCE

Athletes' bodies should be fueled and maintained like high-performance sports cars. They need high-octane fuel at the right time to function and perform optimally. Proper nutrition significantly improves performance and health in athletes. However, nutrition can be a major challenge for most people due to the habitual nature of consuming food and the emotional connection many people share with it. After all, this emotional connection with food is exactly what many advertising companies aim to exploit when developing commercials for fast-food chains. Therefore, it is the responsibility of the performance team, led by a sports nutrition professional when available, to reformulate the players' eating habits so that high performance is prioritized. The more athletes become accustomed to eating in a way that fuels activity demands and enhances recovery, the easier it becomes for them to achieve and maintain a high performance level.

BASIC NUTRITIONAL OVERVIEW

As mentioned, good nutrition habits will ensure that athletes' bodies are properly fueled, providing more available energy to train and compete at a high level. These habits restore nutrients and energy substrates that were diminished during activity, allowing the body to start rebuilding faster. These habits will also help improve body composition, where players are carrying more lean muscle mass and less overall fat, both of which will not only lead to higher levels of performance, as we will discuss, but also have a significant positive impact on player health and wellness.

Carbohydrates

Carbohydrates are the body's preferred fuel source for intense training or sports practice or games, providing fast potential energy to help sustain high outputs of work. They provide 4 calories of energy for every gram burned, and carbohydrates should make up most of what athletes eat every day. Additionally, carbohydrates help provide energy for the brain, which is vital for football players in practice and games as they process the incoming play calls, assess opponent tendencies, and key in on primary external cues. For these reasons, we tell our players to eat carbohydrates at all meals, especially in the times before and after a workout, practice, or game. Some of the best food sources that are high in carbohydrates are listed in table 9.1.

Table 9.1   Common Carbohydrate Sources

Grains and starches	Fruits*	Starchy veggies	Beans and legumes
Bagels (100% whole wheat)	Apples	Corn (sweet corn)	Black beans
Bread (100% whole wheat)	Apricots	Peas (sugar snap)	Black-eyed peas
Brown or white rice	Bananas	Potatoes (regular)	Chickpeas
Cereals (whole grain)	Blueberries	Sweet potatoes	Edamame
Couscous	Dried fruit	Yams	Kidney beans
English muffins	Fruit cups		Lima beans
Muffins	Grapes		Pinto beans
Oatmeal	Nectarines		
Pancakes (whole grain)	Oranges		
Pasta (100% whole wheat)	Peaches		
Pita bread	Pears		
Popcorn	Pineapple		
Quinoa	Strawberries		
Tortillas (wheat)	Watermelon		
Waffles			
Wheat crackers			
Wild rice			

*All colors and types.

Protein

Protein is essential because it is comprised of amino acids, which serve as the building blocks for many different structures in the body. They are especially important for muscle growth. Eating the right amount of protein steadily throughout the day prepares the muscles to repair and rebuild after intense training and competition, allowing athletes to come back stronger and faster than before. Players should aim to get in a quality source of protein at each meal, such as lean meat that is baked, grilled, or broiled, and opt for higher-protein snacks during the day. We recommend that players consume approximately 1 gram of protein per pound of body weight per day, so a 200-pound athlete would aim for 200 grams of protein each day. The best sources of protein are listed in table 9.2.

Table 9.2 Common Protein Sources

Meats*	Dairy	Other
Beef and turkey jerky	Greek yogurt	Beans and legumes
Chicken breast (boneless and skinless)	Low-fat cottage cheese	Eggs or egg beaters
Chicken sausage		Tofu
Eye of round steak	Low-fat milk	Whey protein powder
Ground beef (93/7, 90/10)	String cheese	
Ham		
Pork (tenderloin)		
Shrimp and scallops		
Sirloin steak		
Sushi		
Top and bottom round roast		
Top sirloin steak		
Tuna, salmon, and tilapia		
Turkey bacon		
Turkey breast (boneless and skinless)		
Turkey sausage		

*Limit high-fat, heavy, breaded, and fried meat as much as possible.

Fat

Fats are the primary fuel that your body burns when you are at rest and when you are taking part in low- to moderate-intensity activity. Healthy fats play a role in maintaining heart, joint, and tendon health and help to reduce inflammation in the body. In this way, they may help reduce joint soreness. Fats are also involved in natural testosterone production, which is vital for putting the body in an anabolic muscle-building state. The best healthy fat sources are listed in table 9.3.

Table 9.3 Common Fat Sources

Oils	Nuts and seeds	Other
Canola oil	Almonds	Almond butter
Extra virgin olive oil*	Cashews	Avocados or guacamole
Safflower oil	Chia seeds	Peanut butter
Sunflower oil	Flax seeds	Sunflower butter
	Peanuts	Trail mix
	Pecans	Vinaigrettes
	Pistachios	
	Pumpkin seeds	
	Sunflower seeds	
	Walnuts	

*Best oil to use.

Food Intake Recommendations Before Training or Practice

The goal of food intake before training or practice is to ensure that the body is adequately fueled to support the subsequent work. One of the primary recommendations we make to our players is to eat within 1 hour of the start of training or practice, making sure to pair a carbohydrate source with a protein source. We recommend aiming for approximately 30-60 grams of carbohydrates and 10-20 grams of protein in this preexercise meal.

For workouts lasting less than 1 hour, we recommend primarily consuming "quick carbs" up to 15-30 minutes before exercise from sources like sports drinks, granola bars, and bagels. These carbohydrate sources will be digested quickly. For workouts lasting over an hour, including football practice, we recommend primarily consuming "steady carbs" up to 60 minutes before exercise from sources like oatmeal, whole wheat bread, and fresh fruit. These carbohydrate sources digest slower than "quick carbs" and allow for a better fuel source when exercising over long durations. Table 9.4 provides a brief overview of preworkout nutrition intake recommendations.

Table 9.4 Preworkout Nutrition Intake Recommendations

Quick carbs (15-30 min)	OR	Steady carbs (60 min)*	+	Protein
Bagel Gatorade Gatorade energy chews Gatorade fuel bar Granola bar Plain bread		Fresh fruit Nuts or seeds with fruit Oatmeal PB&J Whole wheat bread (can add peanut butter)		Gatorade RTD shake Greek yogurt Milk Protein bar (20 g)

*Best choice for weight loss.

Food Intake Recommendations After Training or Practice

The goal of food intake after training or practice is to immediately refuel the body to replenish used energy stores (e.g., carbohydrate stores) and repair muscle tissue (e.g., protein structures). We recommend that our players aim for at least 30 grams of protein in addition to 50 grams of carbohydrates, although the specific amounts of each will vary based on weight goals and training intensity. These nutrients may be consumed from a liquid source, such as a postworkout shake or smoothie, or from food sources, like grilled chicken breast eaten with fruit. Once this immediate postworkout refueling has taken place, we then recommend that players eat a meal or a snack within the next 2-hour window following. Table 9.5 provides an overview of postworkout nutrition intake recommendations.

Table 9.5 Postworkout Nutrition Intake Recommendations

Fluid options	OR	Food options	+	Antioxidants
Blended shake* Blended smoothie Chocolate milk (24 oz) Gatorade nutrition shake* Gatorade protein shake Weight-loss shake**		Chicken, steak, or fish and pasta Chicken, steak, or fish and potatoes Chicken, steak, or fish and rice Greek yogurt × 2 and fruit Greek yogurt × 2 and granola bar Protein bar × 2 and fruit		Chia or flax seeds (in shake) Fresh fruit (in shake or whole) Frozen fruit (in smoothie) Spinach or kale (in shake) Tart cherry juice

*For weight gain.

**For weight loss.

Food Intake Recommendations Through Snacking

Snacks are an essential part of every athlete's eating plan. Snacks help provide an athlete's body with a consistent amount of energy and nutrients, keeping them feeling full longer and providing the extra calories needed to build muscle and recover. Snacks that are well-thought-out can help prevent overeating at meals, thereby preventing the feeling of being too full and sluggish. We recommend that athletes include two or three snacks throughout the day between meals, allowing them to consume a fuel intake source approximately every 3-4 hours. For players trying to add more muscle weight, we recommend aiming for high-calorie snacks that are balanced between protein, carbohydrate, and fat calories. For players trying to reduce excess body fat, we recommend choosing snacks that are low in carbohydrates and fat but high in protein. We also classify "anytime snacks," which include fresh fruit, mixed nuts, popcorn, and applesauce; these should be paired with a high-protein source rather than being consumed in isolation. Table 9.6 provides an overview of common snacking sources.

Table 9.6 Common Snacking Sources

High-calorie snacks*	High-protein snacks	Anytime snacks*
Deli meat sandwich (on bagel)	Beef or turkey jerky	Applesauce packet
Gatorade RTD shake × 2 with chicken or egg	Canned chicken or tuna	Fresh fruit
	Deli meat roll-up	Nuts or mixed nuts
Oatmeal with peanut butter	Greek yogurt	Popcorn
PB&J × 2 (on bread or a bagel)	Hard-boiled egg × 2	Small salad
Protein bar × 2 (20 g protein) with hummus	Protein bar (20 g)	Veggies with hummus
	Protein smoothie (blended)	Wheat crackers
Protein shake (blended)	String cheese × 2	
Trail mix	Tuna packet	

*Should be paired with protein.

Fluids

Fluids are an essential part of human life, and the human body is comprised of approximately 60% water. Muscles are comprised of approximately 80% water, so, naturally, fluids play a vital role in athletic performance. In fact, being hydrated may be considered one of the most important ways to improve performance because being dehydrated can have massive consequences on the ability to sustain work and may result in tissue damage or other serious injury. Fluids help the body transport nutrients to muscles and other tissues associated with performing intensive exercise, and adequate fluid intake can help reduce the risk of muscle cramping and overall fatigue. Table 9.7 provides an overview of common hydration sources for athletes.

Table 9.7 Common Hydration Sources

Liquid calories	Liquids with no calories
100% fruit juice	Black coffee
Almond milk	Unsweetened tea
G2	Water
Gatorade	Zero-calorie flavored water
Lactose-free milk	
Low-fat chocolate milk	
Milk (skim, 1%, 2%)	
Protein shake	
Protein smoothie	
Ready-to-drink shake	
V8	

The general hydration strategies that we preach to our players include the following:

- On the days football practice is scheduled, aim to drink approximately 1 ounce of liquid per pound of body weight.
- Aim for two servings (2 cups or 16 oz) at each meal.
- Aim for one or two servings (1-2 cups or 8-16 oz) at each snack.
- If trying to gain body weight, drink liquid calories (e.g., chocolate milk or 100% fruit juice).
- Liquids with carbohydrates and electrolytes, commonly called "sports drinks" (e.g., Gatorade), are best right before, during, or immediately after training or practice. However, due to the high sugar content, these drinks are not encouraged outside of training unless the drink is a zero-calorie electrolyte beverage.

Fluid Intake Recommendations Before Training or Practice

The goal of fluid intake before training or practice is to be adequately hydrated, which is a process that begins several hours before the training session or practice takes place. We encourage our players to always keep a water bottle handy so they are able to drink a steady amount of fluid, rather than waiting until they feel thirsty. Our primary recommendations for fluid consumption before practice or training are to drink 2-3 cups

(16-24 oz) of fluid within a 1- to 2-hour window before the session. On top of that, we recommend consuming another 1-2 cups (8-16 oz) of fluid 30-45 minutes before the session. It's also important for players to weigh themselves before training or practice to be able to assess their rehydration goals after the session, which we will discuss in a moment. Additionally, at some point before training or practice, we recommend that players check their urine colors, which may be compared to a hydration chart or "P-Chart" taped onto the walls of the bathrooms in the training facility.

Fluid Intake Recommendations During Training or Practice

The goal of fluid intake during training or practice is to minimize loss of body water due to sweat. Thus, we suggest that our players drink 6-8 ounces of fluid every 10-15 minutes, when possible. When the total training session duration is less than 60 minutes, water is a sufficient fluid source. However, when training exceeds 60 minutes, which is most common with football practice, we encourage our players to consume a sports drink that has some carbohydrates and electrolytes to help replace some of the nutrients lost from long-duration activity.

Fluid Intake Recommendations After Training or Practice

The goal of fluid intake after training or practice is to rehydrate immediately to replenish lost body water due to sweat. Our post-training recommendation for athletes is to consume 2-3 cups (16-24 oz) of fluid for every pound of body weight lost due to sweating. This is why it is important for players to weigh themselves before training or practice, so they have an accurate goal of how much to rehydrate. So, if a player loses 2 pounds during the session, that player should drink 4-6 cups (32-48 oz) of fluid. The rehydration sources don't have to be limited to water and can include sports drinks, chocolate milk, fruit smoothies, or protein shakes.

Supplementation

Proper supplementation can take athletes' training and performance to the next level, but the sources consumed must be smart, safe, and legally approved in terms of complying with the United States Anti-Doping Agency (USADA). To ensure safety and legality of consumption, it's imperative that coaches and players look for the proper certification stamps on a supplemental product, such as from the National Sanitation Foundation (NSF) Certified for Sport® certification, which implies USADA recognition. Thus, we recommend that our players make sure any supplements are NSF Certified for Sport®. If they are unsure, we tell them to avoid the product. The following is a list of products that are certified by the NSF that can keep you as healthy as possible and should be taken daily as well as their purpose for consumption:

- *Fish oil (omega-3s):* Helps reduce inflammation and improve blood lipid profile, are important for heart health, and can provide omega-3s that help with concussions and head injuries
- *Multivitamin:* Helps fill in the gaps of vitamins and minerals players might not get through diet, especially if they don't eat enough fruits and vegetables
- *Vitamin D:* Important for bone health, muscle contractions, immunity, and mood
- *Probiotic:* May be important for gut and brain health, immunity, and mood

Furthermore, these dietary supplements can be used to support daily muscle recovery and muscle building:

- *Whey protein powder:* Convenient, high-quality protein source that can be added to shakes and smoothies
- *Collagen peptides:* Powder beneficial for joint and tissue repair and maintaining joint and tissue health
- *Creatine:* Helps delay fatigue from lifting and sprinting (allowing more reps) and helps preserve muscle mass

Nutritional Recommendations for Enhancing Recovery and Immune Function

A football player's body is constantly dealing with stress. Training is typically high intensity, football practice is extremely demanding, the in-season period features traveling for away games, and of course the various possibilities of life stressors like academic workload and social stresses are also present. Practicing good eating habits daily can help boost immunity and reduce the risk of getting sick. Practices that may negatively affect immune function include the following:

- Poor eating habits, such as eating fast or fried foods that lack micronutrient (e.g., vitamins, minerals, antioxidants) density
- Maintaining a state of dehydration (not drinking enough fluids)
- Eating significantly less calories than what are being burned during daily activity (undereating)
- Not eating enough fruits and vegetables
- Consuming too much alcohol

Micronutrients include vitamins and minerals, which support growth, recovery, bone health, and proper physiological functioning. Their intake is essential for maintaining healthy immune function. Because the micronutrients in food vary greatly, a variety of foods must be eaten to ensure adequate intake. In healthy individuals, a well-balanced diet will provide sufficient levels of micronutrients, but athletes involved in intense training sessions may require higher intakes of micronutrients to support growth and recovery. Some key vitamins and minerals to support health and performance are the following:

- *Vitamin A:* Supports vision and organ function
- *B vitamins:* Convert nutrients to energy and are necessary for red blood cell formation and nervous system function
- *Vitamin C:* Required for proper nervous system function and collagen production, which is a structural protein in connective tissue like tendons, bones, and cartilage; also supports the immune system
- *Vitamin D:* Promotes healthy immune function and bone mineralization; associated with increased muscle strength
- *Vitamin E:* An antioxidant that protects cells from damage and assists in immune function
- *Vitamin K:* Required for wound healing and bone development
- *Calcium:* Develops strong bones and teeth; supports muscle and blood vessel function
- *Iron:* Helps provide oxygen to working muscles
- *Magnesium:* Assists in over 300 chemical reactions in the body associated with metabolism
- *Sodium:* An electrolyte that aids in fluid balance and maintaining blood pressure
- *Zinc:* Necessary for growth, immune function, and wound healing

Foods that are dense in micronutrients are vital for recovery around training or practice sessions. Therefore, certain food sources promote recovery in football players and others slow recovery. Table 9.8 compares various nutritional sources as classified according to promoting or slowing recovery following exercise. Try to eat less of or limit the foods that slow recovery and eat the foods that promote recovery as often as possible.

Table 9.8 Foods That Slow Recovery Versus Foods That Promote Recovery

Foods that slow recovery	Foods that promote recovery
Alcohol	100% fruit juice
Candy	Any fruit, especially if it is dark in color
Cookies or cake	Any vegetable, especially avocados, sweet potatoes, and leafy greens
Fast food	
Fatty breakfast meats	Brown rice
Fatty meats	Chia seeds
Fried foods	Chicken breast
Heavy gravies	Cinnamon
Heavy pastries	Coffee
Heavy salad dressings	Eggs
Heavy sauces	Extra virgin olive oil
Hotdogs or corndogs	Flax seeds
Ice cream	Garlic
Juices not made from 100% fruit juice	Ginger
Margarine	Greek yogurt
Mayonnaise	Mixed nuts
Salami, pepperoni, or bologna	Oats
Soda	Salmon
Sugary cereals	Spices
Sugary coffee drinks	Tart cherry juice
Sugary desserts	Tea
Sugary energy drinks	Water
White bread	Whole grains

Additionally, various combinations of micronutrients, fluid intake, and nutritional intake can promote recovery. The recovery needs following different forms of activity are summarized in table 9.9.

Table 9.9 Post-Training Recovery Needs

	After weight training (~60 min of activity)	After practice and games (~120+ min of activity)
Muscle damage	Moderate	High
Energy burned	Moderate	High
Carb needs	Reduced (40-50 g)	High (100-200 g)
Protein needs	Moderate (~40-50 g)	Moderate or high (50+ g)
Anti-inflammatory needs	Reduced	High
Supplement needs	Protein and omega-3s	Protein and omega-3s
Fluid replenishment	As needed	Very important
Electrolyte replenishment	Moderately important	Very important

Nutritional Recommendations for Dining Out

It is possible to eat a nutritious meal at restaurants and fast-food places. It's imperative that players consider their body composition goals and what their bodies need. Players should make sure that each meal is complete, meaning the meal is a protein source, a carbohydrate source, and a fruit and vegetable source, with preferably water as fluid. Outside of water, we recommend that players aim for milk, tea, or 100% fruit juice. It's important to limit fried items as much as possible and choose protein sources that are grilled, baked, or broiled. Players should watch out for "empty calories," which come in the form of food items like bread baskets or chips and salsa that are easy to consume in large quantities but low in nutrient density. It's also best to limit heavy-calorie items like cream soups, butter or margarine, thick salad dressings, gravy, and thick sauces. It helps to ask for sauces on the side to control how much is put on the desired food item. Lastly, if ordering a sandwich or burger, we recommend avoiding too many add-ons like bacon, cheese, and onion rings.

RECOVERY FOR PERFORMANCE

Recovery strategies incorporated in the football training process can include any number of modalities to enhance mobility or flexibility, reduce inflammation, promote blood flow and nutrient transport through various massage and heat therapies, or reduce pain in the form of cold therapies.

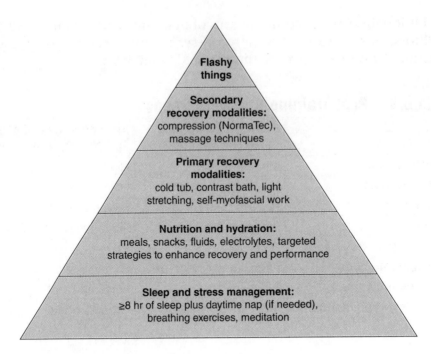

Flashy things

Secondary recovery modalities:
compression (NormaTec), massage techniques

Primary recovery modalities:
cold tub, contrast bath, light stretching, self-myofascial work

Nutrition and hydration:
meals, snacks, fluids, electrolytes, targeted strategies to enhance recovery and performance

Sleep and stress management:
≥8 hr of sleep plus daytime nap (if needed), breathing exercises, meditation

Figure 9.1   Pyramid of nutrition and recovery hierarchy.

While there's nothing inherently wrong with these modalities, they simply cannot compensate for poor nutrition, inadequate hydration, and a lack of quality sleep. Thus, if we were to make a pyramid representing a hierarchy of nutrition and recovery strategies (see figure 9.1), the foundation would be based upon sleep and stress management, with nutrition and hydration fitting directly on top. The rest of the recovery modalities can fall into more supportive roles. Thus, effective recovery strategies do not have to be expensive or overly complicated. Like many aspects of athletic performance, when athletes perform the basics extremely well, significant progress can be achieved.

Optimizing Sleep Habits

Obtaining consistent quality sleep is arguably the most important recovery strategy in a player's toolbox and should underpin the recovery program of every athlete, regardless of age or level of the game. Despite the importance of sleep in optimizing athletic performance and recovery and avoiding injury, athletes and coaches often don't address it adequately.

A typical sleep recommendation is that athletes get 7-9 hours of sleep each day. However, like most things, individual differences exist. Athletes participating in consistent, intense training may need 8-10 hours or even up to 12 hours of sleep each night. This recommendation does not differ if the player is in high school, college, or at the professional level. Thus, when communicating with our players about sleep, we recommend that 8 hours be the minimum goal. Some of the primary performance benefits of sleep include the following:

- Improved reaction time
- Decreased injury risk
- Increased immunity
- Faster sprint times
- Improved accuracy
- Fewer mistakes and mental errors
- Improved body composition
- Increased energy levels
- Improved mood

Importantly, sleep duration is not synonymous with time in bed, especially with the widespread habit of keeping televisions and smartphones present in the bedroom. The blue light emitted from these devices causes a player's brain to stay awake, and scrolling through social media, playing games, or engaging in other common activities can keep the brain stimulated for extended periods of time. It is also common for athletes to experience fear, anxiety, and worry about their playing times, academic stressors, or serious outside life troubles, which may negatively affect their ability to fall asleep and stay asleep. Consequently, implementing strategies like meditation or looking for resources from a psychological professional to reduce anxiety before sleep are recommended as part of a consistent sleep routine to ensure a relaxed state before bedtime. Because of the factors that might affect sleep quality, we suggest that players spend at least 10 hours being physically in bed so that there is some buffer time to account for use of phones, watching television, or anything else. Additionally, we recommend that the players try to step away from screens and engage in another relaxing activity before bed that may be more conducive to carrying the body into a state of deeper sleep for the night. Some of the threats to achieving a good night of sleep include the following:

- Consuming caffeine close to sleep
- Eating heavy or high-fat foods close to sleep
- Eating very sugary foods close to sleep
- Drinking alcohol close to sleep
- Watching too much television or looking at screens close to sleep
- Going to bed in a noisy environment
- A hot room temperature
- Napping too late in the day (e.g., after 3:00 p.m.)

When discussing sleep with our players, we provide a collection of tips to help educate them on how to optimize their sleep each night. These tips include the following:

- Go to bed and wake up at a consistent time each day.
- Decrease screen time before going to bed. Blue light from phones may negatively affect the ability to fall asleep. Try to stop looking at all screens 1 hour before bedtime.
- Read a book or do something without blue light for 15-20 minutes before bedtime.
- Meditate.
- Take a hot or cold shower before going to bed.
- Keep the bedroom as dark as possible.
- Keep the bedroom temperature cool (approximately 68 degrees)—a cool room will help to achieve a deeper state of sleep.
- Ensure bedding is not too warm.
- Foam roll or perform light stretching before bed, or both.
- Perform relaxation breathing while in bed: Inhale for 4 seconds, hold for 4 seconds, and exhale for 4 seconds; repeat for 4-8 cycles.
- Limit caffeine after 12:00 p.m.
- Avoid alcohol, nicotine, and other stimulants in the evening.
- Avoid late naps (after 3:00 p.m.) and longer naps (>30 min).

Eating Before Going to Bed

What is consumed before going to bed can play an important role in the recovery process because it may affect internal body processes while an athlete is asleep. Whether the goal is to gain, maintain, or lose body weight, eating before bed is acceptable as long as it fits within the daily caloric requirements and goals of the athlete. It is worth noting that a high-calorie meal often disrupts sleep, so it's important for athletes to have a plan each day for when to place their largest meals, thereby avoiding having too big of a meal before bed and still attaining their weight goals.

We recommend that athletes consume a small meal or a snack that is high in protein (up to 40 g) before bed to help build and repair muscle and other connective tissues during sleep. When choosing carbohydrate sources, aiming for fiber-rich items like fruits and vegetables can help limit large increases in blood sugar levels, which may contribute to keeping an athlete awake. The fat content of the meal or snack should be low so that calories are kept down because fat has 9 calories per gram while protein and carbohydrates each have 4 calories per gram. Lastly, the meal should include enough fluid to maintain hydration levels, but not so much that the need to urinate multiple times throughout the night disrupts sleep. Based on these recommendations, some examples of nutritious presleep meals include the following:

- Greek yogurt with whey protein mixed in, creating a pudding
- Fruit smoothie with whey protein and milk
- Protein shake (milk or almond milk + powder + peanut butter + banana or oats)

Items to avoid before going to bed include the following:

- Caffeine
- High-fat foods
- Fried foods
- Sugary foods and sweets
- Heavy desserts
- Alcohol

One of the main discussions we have with players is about the consumption of alcohol and how it affects quality of sleep, quality of performance, and quality of life. Alcohol has a very powerful effect on the body. It works as a depressant and is a toxin to the body, so as soon as an athlete consumes alcohol, the body is trying to get rid of it. Sleep is vital to enhancing performance through recovery and restoration from training, and alcohol thwarts these efforts by essentially invoking the opposite effect and damaging the body.

Some of the negative effects that alcohol has on performance include the following:

- Dehydration
- Acceleration of fatigue
- Decreased muscular strength, power, and speed
- Reduced nervous system recovery
- Decreased sleep quality and quantity
- Delayed muscle repair
- Decreased testosterone
- Increased body fat storage
- Compromised immune system and increased risk of illness

Therefore, what an athlete consumes throughout the day and especially before bedtime can have a massive effect on how the training process unfolds. If the athlete is unable to properly recover and build through restorative processes, then all forms of training and practice will prove futile.

CONCLUSION

Nutrition and recovery go hand in hand because an athlete is unable to properly recover if nutrition is suboptimal. The recovery process is constantly in motion, from the pretraining periods to the post-training windows, so proper fueling strategies are vital in the process of fueling performance and rebuilding for the next performance. The most important recovery modality is a full night of sleep, so it is imperative that athletes prioritize their sleep patterns to consistently perform at a high level and stay healthy in the process. The way in which players eat and consume nutrients can positively or negatively enhance their sleep, so they have to have a daily plan of which foods and drinks they will consume at which times of the day to ensure they consume the necessary fuel for optimal body composition, performance, and recovery in the form of sleep. We believe that if we can shift the two habits of nutrition and sleep in a more positive direction, we will have a substantial impact on how our players perform and maintain their health throughout the year.

Chapter 10

Post-Injury Training

When a football player sustains an injury, the player is assessed and cared for by the medical staff, which may include undergoing a surgical procedure. Once the injury is understood and any surgeries have been completed, the player then enters into a stage-based rehabilitative process before being cleared to fully participate in team training activities. However, during the rehabilitative process, there will be a delicate balance between the work done with the sports medicine staff and work performed with the strength and conditioning staff. This balance depends on communication between both departments so that the player is able to continue to develop his body around the injury. Accordingly, there will need to be modifications to certain exercises to help an injured player train so that the desired set of physical stressors and stimuli are provided even if the exercise is different than that being performed by the rest of the team.

This process of post-injury training is typically called the return-to-play (RTP) process. As strength and conditioning coaches, we need to be mindful of the many factors associated with RTP. The most imperative aspect of RTP is protecting the athlete's health and safety, both mentally and physically. The RTP process has complex layers of psychological factors and ethical and legal issues and can require a host of responsibilities for all parties involved. But, again, the top priority is the athlete's health and safety.

A strength and conditioning coach making exercise modifications has to first know the degree of the athlete's injury and avoid exposing the athlete to any unnecessary orthopedic stress or pain around the injury site. It is the strength and conditioning coach's obligation to know which exercises will be appropriate for the athlete. A particular exercise may be contraindicated instead, which means that the exercise should not be used at all due to a specific injury. This chapter will provide examples of modified common exercises used in a strength and conditioning setting to deliver desired training effects during the RTP process or any time a player is dealing with a setback or contraindication.

EXERCISE MODIFICATIONS DURING POST-INJURY TRAINING

One of the most important aspects of preparing a football team to stay healthy and be successful is knowing how to modify exercises, especially if a player has excessive discomfort, pain, or a lack of mobility to properly perform certain exercises. This same mindset must be applied in the RTP process and following rehabilitation to ensure the athlete continues to progress toward full training and full participation.

Before the athlete is asked to engage in modified exercise, he needs to ensure that he is doing the exercise with proper technique. This chapter assumes that the exercise is being properly taught, and if the athlete needs to do an alternative, it is for good reason. We will now discuss the primary problematic body areas associated with injury in the sport of football and how we modify exercises for our players during the post-injury period so that they are able to train as they work to regain their functionality and fitness to return to full performance.

Exercise Modifications for Shoulder Pain or Injury

In football, the shoulder joint can sustain different types of injuries due to collision, overuse, or an acute strained movement, and the most common shoulder injuries are sprains to the acromioclavicular (AC) joint, tears to the shoulder labrum, shoulder impingement, and rotator cuff strains. It is important for us to be able to work around any type of injury in the weight room to put the athlete in the most optimal position to continue to train. The aim is to build strength and resiliency with minimal strain on specific healing structures.

Activation of the Rotator Cuff

One of the first areas of concern for the shoulder joint is the rotator cuff, which is a collection of muscles that help stabilize the shoulder. The rotator cuff muscles are the supraspinatus, subscapularis, infraspinatus, and teres minor, and they exist around the structure of the shoulder blade. The rotator cuff is important to recognize because athletes who complain of shoulder pain may be dealing with an impingement of the joint, which may be alleviated with proper activation of these smaller muscles.

One exercise that we incorporate to help activate the rotator cuff is the side-lying external rotation while holding a weight plate. If this exercise is done correctly, the muscles of the rotator cuff will take on most of the load. But, if the muscles are weak or inhibited, compensations may occur at some of the larger surrounding muscles. This is also said to be one of the most optimal ways to decrease strain in the capsule of the shoulder joint. If a rolled-up towel is accessible, it should be placed on the rib cage and pinned underneath the inside edge of the top arm to allow the back (posterior) rotator cuff muscles to work more efficiently. This is shown in figure 10.1.

Figure 10.1   Apply a rolled-up towel under the arm to decrease strain on the shoulder capsule during resisted side-lying external rotation.

Pressing Exercise Modifications

If pain is experienced when performing the barbell bench press exercise, it can be altered or replaced with a variety of difference exercises. When an athlete is coming back from a shoulder surgery or dealing with great pain on one side, we can have the athlete perform variations of dumbbell pressing and use a lighter dumbbell for the problematic shoulder. This is better than performing a true one-arm press since the injured arm is able to stay active and perform work, hopefully helping reduce any muscle loss on that side. We can also modify technique, such as keeping the arms at an angle of 45 degrees from the sides of the body when lowering the barbell. If the athlete proceeds in a "high-five" angle of the arm or has the arms flared out at 90 degrees, then this may cause an increased risk of pain, most likely from the higher demand placed on the rotator cuff and the biceps tendon. Figure 10.2 shows the difference between these elbow positions.

Figure 10.2　(a) Elbows kept around 45 degrees away from the body and (b) elbows flared at 90 degrees during the bench press.

It's also helpful to ask the player where pain might be occurring through-out the execution of the exercise. Is it occurring as the bar is being lowered? Is it occurring when starting to come out of the bottom position? Or is it occurring while locking out the bar? If the athlete is experiencing the pain at the bottom, then we can place a 4- to 6-inch wooden board on the player's chest, which limits the total range of motion of the movement and may alleviate any painful range of motion. This kind of equipment is readily available from various gym equipment companies and is illustrated in figure 10.3. Another solution is to attach a "shoulder saver" pad on the bar, which is pictured in figure 10.4. This is equivalent to a 4-inch board (or 2-board, which is comprised of two wooden boards that are each 2 in. thick held together with some form of adhesive) and will allow for only one spotter at the bar rather than two spotters.

Figure 10.3 Reduced pressing range of motion by using a wooden board.

Figure 10.4 Reduced pressing range of motion by using a "shoulder saver" pad.

Another alternative for the bench press is to implement an exercise that allows a different pressing angle. For example, if a press from a flat bench is bothering the player's shoulder, then we can try a declined angle, which places the hips higher than the shoulders and keeps the shoulders at a reduced range of motion. Figure 10.5 shows a sample setup for a decline dumbbell press. If the injury or pain is associated with the pectoral (chest) muscles, then we can use an inclined angle to reduce strain on the pectorals. The higher the incline angle, the less stress is placed on the pectoral muscles in favor of proportionately increasing stress on the deltoid muscles.

Figure 10.5 Decline dumbbell press.

These variations can be performed using dumbbells or staying with the barbell. In a team setting, multiple athletes are typically sharing one rack and rotating through, so it may be difficult to stay with the barbell for the modified players, and dumbbells may allow for them to train to the side and stay on track with the flow of the training session. Furthermore, using dumbbells may be even more beneficial for athletes returning from injury because the independent stability requirements of holding an object in each hand allows the athlete to adjust his arms to the most pain-free position, as opposed to a barbell where the arms are fixed to a bar.

Other types of bars for pressing may also be implemented, such as a football bar or a fat-grip bar. The football bar, or modified bench press bar, allows the athlete to hold a neutral position with the hands and wrists while the bar fixes the shoulders at 45 degrees away from the body. This exercise is illustrated in figure 10.6. The fat-grip bar may be used to spread the load differently across the wrists and forearms and, consequently, the shoulders as well. As a result, the thickness of the bar can alleviate some shoulder joint issues due to the difference in muscular activation around these various joints. This exercise is illustrated in figure 10.7.

Figure 10.6   Football bar bench press.

Figure 10.7   Fat-grip bar bench press.

Another way to reduce the range of motion of the press is to incorporate using the ground through a floor press, which is essentially a flat press that is performed while lying down on the floor. The floor reduces the range of motion much like a board press, which allows for the player to minimize the active lengthening of the pectorals and shoulders and can avoid painful ranges of motion. Using dumbbells with this exercise still allows the athlete to move freely and use lighter weight in one hand if needed. The athlete, spotter, and coach must be focused the whole time so the weights do not fall onto the face or body of the lifter. During the exercise, the athlete will control the eccentric path of the movement by coming down slowly to the floor, pausing on the floor for 1 second, and then pressing back up to complete 1 repetition.

An athlete with shoulder pain may also struggle with pressing exercises that require an incline angle, such as the standing barbell overhead press shown in figure 10.8, but may have no pain when pressing directly overhead. Again, one alternative for the barbell overhead press is to incorporate the use of dumbbells, which will allow the athlete more freedom to place his hands in a pain-free position, such as in the seated dumbbell overhead press shown in figure 10.9. If the pain persists, the elbows may be placed in a neutral starting position where the forearms are directly in front of the shoulders with palms facing in toward each other, as seen in figure 10.9. This allows the shoulder to be put in a more advantageous position

Figure 10.8   Standing barbell overhead press.

Figure 10.9   Seated dumbbell overhead press with neutral arm position.

in terms of how it sits in the joint. A machine overhead press may also be implemented, preferably one with a neutral grip, to limit flaring at the elbows.

Pulling Exercise Modifications

Variations of chin-ups and pull-ups are great exercises for improving vertical pulling strength, but they can also cause problems for players with shoulder pain. If pain is present, it may be a certain grip that will cause the athlete pain. The athlete can change hand placement to see if any positions are pain-free, such as going overhand (palms facing away from the body), neutral (palms facing each other), or using a reverse or underhand grip (palms facing toward the body). As the palms rotate more toward the body, the shoulders become less internally rotated when in an overhead position, which may lead to pain-free ranges of motion.

If the magnitude of resistance (e.g., lifting up one's own body weight for a chin-up) is causing pain for the injured shoulder, or the chin-up is a contraindicated exercise, an alternative can be to use a lat pull-down machine or to perform the lat pull-down exercise on a cable machine. These variations will allow the athlete to use less resistance than body weight for a vertical pulling movement.

If the vertical pulling motion is completely contraindicated, then we will have to resort to using horizontal pulling exercises to develop strength in the large muscles of the back. For example, we can implement a neutral grip chest-supported row or a bent-over dumbbell row. Again, if needed, the load lifted can be reduced on the injured side of the body and then progression of load can take place slowly over time until the load on both sides is equal.

During horizontal pulls, it is important to pull the shoulder blades back and down. This not only reduces pressure on the AC joint, but the activation of supporting upper-back muscles is increased to allow more work across the musculature of the back. We want to avoid the shoulders rotating forward too much when pulling because this position can cause a significant decrease in muscle force and may put the athlete at risk for impingement and pain. Extension of the thoracic spine (the area of the spine around the rib cage and up to the base of the neck) is also necessary to accomplish full range of motion of the pull and still optimize the work of the back muscles. The differences between these positions are illustrated in figure 10.10.

Figure 10.10 *(a)* Correct and *(b)* incorrect horizontal pulling posture.

Auxiliary Exercise Modifications

The lateral raise and upright row are great exercises for training hypertrophy of the shoulders and upper back. However, internally rotating the shoulders while elevating them may cause impingement around the rotator cuff. When prescribing these exercises, especially to someone with shoulder pain, it is critical not to go above 90 degrees of shoulder abduction. Another alternative to the upright row is to have the athlete perform a lateral raise with the arms about 30 degrees away from the torso with the thumbs facing up. This allows the joint to have more space through which to move during the exercise.

Olympic Lifting Modifications for Shoulder Issues

For athletes dealing with or coming back from a shoulder issue or injury, Olympic lifts may also need to be modified. When searching for an alternative, it's important to find an exercise that puts the athlete in a similar triple extension pattern and trains rate of force development (RFD) against substantial load. If pain or injury will not allow the athlete to raise the shoulders above 90 degrees from the body pain-free, then the athlete is most likely unable to perform a barbell clean, jerk, or snatch variation. An alternative to these exercises can be to perform a high pull in which the shoulder does not elevate as high along the body, as illustrated in figure 10.11. This will allow the athlete to train the desirable triple extension pattern from the hips through the feet without amplifying shoulder pain.

However, if the pain is present in a high-pull variation, the athlete may perform a barbell power shrug to avoid lifting through the arms altogether, as illustrated in figure 10.12. Here, the shoulders will elevate only at the trapezius muscles in a shrugging movement, but the arms are not bent or lifted up along the sides of the body. Dumbbells may be used to have the athlete freely move the weight in a pain-free path. Another power shrug variation and alternative to Olympic lifting is the hex bar power pull, which lets the shoulders stay closer to a neutral anatomical position along the sides of the body, rather than in front. If the loaded shrugging motion aggravates the shoulder, the next alternative to attain similar training effects would be to perform a dumbbell squat jump, where the body leaves the ground ballistically, but the shoulders are kept still and the work is done through the lower body. Here, it's imperative that each jump be of maximum effort on every repetition to train the desirable RFD and power qualities while putting less strain on the shoulder joint.

Figure 10.11   Barbell high pull.   Figure 10.12   Barbell power shrug.

Lower-Body Strength Training Modifications for Shoulder Issues

Another area of consideration when an athlete is dealing with shoulder pain or injury is how to train the lower extremities for strength without aggravating the shoulder joint. For example, the position and range of motion of the shoulder joint when holding a barbell on the back may be contraindicated because the athlete may not be able to externally rotate or pull the shoulders back to grip the bar and maintain a correct spinal position. In this case, two alternatives to the barbell back squat are the hand-supported safety bar squat, which is illustrated in figure 10.13, and the dumbbell rear-foot elevated split squat. During the hand-supported safety bar squat, the athlete can perform the squat pattern without having to externally rotate the shoulder joint. However, the athlete will end up flexing the shoulders in front of the body at around 90 degrees when reaching the bottom position of the squat, so we must be mindful of whether that will bother the athlete. If pain persists, then the athlete can perform a dumbbell rear-foot elevated split squat, which will allow the arms to stay by the athlete's sides while training the deep hip and knee flexion pattern that is similar to that of a barbell back squat. Another alternative exercise to train a bilateral position that is similar to a barbell back squat is the hex bar deadlift. Again, the arms will be placed along the sides of the body, which will avoid putting the shoulders in a compromised rotated position, and the hex bar shape allows the body to stay more upright so that the movement resembles the concentric phase of a squat when the bar is lifted from the floor.

Figure 10.13   Hand-supported safety bar squat.

Another scenario involves the situation where a player has recently received shoulder surgery and using the recovering shoulder is contraindicated, but the player has been cleared to start training with the team. If that is the case, the coach must find a way to train the lower body without involving the upper extremities as part of the work. This can be accomplished by using exercises such as the belt squat, machine leg press, or barbell hip thrust to challenge the lower body with heavier loads while avoiding the necessity of grasping or holding a bar and straining the shoulder joint. The belt squat and machine leg press are illustrated in figures 10.14 and 10.15, respectively.

The shoulder joint is complex, and exercise alternatives during the post-injury process are crucial because the joint is very mobile but also vulnerable to damage in the sport of football. Therefore, it is crucial to know ways around the pain and how to appropriately progress a shoulder with a previous injury while erring on the side of caution when players are cleared to return to training with the team.

Figure 10.14   Belt squat performed on a Pit Shark machine.

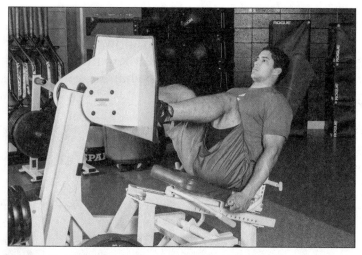

Figure 10.15   Machine leg press.

Elbow, Wrist, and Hand Pain or Injury

Injuries to the elbow, wrist, and hand will involve a similar approach to that taken for injuries around the shoulder joint. The most common injuries that occur in football are due to collision, either directly from another player or with the ground by falling on an outstretched hand. The most common injury for the elbow is a sprain to the ulnar collateral ligament from an inward or hyperextension force. This injury is also found in long snappers due to the overuse of elbow hyperextension when snapping the ball with high effort. Other common injuries that are seen at the elbow may include severe cases like a dislocation or fracture. The most common injuries to the wrist include sprains, fractures, and dislocation or subluxation that results from concussive trauma to the wrist from colliding with opponents or the ground. Hand injuries usually include hyperextension or fractures of the fingers from pulling on jerseys, hand fighting, taking a helmet or facemask impact to the hand, or contacting the ground with a finger or thumb extended while under great load.

Pressing Exercise Modifications

Performing pressing exercises with these types of injuries can be troublesome when using the barbell for a bench press. The pressure from the bar usually causes pain for all these injuries, so alternatives are required. Again, dumbbells may be a useful alternative for an elbow injury because the player can move the weight freely rather than being rigidly locked into a grip on a bar. Further, if range of motion is limited due to pain, then the athlete can be encouraged to stay in a pain-free range. However, the pressure from the dumbbells may still aggravate an elbow, wrist, or hand injury. In this case, it may be possible for the athlete to train using machine-based presses because the exercise may be performed through the shoulder and chest without having to fully wrap the fingers around the handle. This setup is illustrated in figure 10.16, which shows a machine chest press, and also in figure 10.17, which shows the hand placement on an incline machine press. This way, the athlete may find an open-palm position that reduces stress on the fingers, hand, or wrist and still allow for loading a pressing movement.

Figure 10.16 Open-palm position on machine chest press.

Figure 10.17 Open-palm position on incline machine press.

If the athlete is unable to perform any presses due to contraindications of loading the wrist, then the athlete can perform a chest fly exercise on a machine or have a coach or partner assist with manually resisted presses. The machine variation is illustrated in figure 10.18. To achieve the manual resistance, a coach or partner will press down on the athlete's forearm or nearer to the shoulder joint so that the athlete presses against the load applied by the partner, as illustrated in figure 10.19.

Figure 10.18   Machine chest fly.

Figure 10.19   Partner manually resisted chest press.

Pulling Exercise Modifications

When an athlete is dealing with elbow, wrist, or hand pain or injury, pulling exercises should be based on achieving the maximum range of motion and weight the athlete can tolerate. If the athlete can perform a pulling motion but higher loads cause pain, the athlete can perform the exercise with less weight on the problematic side. If the range of motion is an issue, the athlete may be coached to stay in a pain-free range. Furthermore, if the athlete has a hand injury and is unable to grip a bar or handle, the athlete can use a strap around the wrist and the handle when performing a machine-based chest-supported row or dumbbell row. This setup is illustrated in figure 10.20. The next alternative or progression would be to perform manually resisted pulls as shown in figure 10.21. This allows the athlete to pull and work the musculature of the back without having to use the elbow, wrist, or hand.

Figure 10.20   Placement of strap around dumbbell to help hold the weight for athletes with hand injuries.

Figure 10.21   Partner manually resisted horizontal pull.

The coach must consider that even though the elbow, wrist, or hand is injured, it does not mean the shoulder joint has to be significantly limited. There are ways around different injuries that will still allow for progression in training.

Lower-Body Strength Training Modifications for Elbow, Wrist, and Hand Issues

Training the lower body when dealing with an elbow, wrist, or hand injury is similar to that of finding alternatives for the shoulder joint. If the athlete is unable to perform a barbell back squat due to pain or range-of-motion issues, the athlete may try to perform a squat with a safety bar to keep the elbow, wrist, and hand out of more-demanding positions. However, if the athlete is unable to fully extend the elbow or use the injured arm at all, the machine leg press, belt squat, or barbell hip thrust may be incorporated as previously discussed for issues involving the shoulder joint.

Exercise Modifications for Hip and Groin Pain or Injury

In football, hip and groin injuries are not as common as injuries to the knee and ankle, but they do occur in the form of strains, contusions (bruises), tears around the joint capsule (e.g., labral tear), and sometimes hip dislocations. The exercises used to work around these injuries are typically based on limiting the range of motion to a pain-free range. To use the squatting motion as an example, the athlete should be tested on how far down he can go with body weight only. Then, the athlete can be progressed by implementing a box squat, where the athlete will descend under control into a squat pattern to a box set between 16 and 20 inches high. The athlete will be instructed to maintain tension once contacting the box and pause for 1-3 seconds before coming back up to the standing position. This helps the athlete in the isometric phase of the movement and keeps the athlete in a target range of motion.

When load is applied to the box squat, the athlete can begin with a safety bar to distribute the load closer to the center of mass and slowly descend to the box, as illustrated in figure 10.22. During the box phase, the athlete should contract his core to maintain a flat back and not lean back with the bar. The box height used should be recorded, and it is best practice to start with a higher box before progressing to a lower box, such as gradually shifting from 20 inches to 16 inches over time. Another alternative exercise to train the squat pattern at a reduced range of motion would be incorporating the hex bar deadlift. This exercise puts the hip and groin at a better biomechanical advantage that may help decrease or mitigate the presence of pain.

Unilateral movements such as lunge variations may be problematic for hip and groin pain or injury because of the pressure and shearing force on these structures during these movements. If these exercises are bothersome, an alternative would be a low-box step-up using dumbbells. The box height should be set between 10 and 12 inches to reduce pressure on the groin. The athlete will start with his knee over his toe, with a forward body lean and a dumbbell in each hand. Then, he will drive his foot down through the box and reach full hip extension while flexing the other hip at the top of the lift. Other unilateral movements that may be beneficial are the single-leg press and single-leg hip thrust; the latter is illustrated in figure 10.23. These exercises can strengthen the muscles surrounding the hip while maintaining control of the overall ranges of motion.

Figure 10.22　Safety bar box squat.

Figure 10.23　Single-leg hip thrust.

If the athlete is bothered by performing multijoint actions involving a hip hinge pattern (e.g., squat or deadlift variations) or is coming back from a surgery involving the structures surrounding the hip or groin, more isolated machine work may be necessary to reduce the demands on stability and allow reduced loading when required. These modifications may include machines that isolate hip or leg actions, like abduction (outer hip, illustrated in figure 10.24), adduction (groin, illustrated in figure 10.25), leg extension (quadriceps, illustrated in figure 10.26), and leg flexion (hamstrings).

Figure 10.24   Machine hip abduction.

Figure 10.25   Machine hip adduction.

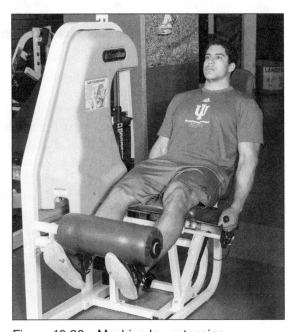

Figure 10.26   Machine leg extension.

Exercise Modifications for Ankle and Knee Pain or Injury

Ankle and knee injuries are some of the most common injuries in football, with knee injuries being some of the most catastrophic, ending seasons or even careers. For the ankle, high and low sprains occur, typically around the lateral (outside) edge of the ankle. The most common knee injuries include tears of the anterior cruciate ligament (ACL), medial collateral ligament, and posterior cruciate ligament. Sprains and tears in the ankles and knees require progression, education, and limitations based on the different severities of each injury. For example, the average time for RTP following an ACL injury and reconstruction is 9-13 months, while some specialists say that it is 2 years before the knee feels "normal" again.

If the athlete is returning from an acute ankle injury and is unable to perform lower-body strength exercises while standing on the ground, machine-based work may be incorporated to strengthen the muscles of the lower body while not having to load the ankle joint. The leg extension and leg curl machines allow strength development while seated or lying, so the ankle is not involved in load-bearing.

If an athlete is coming back from a knee injury or is dealing with knee pain, one exercise that is minimally stressful to the structures of the knee but very effective for developing the muscles of the glutes and hamstrings is the barbell hip thrust. Other variations include the dumbbell hip thrust or single-leg hip thrust, which may help with the adjustment of intensity to that which is desired. Also, the range of motion when performing the exercise may be a concern for knee injuries, so it is imperative to know the athlete is cleared to perform in a knee flexion range between 14 and 30 degrees.

Exercise Modifications for Hamstring Pain or Injury

Hamstring injuries are also very common in football and are typically associated with high-speed sprinting or high-intensity deceleration actions in practice and games. Hamstring injuries will not prevent a player from training with the team, but they will necessitate modifications be made. For example, if the athlete has suffered a hamstring strain near the hip, squatting will become more difficult due to the lengthening of the hamstrings when shifting the hips back at the start of the descent of the squat. However, if the strain is more distal toward the insertion at the knee, the athlete has a much better chance of squatting without pain because of the limited activation of the hamstrings around the knee when squatting into deep knee flexion.

To train the hamstring directly, exercises like the barbell Romanian deadlift can be substituted with a less-intense hip hinge exercise like the 45- or 90-degree back extension. Figure 10.27 illustrates the 45-degree version of the back extension exercise. Back extensions can serve as gentler ways to stimulate the hamstring in a hip extension movement pattern while controlling for intensity of load. Arguably the most commonly used exercise for training the hamstrings by flexing and extending at the knee is the partner Nordic hamstring curl. When an athlete is dealing with a hamstring issue, this exercise may be far too intense in the early stages of post-injury training. If the athlete cannot endure the high eccentric forces of a partner Nordic hamstring curl, the athlete can substitute a roller leg curl (as illustrated in figure 10.28) or stability ball leg curl. These variations bring the intensity down significantly and can allow the athlete to strengthen the knee flexion movement.

Figure 10.27   45-degree back extension.

Figure 10.28   Roller leg curl.

CONCLUSION

In football, it's extremely rare that every athlete will feel 100% healthy. Football is a highly demanding sport, not only due to the collisions that occur but also because the training demands on the athletes are extensive throughout the year. This chapter touched on the most common injuries endured in football and some of the different modifications to common exercises that may be used to help keep players involved and engaged in the training process. These modifications are important to train athletes in the most optimal way possible each day. It's imperative for coaches to have a backup plan to keep every player in a state of development, even when setbacks occur in the form of pain or injuries.

Chapter 11

Complete Conditioning Program

Until this chapter, we have presented our strategy and the training elements football players need to be and stay healthy, perform optimally at the positions and tasks assigned to them, and return to full participation after injury. We also recommended specific testing and monitoring protocols and numerous exercises and drills for each training component and have provided programming guidelines and samples for each.

Now we will pull all those elements together into a complete conditioning program for football. This chapter will provide a road map for a holistic training program that develops the football player as a complete team sport athlete. For organizational purposes, we present our programming guidelines based on the progression of our football training periods across a calendar year, starting with the winter off-season period. Then, we continue chronologically, moving to spring training and practices, summer off-season, and fall training camp and the in-season period. While the specific months assigned to these training periods may not align exactly with your program's annual schedule, they should be similar enough that you can easily adapt them to fit your team's and programming needs.

WINTER CONDITIONING

The winter off-season is a unique training opportunity for football players. After the final game, there is usually some sort of break, anywhere from 2-5 weeks, depending on when the final game was played. While we provide our players with workout programs during this time, we assume our players are somewhat deconditioned after having some extensive time away from our training facilities and organized sessions.

Essentially, winter conditioning is a starting-over period, both physically and mentally. The physical component is based on the likelihood that players have rested their bodies to recover from the season, and the mental component is entering a new year. The bar for competition has been reset in terms of players fighting for playing time next season. Players and coaches are typically highly motivated to get back to work, but we must remember that the season is still a long time away, and training camp won't begin for at least 6-7 months.

This is a unique time to focus on high-quality movement and high-quality output without as much concern about building endurance. Therefore, our emphasis can shift toward raising maximum strength, power, and speed while also putting a premium on body composition, muscular hypertrophy, and tissue integrity. The endurance training components should still be present, but they will not be as comprehensive as they would be in the summer training period since the players will not have a truly competitive season for some time.

In table 11.1, we illustrate a hypothetical workout week for the winter training period. We use a 4-day training split, with each day having a general theme. The training days in this model will typically be Monday, Tuesday, Thursday, and Friday, with Wednesday, Saturday, and Sunday as restoration and recovery days. We like to start the week with lower-intensity work so that we can rev up the engine of the players' bodies, so to speak. Since Saturday and Sunday are recovery-based days, we like to gradually introduce the players into training before we start hitting the higher-intensity work during the rest of the week.

Monday's theme is endurance and upper-body strength. After a dynamic warm-up, we can take the players through some field-based conditioning work in the form of longer tempo runs at relatively low intensities. This will work the aerobic energy system and serve as an extended warm-up for the players when they do it before the weight room session. After the

Table 11.1 Winter Off-Season Complete Conditioning Program, Weeks 1-3

Training day	Day 1	Day 2	Day 3	Day 4
Emphasis	Endurance and upper-body strength	Acceleration, COD and agility, power, and lower-body strength	Top speed technique, reactive power endurance, power, and upper-body strength	Acceleration, COD and agility, power, and lower-body strength
Field-based training	**Extensive tempo runs** Week 1 = 8 total reps Week 2 = 10 total reps Week 3 = 2 sets × 6 reps 1-min rest between reps and 2-min rest between sets OL/DL 60-yd run in 11 sec QB/RB/TE/LB 80-yd run in 13 sec WR/DB 100-yd run in 15 sec **Extensive medicine ball throws** Chest pass throw into wall—25 reps Rotational throw into wall—25 reps Overhead throw into wall—25 reps Slam into the ground—25 reps **Extensive abdominals** McGill curl-up—5 reps each side Toe touches—20 reps Russian twist—15 reps each side V-sits—20 reps	**Resisted sprinting** Light- or heavy-resisted sprinting, with full recovery between reps OL/DL Heavy-resisted sprinting (load 60%-80% body weight)—4 × 10 yd QB/RB/TE/LB Light-resisted sprinting (load 40%-60% body weight)—4 × 10 yd WR/DB Light-resisted sprinting (load 20%-40% body weight)—4 × 10 yd **Acceleration** 2-point sprint, with full recovery between reps OL/DL 2 × 10 yd QB/RB/TE/LB 2 × 15 yd WR/DB 2 × 20 yd **Low push series** Lateral low push—15 yd each way 45-degree low push—15 yd each way **Single-leg landing series** Lateral jump to single-leg landing—2 each way Transverse jump to single-leg landing—2 each way	**Medicine ball throws (10-15 lb)** Chest pass—5 throws Backward over-head—5 throws **Reactive power endurance circuit** Pogo jumps—2 sets A-skip—2 sets High-knee run—2 sets OL/DL = 20 yd; QB/RB/TE/LB = 30 yd; WR/DB = 40 yd per repetition **Top speed technique** Skips for distance—2 sets OL/DL = 20 yd; QB/RB/TE/LB = 30 yd; WR/DB = 40 yd per repetition Curved sprints—4 sets OL/DL = 20-yd curve; All other positions = 40-yd curve Build-up sprints (80% speed)—2 total repetitions OL/DL = 30 yd; All other positions = 40 yd	**Resisted sprinting** Light- or heavy-resisted sprinting, with full recovery between reps OL/DL Heavy-resisted sprinting (load 60%-80% body weight)—4 × 10 yd QB/RB/TE/LB Light-resisted sprinting (load 40%-60% body weight)—4 × 10 yd WR/DB Light-resisted sprinting (load 20%-40% body weight)—4 × 10 yd **Acceleration** 2-point sprint, with full recovery between reps OL/DL 2 × 10 yd QB/RB/TE/LB 2 × 15 yd WR/DB 2 × 20 yd **Jump to bound series** Vertical jump to lateral bound—2 × 3 reps each way Vertical jump to transverse bound—2 × 3 reps each way **Multidirectional acceleration** Half-kneeling hip turn acceleration—2 × 5 yd each way

(continued)

Table 11.1 Winter Off-Season Complete Conditioning Program, Weeks 1-3 *(continued)*

Training day	Day 1	Day 2	Day 3	Day 4
Weight room training	**Primary press** Barbell bench press with 3-sec eccentric Week 1 = 4 sets × 4 reps, finish @ 75% 1RM Week 2 = 4 sets × 3 reps, finish @ 80% 1RM Week 3 = 4 sets × 3 reps, finish @ 85% 1RM *Quarterback alternative:* Dumbbell bench press with 3-sec eccentric—4 sets × 4 reps, finish heavy but with 1-2 reps left in the tank **Primary pull** Neutral grip chin-up with 3-sec eccentric—4 sets OL/DL = 4 reps; QB/RB/TE/LB = 6 reps; WR/DB = 8 reps **Secondary press** Dumbbell one-arm push press—3 sets × 5 reps each arm **Secondary pull** Dumbbell one-arm row—3 sets × 10 reps each arm **Neck and trap** Barbell or dumbbell shrug—2 sets × 10 reps	**Primary lower-body compound** Hex bar deadlift Week 1 = 4 sets × 6 reps, finish @ 70% 1RM Week 2 = 4 sets × 5 reps, finish @ 75% 1RM Week 3 = 4 sets × 4 reps, finish @ 80% 1RM **Power** Barbell countermove-ment jump—4 sets × 2 reps Set 1 = Body weight only; Set 2 = 45 lb; Set 3 = 95 lb; Set 4 = 135 lb **Posterior chain** Barbell hip thrust—3 sets × 10 reps **Single leg** Dumbbell goblet lateral lunge with 3-sec pause—3 sets × 5 reps each leg **Secondary posterior chain** 90-degree back exten-sion with pause (weighted)—3 sets × 8 reps	**Primary press** Barbell close-grip 2-board bench press with pause Week 1 = 4 sets × 8 reps, finish @ 65% 1RM Week 2 = 4 sets × 8 reps, finish @ 70% 1RM Week 3 = 4 sets × 8 reps, finish @ 75% 1RM *Quarterback alterna-tive:* Dumbbell incline bench press (15 degrees) with pause—4 sets × 4 reps, finish heavy but with 1-2 reps left in the tank **Primary pull** Machine seated row—3 sets × 12 reps **Secondary press** Half-kneeling land-mine one-arm press—3 sets × 5 reps each arm **Secondary pull** Machine lat pull-down—3 sets × 10 reps **Neck and trap** Barbell or dumbbell shrug—2 sets × 10 reps	**Primary lower-body compound** Barbell squat Week 1 = 4 sets × 6 reps, finish @ 70% 1RM Week 2 = 4 sets × 5 reps, finish @ 75% 1RM Week 3 = 4 sets × 4 reps, finish @ 80% 1RM **Power** Long-response hurdle jumps—3 sets × 5 hurdles **Posterior chain** Barbell Romanian deadlift with pause—4 sets × 5 reps **Single leg** Barbell reverse lunge with pause—3 sets × 5 reps each leg **Knee flexion** Partner Nordic ham-string curl—2 sets × 4 reps

tempo runs, we can either stay on the field or head into the weight room to perform a warm-up consisting of core work and exercises to warm up the muscles around the shoulder girdle. Then, we perform our upper-body strength session, which includes upper-body hypertrophy work after the primary pressing exercise. Quarterbacks may be given alternative pressing exercises that require more stability or less intensity around the rotator cuff to help preserve shoulder mobility and integrity.

Tuesday and Friday have the same themes of acceleration, change of direc-tion and agility, power, and lower-body strength. Again, we start these ses-sions on the field and emphasize resisted sprinting during the early part of the winter period to start developing horizontal force capabilities. Offensive and defensive linemen will utilize more resistance than any other position due to the nature of their positions and require more weight to acquire gains in relative horizontal strength and power due to their much larger body masses. The "big-skill" positions like tight ends, linebackers, running backs, and quarterbacks will use a relatively moderate load while the wide receivers and defensive backs will use a relatively lighter load for their resisted sprinting. Again, this serves to fulfill positional requirements in terms of the balance between horizontal force ability and training at more conducive speeds.

Resisted sprinting can be followed up with a few repetitions of unloaded sprinting to help maintain coordination of the movement while training to increase strength and power around it. If we were to remove these completely, we might risk players making gains in outputs but losing the ability to coordinate these gains appropriately. Lastly, we can start to introduce some early aspects of multidirectional movement and change of direction by performing multidirectional pushes, jumps, deceleration, bounding, and acceleration from different starting positions.

It's important to note that these field-based exercises may be performed in a circuit, where smaller groups of players go to each exercise as a station and rotate through each station until all the work has been done. Once the work has been completed, the players go into the weight room and perform a warm-up of core work and some remedial exercises around the hip, knee, and ankle joints. Then, they perform a primary compound lift, usually a variation of a squat or deadlift before moving to a primary power exercise. We may superset the primary compound exercise with the primary power exercise where the players move from the compound exercise to the power exercise to complete set 1. They then return to the compound exercise for set 2.

After the primary work is complete, we use auxiliary exercises to develop the muscles of the posterior chain with hinging, bridging, or knee flexion (leg curling) exercises. We develop the muscles surrounding the knee with various single-leg movements like multidirectional lunging, step-ups, single-leg squats, or split squat variations. Lastly, we emphasize the muscles of the foot and ankle complex by utilizing various isometric holds, single-leg balance variations, bent leg calf raises, or extensive in-place plyometric jumping or hopping.

At this time in the year, Thursdays can have a field-based emphasis of top speed technique, reactive power endurance, and power. There will not be any power work performed in the weight room, which will be another upper-body strength session, so the power focus can be on horizontal power on the field. In the example in table 11.1, we have medicine ball throws listed as one option, where the players will explode and attempt to launch the ball as far as possible. The reactive power endurance circuit here is three exercises, but we may choose to use four or even five exercises, depending on how we feel about where our players are in their states of fitness and what we need in the training. Top speed technique work might include an initial foundational drill (e.g., skips for distance) done at a high intensity to allow for continued ramping up of the body before moving into curved sprints, build-up sprints, or other top-speed-oriented activities. For both reactive power endurance and top speed technique work, the linemen will cover the shortest distances, the wide receivers and defensive backs will cover the most distance, and all other positions will fall in between.

In table 11.2, we see how the training will progress as we move into the next training phase (weeks 4-6), which will usually precede the commencement of spring practice. The first major shift in the field training is toward more exposure to change-of-direction and agility training. Spring practice is not as intensive as the in-season practice periods since there are a limited number of practices allowed, and the players will not be practicing every day. Therefore, we can still continue to develop high outputs and devote most of the field-training sessions to increasing power and speed throughout the winter off-season.

Monday becomes less focused on extensive linear running and instead focuses on the endurance capacity of changing direction as well as continuing to reinforce reactive power endurance. For reactive power endurance, we can have the players hold a 10-pound plate overhead to challenge trunk control since the arms will be fixed and also challenge their ability to stay reactive against resistance. Tuesdays and Fridays then shift to change of direction and agility while still maintaining some resisted sprinting to continue building horizontal force and power. The resisted sprinting shifts toward higher speeds for all positions, with distances of each effort increasing for the skill positions.

Unloaded acceleration is still being trained within the change of direction work because every drill will feature a full-speed linear finish. We also tend to set up multiple drill stations so that the players race against each other to increase the intensity of each effort. We introduce agility with basic perceptual-cognitive activities like partner mirror and reaction drills, and we may also incorporate another station that features more position-specific agility work, although this is not listed in the table examples.

Thursday stays true to top speed training, with this example featuring the medicine ball knee punch run exercise as the primer that leads into the build-up sprints. The intensity of the build-up sprints rises to where we communicate to the players to achieve 90% of top speed by the final 10 yards to keep players relaxed and to prevent excessive strain. We have seen players achieve new top speeds by performing build-up sprints in this way due to the efficiency of their running. We then move into tempo interval runs at an increased intensity, aiming to maintain between 80% and 90% speed over longer distances than usual, and we use cut runs to add a deceleration to reacceleration component, making it more physiologically challenging in terms of speed endurance.

The focus in the weight room remains the same, with the exception of the power work progressing to where it becomes more individualized

Table 11.2 Winter Off-Season Complete Conditioning Program, Weeks 4-6

Training day	Day 1	Day 2	Day 3	Day 4
Emphasis	COD endurance, reactive power endurance, and upper-body strength	Acceleration, agility and COD, power, and lower-body strength	Top speed technique and upper-body strength	Acceleration, agility and COD, power, and lower-body strength
Field-based training	**Tempo COD work** 4 total reps (2 turning each way) 45-60 sec rest between reps OL/DL 15-yd shuttle in 5 sec (run 5 yd out, 5 yd back, and 5 yd out again) QB/RB/TE/LB 30-yd shuttle in 7 sec (run 5 yd out, 5 yd back, 10 yd out, and 10 yd back) WR/DB 60-yd shuttle in 13 sec (run 5 yd out, 5 yd back, 10 yd out, 10 yd back, 15 yd out, and 15 yd back) **Reactive power endurance circuit** A-skip with 10-lb plate overhead—2 sets High-knee run with 10-lb plate overhead—2 sets Scissor bounding with 10-lb plate overhead—2 sets OL/DL = 20 yd; QB/RB/TE/LB = 30 yd; WR/DB = 40 yd per repetition	**Resisted sprinting** Light- or heavy-resisted sprinting—full recovery between reps OL/DL Heavy-resisted sprinting (load 40%-60% body weight)—4 × 10 yd QB/RB/TE/LB Light-resisted sprinting (load 20%-40% body weight)—4 × 15 yd WR/DB Light-resisted sprinting (load 10%-20% body weight)—4 × 20 yd **Change-of-direction speed** Perform each with a full-speed 5- to 10-yd finish Cone "N" drill—4 reps (2 each way) Cone "U" drill—4 reps (2 each way) **Agility** "X" box partner reaction drill—4 total reps Partner blind mirror reaction drill—4 total reps	**Top speed technique** Medicine ball (10 lb) knee punch run—2 sets OL/DL = 20 yd; QB/RB/TE/LB = 30 yd; WR/DB = 40 yd per repetition Build-up sprints (90% speed)—2-3 total repetitions OL/DL = 30 yd; All other positions = 40 yd **Tempo interval runs** 4 total reps with 2-min rest between reps OL/DL Cut 40s in 10 sec QB/RB/TE/LB Cut 80s in 13 sec WR/DB Cut 100s in 15 sec	**Resisted sprinting** Light- or heavy-resisted sprinting—full recovery between reps OL/DL Heavy-resisted sprinting (load 40%-60% body weight)—4 × 10 yd QB/RB/TE/LB Light-resisted sprinting (load 20%-40% body weight)—4 × 15 yd WR/DB Light-resisted sprinting (load 10%-20% body weight)—4 × 20 yd **Change-of-direction speed** Perform each with a full-speed 5- to 10-yd finish Cone zigzag run—4 reps (2 each way) 10-5-5 shuttle run—6 total reps from various starting positions (2 reps from 2-point start, 2 reps from half-kneeling start, 2 reps from push-up start) **Agility** Partner mirror reaction drill—4 total reps Run to 90-degree cut on reaction—4 total reps

(continued)

Table 11.2 Winter Off-Season Complete Conditioning Program, Weeks 4-6 *(continued)*

Training day	Day 1	Day 2	Day 3	Day 4
Weight room training	**Primary press** Barbell bench press with chains Week 4 = 4 sets × 4 reps, finish @ 70% 1RM Week 5 = 4 sets × 3 reps, finish @ 75% 1RM Week 6 = 4 sets × 3 reps, finish @ 80% 1RM *Quarterback alternative:* Dumbbell bench press with 3-sec eccentric—4 sets × 4 reps, finish heavy but with 1-2 reps left in the tank **Primary pull** Neutral grip chin-up—4 sets OL/DL = 6 reps; QB/RB/TE/LB = 8 reps; WR/DB = 10 reps **Secondary press** Half-kneeling land-mine one-arm press—3 sets × 4 reps each arm *Quarterback alternative:* Dumbbell one-arm push press—3 sets × 3 reps each arm **Secondary pull** One-arm machine seated row—3 sets × 6 reps each arm **Neck and trap** Barbell or dumbbell shrug—2 sets × 10 reps	**Primary lower-body compound** Hex bar deadlift, concentric only Week 4 = 4 sets × 3 reps, finish @ 75% 1RM Week 5 = 4 sets × 3 reps, finish @ 80% 1RM Week 6 = 4 sets × 3 reps, finish @ 85% 1RM **Primary power** OL/DL Dumbbell squat jump—4 sets × 3 reps QB/RB/TE/LB Barbell squat jump—4 sets × 3 reps WR/DB Depth jump (18 in. box)—4 sets × 3 reps **Single leg** Dumbbell rear-foot elevated split squat—3 sets × 3 reps each leg **Secondary power** Single-leg hurdle hop to box jump (1-1-2)—3 sets × 2 reps each leg **Secondary posterior chain** 45-degree back extension (weighted)—2 sets × 12 reps	**Primary press** Barbell incline bench press (15 degrees) Week 4 = 4 sets × 4 reps, finish @ 70% 1RM Week 5 = 4 sets × 3 reps, finish @ 75% 1RM Week 6 = 4 sets × 3 reps, finish @ 80% 1RM *Quarterback alternative:* Dumbbell incline bench press (30 degrees)—4 sets × 4 reps, finish heavy but with 1-2 reps left in the tank **Primary pull** Dumbbell chest-supported row—3 sets × 8 reps **Secondary press** Dumbbell floor press—3 sets × 12 reps **Secondary pull** Machine lat pull-down—3 sets × 8 reps **Neck and trap** Barbell or dumbbell shrug—2 sets × 10 reps	**Primary lower-body compound** Barbell squat with bands for speed Week 4 = 4 sets × 3 reps, finish @ 70% 1RM Week 5 = 4 sets × 3 reps, finish @ 75% 1RM Week 6 = 4 sets × 3 reps, finish @ 80% 1RM **Primary power** OL/DL = Hex bar power pull—3 sets × 3 reps; All other positions = Plyometric hurdle jumps—4 sets × 5 hurdles **Single leg** Dumbbell step-up—3 sets × 6 reps each leg **Posterior chain** Barbell Romanian deadlift—4 sets × 4 reps **Knee flexion** Partner Nordic hamstring curl—2 sets × 4 reps

toward player position groups. The down linemen perform more power training against higher loads or from paused positions while the skill players are training with the intention of having much higher takeoff speeds or shorter ground-contact times, or both. There is a secondary power exercise that is included on Tuesdays to allow for more power exposure for all positions. This can be an explosive or reactive power exercise, and a different exercise may be used for different positions if the coach chooses.

SPRING PRACTICE CONDITIONING

Moving into spring practice, the players will start practicing skills and football-specific running multiple times per week, so the field training will all be performed during these sessions with the football coaches. The emphasis for the strength and conditioning coaches is to continue to develop players in the weight room during this period. The weight room training can shift to a 3-day full-body template, where upper-body and lower-body exercises are performed in each session. We present a sample 3-day template for 4 weeks of spring training in table 11.3.

Given that the spring period is still much more of a developmental period than a competitive one, we like to continue emphasizing gains in strength and power. So, days 1 and 2 will both feature power training, with day 2 emphasizing explosive strength for the lower body. The training on day 1 will feature a primary lower-body compound lift in addition to a primary power exercise. These may be combined into a superset if the coach desires, where the players finish a set of their primary exercises and then go perform a set of the power exercise. On day 2, the primary lower-body exercise becomes more of a power stimulus as the players are encouraged to push into the ground explosively, resulting in faster movement of the barbell through the range of motion. In our sample template, this is accomplished with a barbell low-box step-up for speed.

The lower-body training on day 3 is more of a true strength day, and it will usually precede the players' most explosive day of practice in the week. So, the strength stimulus can activate the body for the following day of practice as long as fatigue is not excessive. This is why we aim for sets of 3 repetitions on the strength movements for the lower body during this time, rather than 5 or more repetitions, which could cause excessive fatigue.

The upper-body training in the weight room is geared toward building more strength and maintaining hypertrophy, especially in the areas surrounding the players' backs and necks. Practice will expose the players to a higher volume of press-oriented work with actions like punching, striking, pushing, and throwing, so we keep the training in the weight room with a ratio of 2:1 in terms of the pulling-to-pressing work. We want to continue building strength in the pressing movement and allow the press-oriented work in practice to make up for the high-volume pressing that has been removed. We also ensure that we continue building the muscles around the upper back and neck to provide a layer of protection in that area because they are introduced to contact and collision during practice.

After the end of spring practice, the players may have a few more weeks of mandatory training as they head into the last part of the academic year. For these weeks, we will keep a similar approach as the template in table 11.3 to allow their bodies to recover from spring practice. So, we can aim to maintain and hopefully further develop strength as well as hypertrophy before the players leave for a few weeks once their final exams are completed.

Table 11.3 Spring Practice Complete Conditioning Program, Weeks 1-4

Training day	Day 1	Day 2	Day 3
Emphasis	Full-body strength and power		
Field-based training	All done in football practice		
Weight room training	**Primary press** Barbell close-grip 2-board bench press Week 1 = 4 sets × 4 reps, finish @ 75% 1RM Week 2 = 4 sets × 3 reps, finish @ 80% 1RM Week 3 = 4 sets × 3 reps, finish @ 85% 1RM Week 4 = 4 sets × 3 reps, finish @ 90% 1RM *Quarterback alternative:* Dumbbell bench press—4 sets × 4 reps, finish heavy but with 1-2 reps left in the tank **Primary pull** OL/DL = Machine seated row—4 sets × 6-8 reps; All other positions = Neutral grip chin-up (weighted)—3 sets × 6 reps **Secondary pull** OL/DL = Dumbbell one-arm row—3 sets × 6 reps each arm; All other positions = Machine seated row—3 sets × 6 reps **Neck and trap** Barbell or dumbbell shrug—2 sets × 10 reps **Primary lower-body compound** Hex bar deadlift Week 1 = 4 sets × 3 reps, finish @ 75% 1RM Week 2 = 4 sets × 3 reps, finish @ 80% 1RM Week 3 = 4 sets × 3 reps, finish @ 85% 1RM Week 4 = 4 sets × 3 reps, finish @ 90% 1RM **Primary power** Alternating box split jumps—4 sets × 2 reps **Posterior chain** Barbell Romanian deadlift—3 sets × 3 reps	**Primary press** Barbell incline bench press (30 degrees) Week 1 = 4 sets × 4 reps, finish @ 70% 1RM Week 2 = 4 sets × 4 reps, finish @ 75% 1RM Week 3 = 4 sets × 4 reps, finish @ 80% 1RM Week 4 = 4 sets × 4 reps, finish @ 85% 1RM *Quarterback alternative:* Dumbbell incline bench press (30 degrees)—4 sets × 4 reps, finish heavy but with 1-2 reps left in the tank **Primary pull** Machine lat pull-down—3 sets × 6-8 reps **Secondary pull** Suspension trainer pull-up—3 sets × 6 reps **Neck and trap** Barbell or dumbbell shrug—2 sets × 10 reps **Primary lower-body compound** Barbell low-box step-up for speed—3 sets × 3 reps each leg **Primary power** Single-leg box jumps from half-kneeling position—5 reps each leg	**Primary press** Dumbbell incline bench press (15 degrees) Week 1 = 4 sets × 5 reps, finish @ 70% 1RM Week 2 = 4 sets × 5 reps, finish @ 75% 1RM Week 3 = 4 sets × 5 reps, finish @ 80% 1RM Week 4 = 4 sets × 5 reps, finish @ 85% 1RM *Quarterback alternative:* Dumbbell floor press—4 sets × 4 reps, finish heavy but with 1-2 reps left in the tank **Primary pull** Dumbbell chest-supported row—3 sets × 8 reps **Secondary pull** Dumbbell one-arm row—3 sets × 6 reps each arm **Neck and trap** Barbell or dumbbell shrug—2 sets × 10 reps **Primary lower-body compound** Barbell squat Week 1 = 4 sets × 3 reps, finish @ 75% 1RM Week 2 = 4 sets × 3 reps, finish @ 80% 1RM Week 3 = 4 sets × 3 reps, finish @ 85% 1RM Week 4 = 4 sets × 3 reps, finish @ 90% 1RM **Posterior chain** 90-degree back extension (weighted)—3 sets × 10 reps

SUMMER OFF-SEASON CONDITIONING

Once the players come back from their breaks following final exams, summer training officially begins, and it becomes the most important part of the entire calendar year. Typically, we will have about 8 weeks of true summer training, and we need to maximize this time while avoiding the pitfall of doing too much too early. We have seen it before: We have gotten too excited and started pushing the players in the middle of summer training to the point where they are just trying to hold on before the end. This is not what we want. Instead, we want a plan that incorporates all necessary training elements, sequenced progressively and allowing the players to continue to elevate their preparations as the summer leads into fall training camp, without getting them burned out.

On-field training is important during the summer training period because we have to progress the players to where they can handle some aspect of running 5-6 days a week when fall training camp and the in-season period begins. However, if we jump right into this at the beginning, we can risk the players dealing with overuse trauma and soft-tissue injury from the impact on the joints. Also, we cannot be sure players will have maintained an adequate level of training during their weeks away. Some players may have been active and training the entire time while others were mostly sedentary. Thus, we assume most players are deconditioned when they return to us. While it may not be true, we believe that keeping this mindset will allow us to have a more cautious approach and reduce avoidable joint and soft-tissue injuries by not overdoing it before their bodies are ready for a high level of training.

Therefore, during the first 4-week block of summer training, we make the weight room more of a priority across the week, with a 4-day split where 2 days are devoted to upper-body strength and hypertrophy while the other 2 days are for lower-body strength, power, and hypertrophy. The field-based work is done across 3 days throughout the week and takes on a slightly different appearance than that of the winter conditioning period. This is due to more exposure to change-of-direction work to prepare the players for the volume of accelerations and decelerations they will experience in football practices. A sample template is provided in table 11.4.

While the first day of training will again feature extensive tempo running to get the players' bodies activated for the rest of the week, we also include change-of-direction and agility work right off the bat. We keep the nature of this work reduced in volume but expect the players to find a way to bring intention behind every repetition. This helps give them the experience of starting off a week of practice with the expectation that they will lock in mentally and bring high energy physically throughout the season. The extensive tempo running then helps to "flush out" their legs because it is aerobic and enhances blood flow and develops endurance. From here, the players enter the weight room and perform a warm-up for the muscles of the shoulders as well as some core work before moving into an upper-body strength session.

Table 11.4   Summer Off-Season Complete Conditioning Program, Weeks 1-4

Training day	Day 1	Day 2	Day 3	Day 4
Emphasis	COD and agility, endurance, and upper-body strength	Acceleration, COD and agility, reactive power endurance, top speed technique, power, and lower-body strength	Acceleration, COD and agility, and upper-body strength	Lower-body strength and power
Field-based training	**Change-of-direction speed** Cone "N" drill—4 reps (2 each way) Cone "U" drill—4 reps (2 each way) **Agility** Partner mirror reaction drill—4 total reps Partner blind mirror reaction drill—4 total reps **Extensive tempo runs** Week 1 = 8 total reps Week 2 = 10 total reps Week 3 = 2 sets × 6 reps Week 4 = 2 sets × 7 reps 1-min rest between reps; 2-min rest between sets OL/DL 60-yd run in 11 sec QB/RB/TE/LB 80-yd run in 13 sec WR/DB 100-yd run in 15 sec	**Resisted sprinting** Heavy-resisted or light-resisted sprinting with full recovery between reps OL/DL Heavy-resisted sprinting (load 60%-80% body weight)—5 × 10 yd QB/RB/TE/LB Light-resisted sprinting (load 40%-60% body weight)—5 × 15 yd WR/DB Light-resisted sprinting (load 20%-40% body weight)—5 × 15 yd **Change-of-direction speed and agility** Cone zigzag run—6 reps (3 each way) "X" box partner reaction drill—4 total reps Retreat and react—4 total reps **Reactive power endurance circuit** A-skip with 10-lb plate overhead—2 sets High-knee run with 10-lb plate overhead—2 sets OL/DL = 20 yd; QB/RB/TE/LB = 30 yd; WR/DB = 40 yd per repetition **Top speed technique** Medicine ball (10 lb) knee punch run—2 sets OL/DL = 20 yd; QB/RB/TE/LB = 30 yd; WR/DB = 40 yd per repetition Build-up sprints (90% speed)—2 total repetitions OL/DL = 30 yd; All other positions = 40 yd	**Change-of-direction speed** 10-5-5 shuttle—6 reps (3 each way) Cone "90-90" drill—4 reps (2 each way) **Agility** Retreat and react—4 total reps Run to 90-degree cut on reaction—4 total reps **Resisted sprinting** Heavy-resisted or light-resisted sprinting, with full recovery between reps OL/DL Heavy-resisted sprinting (load 60%-80% body weight)—5 × 10 yd QB/RB/TE/LB Light-resisted sprinting (load 40%-60% body weight)—5 × 15 yd WR/DB Light-resisted sprinting (load 20%-40% body weight)—5 × 15 yd	No field training

Training day	Day 1	Day 2	Day 3	Day 4
Weight room training	**Primary press** Barbell bench press with 3-sec pause Week 1 = 4 sets × 4 reps, finish @ 70% 1RM Week 2 = 4 sets × 4 reps, finish @ 75% 1RM Week 3 = 4 sets × 3 reps, finish @ 80% 1RM Week 4 = 4 sets × 3 reps, finish @ 85% 1RM *Quarterback alternative:* Dumbbell incline bench press (15 degrees) with 3-sec eccentric—4 sets × 4 reps, finish heavy but with 1-2 reps left in the tank **Primary pull** 3-way chin-up—4 sets OL/DL = 2 reps each; QB/RB/TE/LB = 3 reps each; WR/DB = 4 reps each **Secondary press** Landmine push press—3 sets × 4 reps *Quarterback alternative:* Dumbbell one-arm push press—3 sets × 3 reps each arm **Secondary pull** One-arm machine seated row—3 sets × 6 reps each arm **Neck and trap** Barbell or dumbbell shrug—2 sets × 10 reps	**Primary compound** Hex bar deadlift, concentric only Week 1 = 4 sets × 3 reps, finish @ 75% 1RM Week 2 = 4 sets × 3 reps, finish @ 80% 1RM Week 3 = 4 sets × 3 reps, finish @ 85% 1RM Week 4 = 4 sets × 3 reps, finish @ 90% 1RM **Primary power** Barbell squat jump—3 sets × 3 reps OL/DL = 95-115 lb; All other positions = 115-135 lb **Single leg** Barbell reverse lunge with pause—2 sets × 5 reps each leg **Posterior chain** Barbell Romanian deadlift—4 sets × 4 reps	**Primary press** Barbell close-grip 2-board bench press Week 1 = 4 sets × 4 reps, finish @ 70% 1RM Week 2 = 4 sets × 4 reps, finish @ 75% 1RM Week 3 = 4 sets × 3 reps, finish @ 80% 1RM Week 4 = 4 sets × 3 reps, finish @ 85% 1RM *Quarterback alternative:* One-arm dumbbell incline bench press (30 degrees)—4 sets × 4 reps each arm, finish heavy but with 1-2 reps left in the tank **Primary pull** Dumbbell chest-supported row—4 sets × 8 reps **Secondary press** Half-kneeling landmine one-arm press—3 sets × 5 reps each arm **Secondary pull** Machine lat pull-down—3 sets × 8-10 reps **Neck and trap** Barbell or dumbbell shrug—2 sets × 10 reps	**Strength and power circuit** Perform each exercise as a circuit, starting back at the first exercise for each set. Barbell squat with pause—4 sets × 3 reps First power exercise—4 sets × 3 reps OL/DL = Dumbbell (25-35 lb) countermovement jump; All other positions = Long-response hurdle jumps Second power exercise—4 sets × 3 reps OL/DL = Barbell (95 lb) squat jump; All other positions = Barbell (45 lb) squat jump Third power exercise—4 sets × 2 reps each side All positions = Single-leg box jumps from half-kneeling position **Posterior chain** 45-degree back extension (weighted)—2 sets × 12 reps **Single leg** Dumbbell goblet lateral lunge—2 sets × 6 reps each leg **Knee flexion** Partner Nordic hamstring curl—2 sets × 4 reps

The field training on day 2 is the most intense field session of the week, featuring elements of acceleration, change of direction, agility, and top speed all in one session. When players start practicing, they will need to be able to operate efficiently in all these domains with a high intensity on a day-to-day basis, so these sessions begin preparing them. We incorporate resisted sprinting during this time to further develop horizontal force capabilities while also emphasizing change-of-direction speed and agility. Top speed is introduced with reactive power endurance circuits and technique drills.

The weight room session that follows involves the players performing a warm-up of core work and exercises around the hip, knee, and ankle joints before engaging in a primary compound exercise. This will typically be some variation of the hex bar deadlift, and the sample template shows the use of the concentric-only variation to reduce eccentric stress to the legs in consideration of the more intense field session that preceded it. Instead, we can emphasize the eccentric phase with higher speeds to further develop deceleration capacity in the weight room by incorporating barbell squat jumps as our primary power exercise. The auxiliary training then puts a focus on single-leg strength, posterior-chain strength, and the strength and integrity of the groin, ankle, and foot.

The weight room emphasis on day 3 is the same as day 1 (upper-body strength and hypertrophy), but the field training emphasizes acceleration rather than endurance. Given that the field training on day 2 was very intense, we take a small step back on day 3, but we still want to ensure we get some exposure to acceleration, change of direction, and agility as these elements form the bulk of the explosive work experienced in football. The change of direction and agility become more intense with a little more volume than day 1, and we then give the players another day of resisted sprinting for their acceleration work. The other aspect of resisted sprinting that we like is how the athletes can perform them with very high effort while at reduced risk of strain since the resistance will put them in a more efficient acceleration position and the speeds are naturally reduced.

Day 4 is the most unique day of the week because we get the players off the field and focus solely on the weight room but still want to develop the capacity to produce high levels of strength and power. So, after a warm-up, we will have the players perform three or four exercises in a strength and power circuit featuring a primary compound lift followed by two or three explosive jumping exercises of various loads. The goal is to give the players some experience along the entire force–velocity spectrum in the vertical plane during each round of the circuit. This will not only challenge them to maintain explosive outputs but also challenges coordination to perform efficiently when faced with various loads and speeds of movement. This is a potent challenge to the players' nervous systems because we encourage them to have maximum intent on every repetition of every exercise in the circuit. This will form the bulk of the training session, so we follow this circuit with some auxiliary training for the posterior chain and single-leg strength.

In the second 4-week block of summer training, we consolidate the weight room training into a 3-day split of full-body strength and power sessions. This is because we want to shift the emphasis to the field sessions, where we add an additional day from the previous block. The field-training emphasis now turns to preparing the players for all forms of running endurance while maintaining the exposure to acceleration, change of direction, agility, and top speed. We also want to shift toward more position specificity because this will be the final phase of off-season training before fall training camp begins. We present a sample template of this block in table 11.5.

Table 11.5   Summer Off-Season Complete Conditioning Program, Weeks 5-8

Training day	Day 1	Day 2	Day 3	Day 4
Emphasis	Endurance, power, and full-body strength	COD and agility and top speed technique	Position-specific endurance, power, and full-body strength	Position-specific COD and agility, top speed technique, power, and full-body strength
Field-based training	**Change-of-direction speed** Cone "90-90" drill—4-6 reps (2-3 each way) **Agility** OL/DL = Partner mirror reaction drill—4 total reps; All other positions = Open field tag—4 total reps **Extensive tempo runs**—4 sets × 4 reps Weeks 5-6 = 1-min rest between reps, 2 min between sets Weeks 7-8 = 45-sec rest between reps, 90 sec between sets OL/DL 60-yd run in 10 sec QB/RB/TE/LB 80-yd run in 12 sec WR/DB 100-yd run in 14 sec	**Field-training circuit** Go through each exercise in sequence then repeat for another round. **Tempo interval runs**—4 total reps and 1-min rest between reps OL/DL Cut 40s in 11 sec QB/RB/TE/LB Cut 80s in 13 sec WR/DB Cut 100s in 15 sec **Change of direction or heavy-resisted sprinting**—4 total reps OL/DL = Heavy-resisted sprinting (load 80%-100% body weight)—10 yd; All other positions = 30-yd shuttle (5 yd out, 5 yd back, 10 yd out, 10 yd back) **Agility**—4 total reps OL/DL = Retreat and react; All other positions = Cone tunnel open field tag **Position-specific drill**—4 total reps Should resemble the work done during individual periods in practice.	**Position-specific endurance** Array of positional movements performed on air, covering 10-20 yd per repetition for a determined number of total repetitions. Perform every repetition at game speed, taking 30-40 sec rest in between each repetition. Week 5 = 15 total reps Week 6 = 20 total reps Week 7 = 25 total reps Week 8 = 30 total reps	**Position-specific drills** Choose 2-3 drills that resemble the work the player does in practice and perform 4-6 total repetitions of each. **Agility** OL/DL = Open field tag—4 total reps; All other positions = Double-blind open field tag—4 total reps **Top speed technique** Build-up sprints (90% speed)—2-3 total reps OL/DL = 30 yd; All other positions = 40 yd

(continued)

Table 11.5   Summer Off-Season Complete Conditioning Program, Weeks 5-8 *(continued)*

Training day	Day 1	Day 2	Day 3	Day 4
Weight room training	**Primary press** Barbell close-grip 2-board bench press—4 sets × 3 reps, finish heavy but with 1-2 reps left in the tank *Quarterback alternative:* Dumbbell bench press—4 sets × 6 reps, finish heavy but with 1-2 reps left in the tank **Primary pull** Neutral grip chin-up (weighted)—4 sets OL/DL = 4 reps; QB/RB/TE/LB = 6 reps; WR/DB = 8 reps **Secondary press** Dumbbell two-arm push press—3 sets × 5 reps *Quarterback alternative:* Half-kneeling landmine one-arm press—3 sets × 6 reps each arm **Primary lower-body compound** Barbell squat—4 sets × 3 reps, finish heavy but with 1-2 reps left in the tank **Primary power** <u>OL/DL</u> Dumbbell squat jump—4 sets × 3 reps <u>QB/RB/TE/LB</u> Depth jump (18 in. box)—4 sets × 3 reps <u>WR/DB</u> Plyometric hurdle jump to box jump—4 sets × 3 reps **Posterior chain** Barbell Romanian deadlift for speed—4 sets × 3 reps	No weight room training	**Primary press** Barbell incline bench press—4 sets × 8 reps, finish heavy but with 1-2 reps left in the tank *Quarterback alternative:* Dumbbell incline bench press (15 degrees)—4 sets × 10 reps **Primary pull** Dumbbell chest-supported row—3 sets × 12 reps **Secondary pull** Dumbbell one-arm row—3 sets × 5 reps each arm *Quarterback alternative:* Half-kneeling land-mine one-arm press—3 sets × 8 reps each arm **Neck and trap** Barbell or dumbbell shrug—2 sets × 10 reps **Primary lower-body compound** Barbell step-up for speed—4 sets × 3 reps **Primary power** WR/DB = Barbell countermovement jump—4 sets × 2 reps each leg; All other positions = Barbell hang power clean—4 sets × 2 reps All done for speed, fluid movement, and technique. **Posterior chain** 90-degree back extension (weighted)—2 sets × 8 reps	**Primary press** Dumbbell incline bench press (15 degrees)—4 sets × 5 reps, finish heavy but with 1-2 reps left in the tank **Primary pull** Neutral grip chin-up (weighted)—4 sets OL/DL = 4 reps; QB/RB/TE/LB = 6 reps; WR/DB = 8 reps **Neck and trap** Barbell or dumbbell shrug—2 sets × 10 reps **Lower-body strength and power circuit** Perform each exercise as a circuit, starting back at the first exercise for each set. Dumbbell rear-foot elevated split squat for speed—4 sets × 2 reps each leg First power exercise—4 sets OL/DL = Box counter-movement jump with dumbbell (25-35 lb)—3 reps; All other positions = Plyometric hurdle jumps—4 hurdles Hex bar (95 lb) counter-movement jump—4 sets × 3 reps Band-assisted jump—4 sets × 3 reps **Knee flexion** Partner Nordic hamstring curl—2 sets × 4 reps

The field training on day 1 remains similar to the previous block, but the agility training becomes more complex, and the tempo running becomes faster on each repetition. The weight room session is then full body, where two presses and one pull are performed for the upper body. The lower-body exercises focus on maximum strength, with either a squat or deadlift variation as the primary compound movement and a primary power exercise based on player position groups. In the strength training, we encourage the players to go as heavy as they can while leaving 1-2 repetitions in the tank, meaning they could have easily achieved those repetitions if they had continued the set. Since our primary training emphasis now shifts to the work done on the field, this self-regulation allows us to fluctuate the loads used in the weight room, depending on the fatigue accumulated from the field sessions.

The training on day 2 is typically a team running session, where the entire day's work is done on the field. We do not visit the weight room on this day. We keep a similar format to day 2 from the previous block in terms of various forms of running, but we make longer running efforts more of a priority with tempo interval runs and begin adding in position-specific drills. These drills will resemble the work done during individual periods of football practice, so we find it helpful to consult with our football coaches on how they should be designed. Additionally, the exercises are not just performed as various stations, they are performed as a circuit for two rounds. So, in this example, we have the players start at the tempo interval runs and then move to the other exercises before starting over again at the tempo interval runs for a second round. Much like the strength and power circuits in the weight room, we are challenging the players' abilities to maintain high outputs of running-based efforts in the face of fatigue and delivering a potent stimulus for the nervous system.

Field training on day 3 shifts back to primary endurance, but this time we want to emphasize repeated sprint ability with position specificity. So, we will incorporate positional movements that cover shorter distances (e.g., <30 yd) but for high volumes (e.g., up to 30 total repetitions). One example would be having wide receivers perform routes on air from the 20-yard line going into the end zone, where they perform a route, simulate a catch, and then burst into the end zone to score before jogging back to the starting line for the next repetition. We encourage the players to use maximal effort on every repetition, so even though they will naturally slow down as fatigue builds, we want them to move at game speed for every repetition. The players then head into the weight room, where the session focuses on one press and two pulls for the upper body and a more explosive theme for the lower body. The primary compound exercise for the lower body will be performed to drive through the ground with speed and then we will incorporate a loaded power exercise, like variations of the barbell clean. This will give the players a consistent maximum power stimulus since the field training was endurance-oriented in nature.

On day 4, we can expect to give the players the most fatiguing session of the week. We do this by design since we know that the players will be off for the weekend over the next 2 days, so we want to give them a potent stimulus from which to recover before beginning the next week. The on-field session incorporates position-specific change-of-direction drills with agility training, all of which are performed for maximum intensity, so we give the players the necessary recovery time between efforts. We also include top speed technique work on this day to give the players a maximum effort speed stimulus, but we keep the volume minimal, typically only 2-3 total repetitions. Our goal is for the players to experience a very high running speed but not keep them there so long that we risk any loss of technique or soft-tissue injury. The weight room session features some minimal upper-body training, typically just one press and one pull along with some work for the neck and upper back, but we maintain the strength and power circuit for the lower body. In this block, we want the exercises in the circuit to shift more toward velocity overall, so we might incorporate plyometrics and band-assisted jumps while reducing the weights for the loaded jump efforts.

Our goal throughout the summer phase is to gradually progress the players to where we can build a nice bridge as they enter fall training camp. We do this by exposing them to consistent on-field training throughout the week and working across the spectrums of various speeds, loads, and movements that the players might experience as they enter sports practice.

FALL TRAINING CAMP CONDITIONING

Following the summer training period, the players will typically have a week off before the fall training camp period begins. At this point, we want to take a back seat and allow the training camp practices themselves to be the greatest training stimulus. We know from experience that football coaches will be highly energized and ready to get the players going, so the intensity of practice is usually very high from the first day. In addition, we recognize the existence of high levels of psychological stress associated with learning the playbook, competing for playing time, and adjusting to the balance of being a student-athlete. So, the training that we incorporate during the training camp period is the least-demanding training we will give the players all year. We provide a sample template for training camp practice in table 11.6.

Like any in-season period, football practice will serve to meet the needs of the on-field training sessions. In the weight room, we maintain a 3-day split, where day 1 is the most intensive and the other days taper down as the week unfolds. This will emulate what we do during the in-season period because intrasquad scrimmages typically take place at the end of the week during training camp, and we treat them as designated game days. So, day 1 will feature maximum strength work for the upper and lower body. We keep it very simple—one press, one pull, a primary lower-body compound

Table 11.6 Training Camp Practice Complete Conditioning Program, Weeks 1-3

Training day	Day 1	Day 2	Day 3
Emphasis	Full-body strength and power		
Field-based training	All done in football practice		
Weight room training	**Primary press** Barbell close-grip 2-board bench press Week 1 = 4 sets × 4 reps, finish @ 75% 1RM Week 2 = 4 sets × 3 reps, finish @ 80% 1RM Week 3 = 4 sets × 3 reps, finish @ 85% 1RM *Quarterback alternative:* Dumbbell bench press—4 sets × 4 reps, finish heavy but with 1-2 reps left in the tank **Primary pull** OL/DL = Machine seated row—4 sets × 6-8 reps; All other positions = Reverse grip chin-up (weighted)—3 sets × 6 reps **Neck and trap** Barbell or dumbbell shrug—2 sets × 10 reps **Primary lower-body compound** Barbell squat Week 1 = 4 sets × 3 reps, finish @ 75% 1RM Week 2 = 4 sets × 3 reps, finish @ 80% 1RM Week 3 = 4 sets × 3 reps, finish @ 85% 1RM **Posterior chain** Barbell Romanian deadlift—3 sets × 3 reps	**Primary press** Barbell incline bench press (30 degrees) Week 1 = 4 sets × 4 reps, finish @ 70% 1RM Week 2 = 4 sets × 4 reps, finish @ 75% 1RM Week 3 = 4 sets × 4 reps, finish @ 80% 1RM *Quarterback alternative:* Dumbbell incline bench press (30 degrees)—4 sets × 6 reps, finish heavy but with 1-2 reps left in the tank **Primary pull** Machine lat pull-down—3 sets × 6-8 reps **Neck and trap** Barbell or dumbbell shrug—2 sets × 10 reps **Primary lower-body compound** Barbell step-up for speed—3 sets × 3 reps each leg	**Primary press** Dumbbell incline bench press (15 degrees) Week 1 = 4 sets × 5 reps, finish @ 70% 1RM Week 2 = 4 sets × 5 reps, finish @ 75% 1RM Week 3 = 4 sets × 5 reps, finish @ 80% 1RM **Primary pull** Suspension trainer pull-up (weighted)—4 sets × 6 reps **Neck and trap** Barbell or dumbbell shrug—2 sets × 10 reps **Lower-body mobility and recovery** Foam rolling, mobility exercises, stretching

exercise, and some auxiliary work for the neck, upper back, and posterior chain. Day 2 is similar for the upper body, and the lower body features only one exercise, which is typically a compound exercise done for speed of movement. On day 3, we maintain similar upper-body training but take advantage of the training time to perform some recovery work for the lower body, including foam rolling or self-massage, mobility exercises, and stretching. Our primary goal during training camp is to maintain strength levels and reduce any unnecessary stress on the players where we can.

IN-SEASON CONDITIONING

As we progress to the in-season period, the work we provide for the players is all in the weight room. At this point, we will have an idea of what our depth chart looks like, meaning we know who the starting players and the developmental players, who likely won't get playing time, will be. The players who contribute the most during games will travel to away games, so we have to ensure that we are not overstressing these players with in-season training. The backup players who do not play as much can have more exposure to strength and conditioning during the season since they will not be as stressed during practices and games. So, we have 2 days devoted to full-body strength and power for the full team. Then, we have a day devoted to extra upper-body hypertrophy for the offensive and defensive linemen, running backs, tight ends, and linebackers who contribute the most in practice and games. Lastly, we have a final training day at the end of the week that is a full-body strength and power session for the backup players who need more development. A sample template for the first 4 weeks of the season is laid out in table 11.7. Tables 11.8 and 11.9 offer sample templates for the second and third four-week blocks of the season, respectively.

Again, like the fall training camp period, our most stressful weight room day will be day 1, which is performed the day after the game. Even though it is the most intense training day of the week in terms of exposure to strength training, it is still far less demanding than any training session we would have done previously during the year. We want to get this work done closer to the previous game so that we have plenty of time to recover from it before the next game. This is the day that we will perform our heavy primary compound exercise for the lower body, which we like to alternate between a split position and squat position each week. This format remains in place throughout the season, which allows us to spread the stress of the strength training across the hips in a way that is variable and avoids too much monotony over the course of 12-13 weeks of the in-season period. We also perform our most hamstring-intensive work on this day to avoid too much soreness in the hamstrings later in the week.

In our program, day 1 falls on a Sunday and follows a Saturday game day. Monday is a day off, and we will then bring in the linemen, running backs, tight ends, and linebackers for their next weight room session on Tuesday. This same group will have a bonus upper-body hypertrophy training session on Thursday. We will have the major contributing wide receivers, defensive backs, and quarterbacks come in on Wednesday since they will not have a Thursday session. This allows their training to be spread out more across the week. This group will only have two weight room training sessions each week—Sunday and Wednesday. The backup players at these positions will also come in on Wednesday for their day 2 workouts and then again on Friday for another developmental training session. So, the backup players will train 3 days each week—Sunday, Wednesday, and

Friday. There are many ways that coaches can break up the week, and this is just one example based on our program.

The training session on day 2 will continue with upper-body strength training and emphasize more explosive work for the lower body rather than heavy strength work. Crisp, fast, and fluid movement is the goal for these exercises. The hypertrophy session on day 3 for the linemen, running backs, tight ends, and linebackers will focus on extra stimulation of the upper body to continue increasing muscle size to help provide figurative "armor" against the high frequency of contact and collision for these positions. The developmental squad training session at the end of the week is another strength-oriented session with the inclusion of power as the season progresses. These players will be getting less practice repetitions and won't be playing in games, so we have to ensure that they are still receiving some explosive training. This is illustrated in table 11.8 as well as table 11.9, in which circuits of jumps and plyometrics are included on this training day.

During the season, we keep the overall template intact so that we are not adding to our players' competitive stressors. Ideally, if we decide to change or add a new stimulus, we will aim to do so during the scheduled bye week, provided it occurs somewhere in the middle of the season. However, we want to keep the movements very familiar for the players throughout the season and allow for practices and games to provide the natural variation of load. In addition, although we can aim to progress and train at heavier loads in our primary strength exercises, there will be times that we have to back off or remove exercises entirely based on what is occurring with the team in real time as we get through each game. If players are beat up, injured, or mentally stressed, we will have to consider adjusting our training accordingly. The most important training stimulus any football player can get is practicing and playing the sport of football, so we always have to protect that.

CONCLUSION

This chapter presented just one of the many ways to prepare a football team physically for a competitive season. The approach we outlined here is based on what we have done in the past, but we are constantly seeking to improve our program. Whatever program you use, it is essential to address all the conditioning areas covered in this book, proceed progressively, and closely monitor how players respond. Be ready to adapt as things change in real time, but be consistent and retain the pillars on which the program is based. It is fine to take a slightly different route, but do not abandon the road map you are most confident will get you to the desired destination. In other words, if you get the big rocks in place and stay true to those, the pebbles will tend to fall in line.

Table 11.7 In-Season Complete Conditioning Program, Weeks 1-4

Training day	Day 1	Day 2	Day 3	Day 4
Emphasis	Full team: Full-body strength	Full team: Full-body strength and power	Starting players OL/DL/RB/TE/LB: Upper-body hypertrophy	Developmental players: Full-body strength and power
Field-based training	All done in football practice			
Weight room training	**Primary press** Barbell bench press Week 1 = 4 sets × 4 reps, finish @ 70% 1RM Week 2 = 4 sets × 3 reps, finish @ 75% 1RM Week 3 = 4 sets × 2 reps, finish @ 80% 1RM Week 4 = 4 sets × 2 reps, finish @ 85% 1RM *Quarterback alternative:* Dumbbell incline bench press (15 degrees)—4 sets × 6 reps, finish heavy but with 1-2 reps left in the tank **Primary pull** Dumbbell chest-supported row—3 sets × 6 reps **Neck and trap** Barbell or dumbbell shrug—2 sets × 10 reps **Primary lower-body compound** Barbell squat (4 sets × 3 reps) or dumbbell rear-foot elevated split squat (4 sets × 3 reps each leg), finish heavy but with 1-2 reps left in the tank Week 1 = Dumbbell rear-foot elevated split squat Week 2 = Barbell squat Week 3 = Dumbbell rear-foot elevated split squat Week 4 = Barbell squat **Knee flexion** Partner Nordic hamstring curl—2 sets × 4 reps **Posterior chain** Barbell Romanian deadlift—4 sets × 3 reps	**Primary press** Barbell incline bench press (15 degrees) Week 1 = 4 sets × 4 reps, finish @ 70% 1RM Week 2 = 4 sets × 3 reps, finish @ 75% 1RM Week 3 = 4 sets × 2 reps, finish @ 80% 1RM Week 4 = 4 sets × 2 reps, finish @ 85% 1RM *Quarterback alternative:* Half-kneeling landmine one-arm press—3 sets × 4 reps each arm **Primary pull** Machine seated row—3 sets × 8 reps **Secondary pull** Neutral grip chin-up (weighted if possible)—2 sets × 6 reps *Quarterback alternative:* Dumbbell one-arm row—2 sets × 5 reps each arm **Neck and trap** Barbell or dumbbell shrug—2 sets × 10 reps **Primary power** OL/DL = Barbell hang power clean for speed—3 sets × 2 reps; All other positions = Hex bar (95-135 lb) countermovement jump—3 sets × 2 reps **Posterior chain** 90-degree back extension (weighted)—2 sets × 8 reps	**Primary press** Dumbbell incline bench press (15 degrees)—3 sets × 6 reps, finish heavy but with 1-2 reps left in the tank **Back superset** Machine seated row—3 sets × 12 reps Dumbbell incline rear delt raise—3 sets × 12 reps **Shoulders and arms circuit** Barbell curl—3 sets × 30 sec Band triceps push-down—3 sets × 30 sec Dumbbell shrug—3 sets × 30 sec	**Primary press** Barbell incline bench press (15 degrees)—4 sets × 10-12 reps, finish heavy but with 1-2 reps left in the tank **Primary pull** Neutral grip chin-up—3 sets OL/DL = 6 reps; QB/RB/TE/LB = 8 reps; WR/DB = 10 reps **Shoulders and arms circuit** Barbell curl—3 sets × 30 sec Band triceps push-down—3 sets × 30 sec Dumbbell shrug—3 sets × 30 sec **Primary lower-body compound** Barbell reverse lunge—4 sets × 4 reps each leg, finish heavy but with 1-2 reps left in the tank **Posterior chain** 90-degree back extension (weighted)—2 sets × 8 reps **Knee flexion** Partner Nordic hamstring curl—2 sets × 4 reps **Secondary posterior chain** Single-leg hip thrust with dumbbell—2 sets × 8 reps each leg

Table 11.8 In-Season Complete Conditioning Program, Weeks 5-8

Training day	Day 1	Day 2	Day 3	Day 4
Emphasis	Full team: Full-body strength	Full team: Full-body strength and power	Starting players OL/DL/RB/TE/LB: Upper-body hypertrophy	Developmental players: Full-body strength and power
Field-based training	All done in football practice			
Weight room training	**Primary press** Barbell close-grip 2-board bench press Week 5 = 4 sets × 4 reps, finish @ 70% 1RM Week 6 = 4 sets × 3 reps, finish @ 75% 1RM Week 7 = 4 sets × 2 reps, finish @ 80% 1RM Week 8 = 4 sets × 2 reps, finish @ 85% 1RM *Quarterback alternative:* Dumbbell floor press—3 sets × 8 reps, finish heavy but with 1-2 reps left in the tank **Primary pull** Machine seated row—3 sets × 8 reps **Neck and trap** Barbell or dumbbell shrug—2 sets × 10 reps **Primary lower-body compound** Barbell squat (4 sets × 3 reps) or dumbbell rear-foot elevated split squat (4 sets × 3 reps each leg), finish heavy but with 1-2 reps left in the tank Week 5 = Dumbbell rear-foot elevated split squat Week 6 = Barbell squat Week 7 = Dumbbell rear-foot elevated split squat Week 8 = Barbell squat **Knee flexion** Partner Nordic hamstring curl—1 set × 4-6 reps **Posterior chain** Barbell Romanian deadlift—3 sets × 3 reps	**Primary press** Dumbbell incline bench press (30 degrees) Week 5 = 4 sets × 4 reps, finish @ 70% 1RM Week 6 = 4 sets × 3 reps, finish @ 75% 1RM Week 7 = 4 sets × 2 reps, finish @ 80% 1RM Week 8 = 4 sets × 2 reps, finish @ 85% 1RM *Quarterback alternative:* Dumbbell bench press—3 sets × 8 reps, finish heavy but with 1-2 reps left in the tank **Primary pull** Suspension trainer pull-up (weighted)—3 sets × 6 reps **Secondary pull** Machine lat pull-down—2 sets × 6 reps *Quarterback alternative:* Dumbbell one-arm row—2 sets × 6 reps each arm **Neck and trap** Barbell or dumbbell shrug—2 sets × 10 reps **Primary power and strength** OL/DL = Barbell hang power clean for speed—3 sets × 2 reps; RB/TE/LB = Hex bar (95-135 lb) countermovement jump—3 sets × 2 reps; QB/WR/DB = Dumbbell rear-foot elevated split squat—3 sets × 4 reps each leg	**Primary press** Barbell incline bench press (15 degrees)—4 sets × 6 reps, finish heavy but with 1-2 reps left in the tank **Back circuit** Suspension trainer pull-up—3 sets × 5 reps Neutral grip chin-up—3 sets × 5 reps Machine seated row—2 sets × 10 reps **Shoulder circuit** Dumbbell standing side raise—2 sets × 10 reps Dumbbell incline rear delt raise—2 sets × 20 reps **Arm circuit** Choice of biceps exercise—3 sets × 10 reps Choice of triceps exercise—3 sets × 10 reps	**Primary press** Barbell incline bench press (15 degrees) with 3-sec pause—4 sets × 3 reps, finish heavy but with 1-2 reps left in the tank **Back circuit** Suspension trainer pull-up—2 sets × max reps Neutral grip chin-up—2 sets × max reps Machine seated row—2 sets × 12 reps **Jump and plyometric circuit** Countermovement jump—2 sets × 5 reps Tuck jumps—2 sets × 5 reps Plyometric low-hurdle jumps (5 hurdles)—4 times through **Primary compound** Barbell squat Week 5 = 4 sets × 4 reps, finish @ 75% 1RM Week 6 = 4 sets × 4 reps, finish @ 80% 1RM Week 7 = 4 sets × 3 reps, finish @ 85% 1RM Week 8 = 4 sets × 3 reps, finish @ 90% 1RM **Primary power** Barbell (95 lb) squat jump—4 sets × 2 reps **Posterior chain** 45-degree back extension (weighted)—3 sets × 10 reps

Table 11.9 In-Season Complete Conditioning Program, Weeks 9-12

Training day	Day 1	Day 2	Day 3	Day 4
Emphasis	Full team: Full-body strength	Full team: Full-body strength and power	Starting players OL/DL/ RB/TE/LB: Upper-body hypertrophy	Developmental players: Full-body strength and power
Field-based training	All done in football practice			
Weight room training	**Primary press** Barbell bench press Week 9 = 4 sets × 3 reps, finish @ 65% 1RM Week 10 = 4 sets × 3 reps, finish @ 70% 1RM Week 11 = 4 sets × 3 reps, finish @ 75% 1RM Week 12 = 4 sets × 3 reps, finish @ 80% 1RM *Quarterback alternative:* Dumbbell incline bench press (15 degrees)—4 sets × 6 reps, finish heavy but with 1-2 reps left in the tank **Primary pull** Dumbbell chest-supported row—3 sets × 6 reps **Neck and trap** Barbell or dumbbell shrug—2 sets × 10 reps **Primary lower-body compound** Barbell squat (4 sets × 3 reps) or dumbbell rear-foot elevated split squat (4 sets × 3 reps each leg), finish heavy but with 1-2 reps left in the tank Week 9 = Dumbbell rear-foot elevated split squat Week 10 = Barbell squat Week 11 = Dumbbell rear-foot elevated split squat Week 12 = Barbell squat **Knee flexion** Band-assisted partner Nordic hamstring curl—1 set × 4-6 reps **Posterior chain** Barbell Romanian deadlift—3 sets × 3 reps	**Primary press** Dumbbell incline bench press (30 degrees) Week 9 = 4 sets × 3 reps, finish @ 65% 1RM Week 10 = 4 sets × 3 reps, finish @ 70% 1RM Week 11 = 4 sets × 3 reps, finish @ 75% 1RM Week 12 = 4 sets × 3 reps, finish @ 80% 1RM *Quarterback alternative:* Half-kneeling landmine one-arm press—3 sets × 4 reps each arm **Primary pull** Machine seated row—3 sets × 6 reps **Secondary pull** Neutral grip chin-up (weighted if possible)—2 sets × 6 reps *Quarterback alternative:* Suspension trainer pull-up—2 sets × 6 reps **Neck and trap** Barbell or dumbbell shrug—2 sets × 10 reps **Primary compound** Barbell step-up for speed—3 sets × 2 reps each leg **Primary power** Single-leg hurdle hop to box jump (1-1-2)—3 sets × 2 reps each leg	**Back circuit** Machine lat pull-down—3 sets × 8 reps Machine seated row—3 sets × 8 reps Dumbbell one-arm row—3 sets × 8 reps each arm **Trap and shoulder circuit** Dumbbell shrug—2 sets × 12 reps Dumbbell incline rear delt raise—2 sets × 12 reps **Arm circuit** Choice of biceps exercise—3 sets × 10 reps Choice of triceps exercise—3 sets × 10 reps	**Primary press** Barbell close-grip 2-board bench press—4 sets × 4 reps, finish heavy but with 1-2 reps left in the tank **Back circuit** Neutral grip chin-up—2 sets × max reps Machine lat pull-down—2 sets × 12 reps Machine seated row—2 sets × 12 reps **Jump and plyometric circuit** Countermovement jump—2 sets × 5 reps Tuck jumps—2 sets × 5 reps Plyometric low-hurdle jumps (5 hurdles)—4 times through **Primary compound** Barbell squat Week 9 = 4 sets × 3 reps, finish @ 80% 1RM Week 10 = 4 sets × 3 reps, finish @ 85% 1RM Week 11 = 4 sets × 2 reps, finish @ 90% 1RM Week 12 = 4 sets × 2 reps, finish @ 95% 1RM **Knee flexion** Stability ball leg curl—2 sets × 10 reps

References

Chapter 1

1. Siff, M.C. (2003). *Supertraining*. Denver: Supertraining Institute.
2. Kiely, J. (2018). Periodization theory: Confronting an inconvenient truth. *Sports Medicine, 48*(4), 753-764.

Chapter 3

1. Issurin, V. (2008). *Block periodization: Breakthrough in sport training*. Muskegon, MI: Ultimate Athlete Concepts.
2. Clark, K.P., Rieger, R.H., Bruno, R.F., and Stearne, D.J. (2019). The National Football League combine 40-yd dash: How important is maximum velocity? *Journal of Strength and Conditioning Research, 33*(6), 1542-1550.

Chapter 4

1. Sheppard, J.M., and Young, W.B. (2006). Agility literature review: Classifications, training and testing. *Journal of Sports Sciences, 24*(9), 919-932.
2. DeWeese, B.H., and Nimphius, S. (2016). Program design and technique for speed and agility training. In G.G. Haff and N.T. Triplett (Eds.), *Essentials of strength training and conditioning* (4th ed., pp. 521-558). Champaign, IL: Human Kinetics.
3. Valle, C. (2020, April 17). Ground contact times in sports performance training. SimpliFaster. Retrieved October 25, 2021, from https://simplifaster.com/articles/ground-contact-times
4. Graham-Smith, P., Atkinson, L., Barlow, R., and Jones, P. (2009). Braking characteristics and load distribution in 180 degree turns. In *Proceedings of the 5th annual UKSCA conference* (Vol. 2009).
5. Verkhoshansky, Y.V., and Verkhoshansky, N. (2006). *Special strength training: A practical manual for coaches*. Muskegon, MI: Ultimate Athlete Concepts.
6. Ford, P.R., Ward, P., Hodges, N.J., and Williams, A.M. (2009). The role of deliberate practice and play in career progression in sport: The early engagement hypothesis. *High Ability Studies, 20*(1), 65-75.

Chapter 5

1. Suchomel, T.J., Nimphius, S., and Stone, M.H. (2016). The importance of muscular strength in athletic performance. *Sports Medicine (Auckland, N.Z.), 46*(10), 1419-1449. https://doi.org/10.1007/s40279-016-0486-0
2. Wagle, J.P., Taber, C.B., Cunanan, A.J., Bingham, G.E., Carroll, K.M., DeWeese, B.H., Sato, K., and Stone, M.H. (2017). Accentuated eccentric loading for training and performance: A review. *Sports Medicine (Auckland, N.Z.), 47*(12), 2473-2495. https://doi.org/10.1007/s40279-017-0755-6
3. Toigo, M., and Boutellier, U. (2006). New fundamental resistance exercise determinants of molecular and cellular muscle adaptations. *European Journal of Applied Physiology, 97*(6), 643-663. https://doi.org/10.1007/s00421-006-0238-1
4. Brady, C.J., Harrison, A.J., Flanagan, E.P., Haff, G.G., and Comyns, T.M. (2019). The relationship between isometric strength and sprint acceleration in sprinters. *International Journal of Sports Physiology and Performance*, 1-8. https://doi.org/10.1123/ijspp.2019-0151

5. Sheppard, J.M., and Triplett, N.T. (2016). Program design for resistance training. In G.G. Haff and N.T. Triplett (Eds.), *Essentials of strength training and conditioning* (4th ed., p. 452). Champaign, IL: Human Kinetics.
6. Chapman, P.P., Whitehead, J.R., and Binkert, R.H. (1998). The 225-lb reps-to-fatigue test as a submaximal estimate of 1RM bench press performance in college football players. *Journal of Strength and Conditioning Research*, 12(4), 258-261.
7. Lander, J. (1984). Maximum based on reps. *NSCA J*, 6(6): 60-61.
8. Mayhew, J.L., Ball, T.E., Arnold, M.E., and Bowen, J.C. (1992). Relative muscular endurance performance as a predictor of bench press strength in college men and women. *Journal of Strength and Conditioning Research*, 6(4), 200-206.
9. Morales, J., and Sobonya, S. (1996). Use of submaximal repetition tests for predicting 1-RM strength in class athletes. *Journal of Strength and Conditioning Research*, 10(3), 186-189.
10. Mann, J.B., Thyfault, J.P., Ivey, P.A., and Sayers, S.P. (2010). The effect of autoregulatory progressive resistance exercise vs. linear periodization on strength improvement in college athletes. *Journal of Strength and Conditioning Research*, 24(7), 1718-1723. https://doi.org/10.1519/JSC.0b013e3181def4a6
11. Randell, A.D., Cronin, J.B., Keogh, J.W., Gill, N.D., and Pedersen, M.C. (2011). Effect of instantaneous performance feedback during 6 weeks of velocity-based resistance training on sport-specific performance tests. *Journal of Strength and Conditioning Research*, 25(1), 87-93. https://doi.org/10.1519/JSC.0b013e3181fee634

Chapter 6

1. Schoenfeld, B.J. (2010). The mechanisms of muscle hypertrophy and their application to resistance training. *Journal of Strength and Conditioning Research*, 24(10), 2857-2872.
2. Noakes, T.D.O. (2012). Fatigue is a brain-derived emotion that regulates the exercise behavior to ensure the protection of whole body homeostasis. *Frontiers in Physiology*, 3, 82.
3. Kraemer, W.J., and Ratamess, N.A. (2005). Hormonal responses and adaptations to resistance exercise and training. *Sports Medicine*, 35, 339-361.
4. Sheppard, J.M., and Triplett, N.T. (2016). Program design for resistance training. In G.G. Haff and N.T. Triplett (Eds.), *Essentials of strength training and conditioning* (4th ed., pp. 439-470). Champaign, IL: Human Kinetics.
5. Martins-Costa, H.C., Lacerda, L.T., Rodrigo, C.R.D., Lima, F.V., et al. (2022). Equalization of training protocols by time under tension determines the magnitude of changes in strength and muscular hypertrophy. *Journal of Strength and Conditioning Research*, 36(7), 1770-1780.
6. Kelly, S.B., Brown, L.E., Coburn, J.W., Zinder, S.M., et al. (2007). The effect of single versus multiple sets on strength. *Journal of Strength and Conditioning Research*, 21(4), 1003-1006.

Chapter 7

1. Komi, P.V. (2003). Stretch-shortening cycle. *Strength and Power in Sport*, 2, 184-20

Chapter 8

1. Morris, B., and Williams, R. (2013). *American football physical preparation*. Self-published.

Index

About the Editor

Aaron Wellman is the senior assistant athletic director for football performance at Indiana University. He has over 25 years of experience in football strength and conditioning.

Wellman started his career as a graduate assistant with Indiana University before being elevated to assistant strength and conditioning coach. After his initial stint at Indiana, he served as an assistant strength and conditioning coach at Michigan State University and went on to lead strength and conditioning programs at Ball State University, San Diego State University, and the University of Michigan. Prior to returning to Indiana University, Wellman worked as an assistant for one year at the University of Notre Dame before spending the subsequent four years in the National Football League (NFL) as the head strength and conditioning coach for the New York Giants.

Wellman earned his bachelor's degree in exercise science, added master's degrees in applied sport science and nutrition science, and earned his PhD in 2018 from Bond University in Queensland, Australia. He is certified as a master strength and conditioning coach by the Collegiate Strength and Conditioning Coaches Association (CSCCa), holds the certified strength and conditioning specialist (CSCS) and personal trainer (NSCA-CPT) designations from the National Strength and Conditioning Association (NSCA), and is certified as a specialist in performance nutrition by the International Sports Sciences Association (ISSA).

About the Contributors

Cameron Josse is a certified strength and conditioning specialist (CSCS), a certified physical preparation specialist (CPPS), and is certified as a Functional Range Conditioning mobility specialist (FRCms). He is an athletic performance coach for football at Indiana University. He previously was associate director of football performance at University of North Carolina at Charlotte and director of sports performance at DeFranco's Training Systems in New Jersey.

Peter Remmes is certified by the Collegiate Strength and Conditioning Coaches Association and holds the certified strength and conditioning specialist (CSCS) designation from the National Strength and Conditioning Association. He is a sport performance coach for football at Texas A&M University. He previously worked as an athletic performance coach at Indiana University and an assistant strength and conditioning coach at University of Iowa and Florida State University.

Justin Collett is a certified strength and conditioning specialist (CSCS). He is an athletic performance coach for football at Indiana University and previously worked as head strength and conditioning coordinator and offensive line coach at Maryville College in Tennessee.

Jordan Hicks is a certified strength and conditioning specialist (CSCS). He is an athletic performance coach for football at Indiana University. He previously worked as the head football strength and conditioning coach at Utah State University, assistant director of sport performance at University of Utah, and director of strength and conditioning at University of North Alabama.